JE

Moses Mendelssohn

JERUSALEM

OR ON RELIGIOUS POWER

AND JUDAISM

TRANSLATED BY

Allan Arkush

INTRODUCTION

AND COMMENTARY BY

Alexander Altmann

BRANDEIS UNIVERSITY PRESS

Published by University Press of New England

Hanover and London

BRANDEIS UNIVERSITY PRESS
Published by University Press of New England
Hanover, NH 03755

Printed in the United States of America 10 9 8 7 6
CIP data appear at the end of the book

*The publisher gratefully acknowledges the support of the
Translations Program of the National Endowment of
the Humanities in the publication of this book.*

CONTENTS

TRANSLATOR'S PREFACE

THERE exist three previous translations of Moses Mendelssohn's *Jerusalem* into English: M. Samuels (London, 1838), I. Leeser (Philadelphia, 1853), and A. Jospe (New York, 1969). The merit of these translations is not in dispute and is gratefully acknowledged. However, a new, more philosophically exact rendition of *Jerusalem* is an urgent desideratum. Recent progress in Mendelssohn research has sharpened our awareness of the subtle shades of meaning in the text. The precision in terminology which characterizes the entire work has become manifest.

The present translation is based on the *editio princeps* (Berlin, 1783). Its aim is complete fidelity to the text without detriment to the character of the English language. The temptation to "improve" the clarity of Mendelssohn's thought by paraphrasing it has been carefully resisted. No attempt has been made to make Mendelssohn sound contemporary. The reader is entitled to a translation that authentically reflects a distinguished eighteenth-century text in all its preciseness. It is for the reader to judge whether this goal has been achieved.

ALLAN ARKUSH

INTRODUCTION

INTRODUCTION

I

As THE subtitle of the work indicates, Moses Mendelssohn's *Jerusalem* (Berlin, 1783) consists of two sections, one discussing the question of "Religious Power," the other outlining his conception of "Judaism." What binds these two seemingly disparate parts together is the aim of the book as a whole, Mendelssohn's endeavor to show that there is no contradiction between his earlier rejection of "religious power" and his continued adherence to "Judaism." *Jerusalem* reaffirms (in Section I) his strong conviction that neither religion nor the state is authorized to coerce the consciences of men, and seeks to show (in Section II) that Judaism honors this principle. In order to substantiate this claim, he offers an analysis of the various aspects that compose the Jewish religion. In so doing he presents the first attempt at a philosophy of Judaism in the modern period and places it squarely within the context of an important issue of his time, the relation of church and state. The boldness with which Mendelssohn stated his plea for liberty of conscience, unrestricted toleration, and civic equality irrespective of creed makes *Jerusalem* a classical document of the new age that was ushered in by the American Revolution and was about to stir in France, while Germany was a mere onlooker. Count Mirabeau, writing about Mendelssohn's work in

1787, one year after his death, enthusiastically described it as animated by the same spirit as the one that had informed Turgot's liberal philosophy and was expressed in the preamble to the newly proclaimed constitution of Virginia.[1] It may be noted that Mendelssohn wrote *Jerusalem* in the same year (1782) in which Thomas Jefferson produced his *Notes on Virginia*.

Allusion has been made to the intimate connection between Mendelssohn's *Jerusalem* and an earlier work of his in which he had already taken a stand on the issue of toleration and liberty of conscience. That work was the "Preface" (*Vorrede*) to his re-edition, in German translation, of *Vindiciae Judaeorum* (London, 1656; 1708), an extremely learned and deeply moving treatise by Menasseh ben Israel, the famous Amsterdam rabbi, philosopher, and humanist (1604–57).[2] By writing his "Defense of the Jews" Menasseh had sought to dispel, once and for all, the crude prejudices that, in his time, stood in the way of the resettlement of the Jews in England, a country from which they had been expelled in 1290.[3] What motivated Mendelssohn to present this historical document to his German contemporaries was the hope that it would reinforce the cause of Jewish civil admission which had recently been argued in Christian Wilhelm Dohm's powerful treatise *On the Civil Improvement of the Jews* (Berlin, 1781). He fittingly described his own publication as an "Appendix" to Dohm's work.[4] Public debate on the merits of Dohm's proposals was in its infancy, and Mendelssohn felt it most desirable to keep it alive.[5] His "Pref-

1. Honoré Gabriel Victor Riqueti, Comte de Mirabeau, *Sur Moses Mendelssohn, sur la réforme politique des Juifs: et en particulier sur la révolution tentée en leur faveur en 1753 dans la Grande Bretagne* (London [Strasburg], 1787; nouv. éd., Leipzig, 1853), pp. 23–28.

2. *Manasseh Ben Israel Rettung der Juden aus dem Englischen übersetzt nebst einer Vorrede von Moses Mendelssohn. Als ein Anhang zu des Hrn. Kriegsraths Dohm Abhandlung: Ueber die bürgerliche Verbesserung der Juden* (Berlin and Stettin, 1782).

3. See Lucien Wolf, *Menasseh ben Israel's Mission to Oliver Cromwell* (London, 1901).

4. See note 2.

5. See Mendelssohn's letter to Friedrich Nicolai dated February 8, 1782, *JubA* XIII, 31; cf. Altmann, *Essays*, p. 154.

ace"—an essay aglow with anticipations of a new dawn in history—was meant to put Menasseh's arguments in true perspective and to measure the modern prejudices against the medieval ones. He had clearly perceived the strange anomaly that the Age of Enlightenment had produced a new version of what today is called anti-Semitism.[6]

The Preface discusses, in addition, the eminently practical question of the extent of Jewish autonomy in the envisaged framework of citizenship, and it was in connection with Dohm's proposals relevant to this issue that Mendelssohn expressed certain misgivings. He disapproved, in particular, Dohm's suggestion that the Jewish "colony" should be permitted to retain the right of excommunication, which was a prerogative of all religious societies. He made the point that from the principles of natural law no semblance of authority for coercing men's minds could be derived.[7] He insisted, moreover, that the notion of ecclesiastical power was absurd and self-contradictory. It destroyed the very character of religion. "True, divine religion arrogates to itself no power over opinions and judgments . . . it knows only the power to win over by arguments, to persuade and create felicity by persuasion. True, divine religion need employ neither arms nor fingers by which to take hold of believers. It is all mind and heart."[8] Dissidents are not to be barred from participation in religious devotions: "Reason's house of worship has no need of locked doors. It does not have to guard anything inside nor does it have to prevent any one from entering."[9] Excommunication is the very opposite of the spirit of religion. Even assuming that disciplinary measures of the milder sort (the so-called "minor ban") will not adversely affect the dissident's civil status—an assumption which Mendelssohn does not share—they are in themselves irreconcilable with the nature of true religion. Mendelssohn concludes his Preface with a fervent appeal

6. For a comprehensive analysis of modern anti-Semitism see Jacob Katz, *From Prejudice to Destruction: Anti-Semitism, 1700–1933* (Cambridge, Mass., 1980).

7. *GS*, III, 194f.

8. Ibid.

9. *GS*, III, 198.

to the rabbis and elders of the Jewish nation to renounce the weapon of excommunication (*herem*) as unworthy of their faith.

The Preface denies also the state's right of coercion in matters of conscience. No positive legislation, he maintains, can confer coercive rights for which natural law offers no grounds. Nor is the state permitted to discriminate between members of different faiths by making their civil status dependent on religious conformity. No "opinion" can serve as a legal title to either civil privilege or civil degradation. Mendelssohn's arguments will be fully elaborated in *Jerusalem* and there is therefore no need to restate them at this point.

The forceful denial of ecclesiastical power and civil discrimination which the Preface contains pleased some and annoyed others. Mendelssohn himself recorded some of the reactions he had noticed.[10] The sharp rebuttal ("All this is new and harsh") which he had encountered in the prestigious *Göttingische Anzeigen*[11] in no way dampened his ardor. On the contrary, it provoked a pointed rejoinder in *Jerusalem,* in stark contrast to the caution which his friend, Professor Eberhard in Halle, had counseled.[12] A private letter addressed to him by Friedrich Eberhard von Rochow, a prominent educator,[13] warmly approved of his characterization of true religion but wondered whether it did not imply a certain readiness to recognize Christianity as the shortest road to blessedness and civil equality. Clearly, many readers of the Preface inferred from its tone and temper that Mendelssohn's stress on forbearance, love, and tolerance as the essence of religion indicated what they considered a growing closeness to Christian principles. They disregarded his explicit references to the Jewish tradition (1 Kings 8:41f.; b. Hullin 5a) for the purpose of showing its tolerant ethos, and they failed to perceive that in his view the "true, divine religion" (the religion

10. See *JubA* XIII, 63; *Jerusalem* (present edition), pp. 78–81.
11. See Commentary, 80, 33–81, 3.
12. *JubA* XIII, 102.
13. *JubA* XIII, 42–48.

of reason, or natural religion) formed the sole credal element of Judaism, a point he had expressed as early as 1770 in a letter to his friend Elkan Herz[14] and was to elaborate in *Jerusalem*. Since, however, his religious position had not been spelled out in the Preface, some faint possibility of misreading him did exist. It provided the misty atmosphere in which phantoms could take shape, and the incentive for writing an anonymous little tract that urged him to convert to Christianity. It was this particular publication that compelled him to write *Jerusalem*, and it did so not because of its challenge that he convert but for a far weightier reason, its charge of inconsistency.

That brochure of forty-seven octavo pages bears the title "The Searching for Light and Right in a Letter to Mr. Moses Mendelssohn Occasioned by his Remarkable Preface to Menasseh ben Israel" (Berlin, 1782).[15] As modern research has finally established,[16] the unnamed author was August Friedrich Cranz, a gifted writer with a satirical bent who resided in Berlin and whose reputation was diminished on account of some rather scandalous pieces he had published. He had a profound admiration for Mendelssohn, and his public epistle to him was motivated by a genuine desire to promote the fulfillment of the old prophecy that in the hoped-for future there would be one shepherd and one flock. From a revered teacher he had imbibed respect for the Jews, coupled with some evangelical zeal, and the rest followed naturally. He feared that an appeal to Mendelssohn bearing his name was unlikely to win much attention, let alone elicit a reply. Hence his decision to publish his work anonymously. Yet to make

14. *JubA* XIX, 151, quoted in part by Fritz Bamberger, "Mendelssohn's Concept of Judaism," in Jospe, ed., *Studies*, p. 353.

15. *Das Forschen nach Licht und Recht in einem Schreiben an Herrn Moses Mendelssohn auf Veranlassung seiner merkwürdigen Vorrede zu Manasseh Ben Israel* (Berlin, 1782); reprinted in *JubA* VIII.

16. See Jacob Katz, "To Whom Was Mendelssohn Replying in His 'Jerusalem'?" in *Zion*, XXXVI. 1–2 (1971), 116f., where his earlier assumption of Sonnenfels's authorship based on the discovery of Münter's letter (*Zion*, XXIX. 1–2 [1964], 112–32; *Scripta Hierosolymitana*, XXIII [1972], 214–43) is revised; Altmann, *Mendelssohn*, pp. 502–13.

doubly sure that Mendelssohn would take it seriously he signed it at the end "Your most sincere admirer S****, Vienna, June 12, 1782," using a strategy designed to give the impression that the author was none other than the celebrated Viennese statesman, philosopher, and patron of the arts Joseph Baron von Sonnenfels who was known to have the highest regard for Mendelssohn and whom the latter held in much esteem. The deception worked. Mendelssohn was sure that it was Sonnenfels who had written the brochure and he saw no possibility of ignoring the challenge. That he so believed is attested by a letter written on October 3, 1782 by the young Danish theologian Friedrich Münter, who had visited Berlin from August 22 until September 12 of that year. Reporting on his experiences in the Prussian capital, he remarked: "I had many conversations with Moses Mendelssohn but he was far too busy responding to Sonnenfels's question why he had not yet become a Christian to make it possible for me to see him more often." How long the deception persisted is not entirely clear. A letter from Eberhard to Mendelssohn dated April 19, 1783 mentions Cranz as the author,[17] and it may be assumed that the truth became known much earlier. Mendelssohn, nevertheless, preferred publicly to ignore Cranz's authorship. In a letter written at the beginning of April, 1783–the book appeared in the second half of that month–he referred to his treatise as a work occasioned by a piece of writing that "purports to have been written in Vienna."[18]

The last-mentioned letter (which was addressed to the illustrious Prague pedagogue Ritter von Schulstein) contains a statement of the reason that made it imperative for Mendelssohn to answer the "Viennese" brochure: "In *Jerusalem* I defend myself against an attack made upon my principles." In order to comprehend this remark we have to take a closer look at Cranz's work. Mention has already been made of its outspoken effort to convert Mendelssohn to Christianity. A characteristic passage making this

17. *JubA* XIII, 102.
18. *JubA* XIII, 97f.; *Jerusalem*, p. 51.

suggestion is quoted in *Jerusalem*.[19] Cranz obviously felt that the time was ripe for renewing Lavater's attempt but, as is clear from other passages, he put a distance between himself and the "indiscreet" Swiss clergyman who had lamentably failed. Everybody, he wrote, had admired the skillful way in which Mendelssohn had dodged rather than confronted the issue then, and there had been universal understanding for the reserve and reticence with which he had stated his case. Now, however, the situation was different. For a brief moment, by what he had revealed in the Preface, Mendelssohn had shed the mask that hid his face and the public had a right to expect a further clarification as to where he stood. He had affirmed his loyalty to the "faith of his fathers" when replying to Lavater. But what did he mean by that faith? Was not Christianity the very faith of his fathers in a wider sense, a faith "purified of the onerous statutes of the rabbis and augmented by new elements" that in fact represented the "fulfillment of Old Testament prophecies"? Did Christianity not embrace the old faith, its worship of the one God, the law of Moses as fulfilled, and the gathering of all nations into one flock under the scepter of the Messiah?

The faith of the fathers in the narrower sense, Cranz continued, was confined to the specifically Jewish "church system" which contained the "statutory ecclesiastical law" that separates the Jews from all other nations of the earth. "From this latter special faith, my dear Mr. Mendelssohn, you have torn yourself away in your remarkable Preface by plainly depriving the Synagogue of its principal force, denying as you do its right to exclude from the community of the holy those who fall away from the faith of their fathers and to invoke the ban and the curse upon heretics." There follows a long section from which Mendelssohn himself adduces the most relevant sentences in *Jerusalem*.[20] Their upshot is that by rejecting religious power (the right of excommunication) Mendelssohn had removed the "cornerstones" of the Mosaical system,

19. *Jerusalem*, pp. 86f.
20. Ibid., 84f.

which was one built on fear of punishment. Having professed principles of reason that undermined the power structure of the Jewish "ecclesiastical law," how could he still remain an adherent of the faith of his fathers in the narrow sense of this term?

In his *Jerusalem* Mendelssohn refers in the first place to Cranz's characterization of Judaism as a churchly system armed with the "sword of the curse" and severely punishing transgressors of the law. It is this "objection" that, as he admits, "cuts me to the heart" and requires an answer. When presenting his picture of the true, divine religion in the Preface, he had indeed tried to link it to certain elements in the Jewish tradition but had ignored what was now held up to him as evidence to the contrary. This was an "attack made upon [his] principles" since the evidence produced seemed to shatter the validity of his presentation of Judaism as a religion in harmony with the principles of toleration and liberty of conscience. That rosy picture had, in fact, already been ruthlessly questioned by his friend August Hennings, an avowed disciple of Voltaire's.[21] As for Cranz's attitude to the Jewish religion, it represents a curious mixture of Deistical and traditional features. It adopts, on the one hand, the Deists' portrayal of the Old Testament as a harsh and cruel legislation and clings, on the other hand, to the inherited view which sees in the New Testament the fulfillment of the Old. According to the radical Deists,[22] Christianity was a brand new, independent religion which owed nothing to Judaism. Mendelssohn was well aware of Cranz's traditionalist stance, for in reply to his evangelical overtures—to which he pays but secondary and fleeting attention—he uses the striking simile of the two floors in the same building.[23] While he makes short shrift of the "suggestion" that he convert to the Christian faith, he does take the "attack" seriously. He does not seem to have been thrown off balance, but he obviously realizes that Cranz

21. *JubA* XIII, 35–40.

22. Cf. Commentary, 87, 14–23; 131, 2–3; Wolfhart Pannenberg, *Wissenschaftstheorie und Theologie* (Frankfurt a.M., 1973), p. 386, note 714.

23. *Jerusalem*, p. 87.

presented him with a problem. That problem was seemingly compounded by the fact that the anonymous brochure contained also a brief postscript (*Nachschrift*) in the form of yet another letter (five pages) addressed to Mendelssohn and signed "Your most devoted Mörschel." The author, Daniel Ernst Mörschel, was an army chaplain who had tried his hand at an anthology of hymns and at a reader for school children.[24] His purpose in approaching Mendelssohn was different from Cranz's. He wanted to know where Mendelssohn stood in respect of belief in revelation. From certain passages in the Preface he had inferred that Mendelssohn was neither Jew nor Christian but disbelieved all revelation, in short, was a Deist. He did not say so in blunt terms but hinted at his suspicion and asked for clarification.

Mörschel's importunate request, which is referred to in *Jerusalem*[25] with good-humored irony, actually proved helpful to Mendelssohn. It gave him the cue, as it were, for outlining the basic distinction between Judaism as a rational creed and Judaism as a revealed legislation. In fact, the major part of Section II consists of subject matter relevant to Mörschel's question, while the answer to Cranz is given only briefly toward the end of the book.

Mörschel's postscript is dated "Berlin, September 3rd, 1782," and the brochure must have appeared immediately afterwards, for when Münter, who left Berlin on September 12, visited Mendelssohn, the latter was already busy with his reply.[26] We have no information about the progress in the writing of *Jerusalem* but, fortunately, we possess the original plan (two folio pages) of the book drafted in Mendelssohn's own hand and, attached to it, another autograph (two folio pages) containing excerpts from two works he consulted, Israel Gottlieb Canz's *Disciplinae morales omnes* (Leipzig, 1739) and Thomas Hobbes's Latin edition of *Leviathan* (Amsterdam, 1668).[27] The draft of the plan vividly re-

24. See *JubA* VIII, xxiv.
25. Pp. 87–89.
26. Cf. above, p. 8.
27. The four folio pages of the autograph and a facsimile of page 1 are

flects Mendelssohn's first reaction upon reading "The Searching
for Light and Right." It was far angrier than the final form of
Jerusalem would lead one to assume, and had his frame of mind
persisted, we might have found some fairly strong polemical utter-
ances about Christianity in the book. In reply to the "Searcher's"
suggestion that he convert, he employs already here the simile of
the two floors in the same building which later so intrigued Kant,[28]
but he adds, in a simultaneous answer to the attack, that Christianity, not Judaism, coerces the conscience; that the former, not
the latter, represents what Cranz had called "'the servitude of iron
churchly bonds." Christianity, he says, has transformed the thirty-
nine corporal floggings of the Mosaic law into as many spiritual
ones, a reference to the thirty-nine articles of the Anglican Church
which have to be subscribed to by the clergy under oath and
concerning which there is a spirited passage in *Jerusalem*.[29] The
phrase "Christianity is a yoke in spirit and in truth" is omitted
there. He condemns the post-Reformation Church for still arrogating to itself privileges which, on grounds of reason, cannot be
admitted and he adds: Not so Judaism. His original strategy obviously was to shift the blame—the charge of intolerance—to
Christianity as the more guilty offender but, in the end, he refrained from doing so.

From the autograph we also learn that, originally, *Jerusalem*
was to comprise three parts. The first was to delineate the respective realms of authority belonging to church and state. The position Mendelssohn took was from the very start in opposition to
both Hobbes and Locke. The phrase "Borderline disputes . . .
have caused immeasurable evils," which reappears in the opening
section of the book, is taken from Canz.[30] The second part was

---

reproduced in *JubA* VIII. An English translation of the Draft was published
in Altmann, *Mendelssohn*, p. 515f. and appears as an Appendix in the present
edition. The autograph (which was never published before) is owned by
Professor Fritz Bamberger, New York, with whose kind permission it was
reproduced in *JubA* VIII.

28. See Commentary, 87, 4–14.
29. Pp. 63–70.
30. See Commentary, 33, 9–23.

meant to develop Mendelssohn's theory of natural law insofar as it had a bearing on the origin and limits of coercive rights; it also was to show the illegitimacy of religious oaths. Part 3 was to contain the answer to the assertion that Mendelssohn's rational principles ran counter to the Jewish religion. A number of additional themes that were to play a significant role in the book are merely named in the bottom margin of the page.

The draft bears no title. It seems that Mendelssohn hit upon the name "Jerusalem" only when the book was about to leave the press. Eberhard's letter of April 19, 1783 merely refers to "what you write against Cranz."[31] In his letter to Schulstein written at the beginning of April, 1783[32] Mendelssohn himself mentions only the subtitle, but a letter to Redlich in Vienna written on April 4 for the first time quotes the full title.[33] The book appeared in the second half of April, 1783.[34]

II

Jerusalem is the work of a man who had achieved a unique and highly personal blend of the rabbinic culture in which he had grown up and continued to feel at home and the European Enlightenment in which he had immersed himself with dazzling success. It is hard to say which of these two elements predominated in his inner life. To study *Jerusalem* is to try to read Mendelssohn's mind. Never before had he made such a full and explicit statement about Judaism. And never before had he expressed his enlightened stance about religion and liberty of conscience as forcefully as here. To some it appeared that the two sections of *Jerusalem* represented the coexistence of two separate halves of his personality rather than a unified whole. Yet this is a view unsupported by the available evidence. He was neither a "sophist" in Section I nor a *Stockjude* (an "arrant Jew") in the second part.[35] Both sections are closely interrelated. As for Section I, though a

31. *JubA* XIII, 102.
32. *JubA* XIII, 98.
33. *JubA* XIII, 99.
34. See the letter to Christian Garve, *JubA* XIII, 103.
35. Cf. *JubA* XIII, 179.

model of logical deduction, it bears all the marks of a Jewish composition. It flows from an ultimately Jewish concern aiming as it does at the removal of oppressive laws that deny the Jew civil equality. The issue of Jewish rights had occupied his mind throughout his life[36] and he had actively intervened as spokesman for his brethren on more than one occasion.[37] He saw the age-old denial of these rights as coming from the Church rather than from the State. He was contemptuous of ecclesiastical law, which even in its most advanced form continued to advocate restrictions on the toleration of Jews.[38] There had been high-minded nonecclesiastical advocates of toleration before, men like Locke, Reimarus, Lessing, Iselin and, recently, Dohm, yet none of them had spoken with a passion comparable to his, and none had made an effort to demonstrate the illicit nature of curbs on toleration as he did in his *Jerusalem*, where the whole array of natural law is put in the service of his idea of liberty. As a document of an all-out effort, *Jerusalem* stands alone, and it will remain a classic in this field for centuries to come. It will also stand as a testimony to Mendelssohn's Jewishness, the source of his passion and ethos.

Moreover, the whole tenor of Section I is imperceptibly linked to the philosophy of Judaism as perceived by Mendelssohn and stated at length in Section II. The attack on religious oaths[39] has its parallel in the terse statement made in Section II: "Hence, ancient Judaism has no symbolic books, no *articles of faith*. No one has to swear to symbols or subscribe, by oath, to certain articles of faith. Indeed, we have no conception at all of what are called *religious oaths;* and according to the spirit of true Judaism, we must hold them to be inadmissible."[40] It almost looks as if the "inadmissible" character of oaths of this kind according to the Jewish view furnished the grounds, or supplied the sentiment, for the spirited attack upon this widely accepted Christian practice.

36. See *JubA* XI, 338; VII, 8.
37. See Altmann, *Mendelssohn,* pp. 421–49.
38. See Altmann, *Die trostvolle Aufklärung,* pp. 268–75.
39. See note 29.
40. *Jerusalem,* p. 100.

Most certainly the Jewish stance proved helpful to Mendelssohn in his impressive reasoning against the legality of the procedure as found in Section I. We have here an instructive example of the inner relatedness of Sections I and II. Another case in point is the denunciation, in Section I, of salaries paid for religious services which, again, is inspired by a principle that held sway in ancient rabbinic Judaism. Its suspension in subsequent times could be safely ignored by Mendelssohn because, as Section II repeatedly emphasizes, his concern is with the "true," "original" Judaism. In his review of *Jerusalem*, Johann David Michaelis, the noted Göttingen Orientalist, further explained the rabbinic position which Mendelssohn had cited, and he drew attention to the remarkable fact that even when discoursing on matters of natural law Mendelssohn was guided by his native rabbinic tradition.[41] Furthermore, natural religion, which, in Section I, is said to form the core of all positive faiths and, as a moral force, to qualify for special protection by the state,[42] turns out, on closer inspection, to be identical with the credal part of Judaism as defined in Section II. For the three "fundamental principles" (God, providence, future life) which Section I attributes to natural religion more or less correspond to the three "basic principles" of Judaism as formulated by Joseph Albo and referred to in Section II. The latter are described by Mendelssohn as akin to the famous *notitiae communes* spelled out by Herbert of Cherbury, the father of the doctrine of natural religion. It is obvious, therefore, that far from being in opposition to Section II, the first part reflects in large measure Mendelssohn's view of Judaism. He is as much of a *Stockjude* here as there.

Mendelssohn's denial of the legitimacy of excommunication might seem to suggest that, in this instance, he does put himself in opposition to rabbinic law. It should be noted, however, that at the end of the Preface to *Vindiciae Judaeorum*, where he appeals

41. *Orientalische und exegetische Bibliothek*, XXII (1783); see *JubA* VIII, lxv.
42. *Jerusalem*, p. 63.

to the rabbis and elders of his nation to forgo this practice, he makes it abundantly clear that in his view the ban was not an authentically Jewish institution but had been introduced in imitation of Christian usage. This opinion is obviously an erroneous one,[43] but it must be assumed that it was honestly held by Mendelssohn. It was part and parcel of his conviction that a line had to be drawn between "ancient" Judaism, which was the pure pristine faith, and the disturbing subsequent accretions that marred the erstwhile beauty of the Jewish religion. It is this essentially Deistic outlook which accounts for the position he took.

If, as we saw, Section I is permeated by Jewish motivations and elements of thought, Section II is shot through with philosophical ingredients. Indeed, the presentation of Judaism is determined throughout by a philosophical frame of mind. It is clear that what Mendelssohn attempts is a phenomenology of the Jewish religion in the constructive, not in the descriptive, sense. What he offers is not a picture of Judaism as it had crystallized historically and was still largely intact in his period but an idealized image of the faith as he believed it to have existed in the ancient past. This image of the original Judaism was meant to serve as a blueprint for the anticipated era of civil admission. This reconstruction of the true Judaism was entirely in tune with the Deistic reading of present-day religion as overlaid with alien elements and therefore in need of having its true character restored. The critique of this Deistic account of religious history, which took such brilliant shape in Hegel, did not yet loom on the horizon. It required critical sense and a deeper appreciation of religious motivations than the period of the Enlightenment was capable of. For Mendelssohn, a true child of his age, though far more critical of the Enlightenment than most of his contemporaries,[44] the history of religion, including Judaism, was a process of degeneration. In Section II of *Jerusalem* he stresses again and again the corrup-

43. See Altmann, *Essays,* pp. 177f., 187f.
44. See Altmann, "Moses Mendelssohn on Education and the Image of Man," in Jospe, ed., *Studies,* pp. 387–91.

tions that had taken place.[45] The vicissitudes of Jewish history are portrayed by him as a series of deviations from the authentic path starting from the incident of the golden calf and continued by such events as the people's clamoring for a king at the time of Samuel and subsequent breaches of the ideal unity of life and doctrine. The innovation of committing the oral law to script is presented as an instance of such fatal change. In typical Enlightenment fashion he attributes the more flagrant violations of ancient practice to the "folly" of men.

Yet there is a strange paradox in his attitude to the changes wrought. While he deplores the transformations and seemingly yearns for the ancient way, we sense that he is by no means unhappy with some of them. As a passionate advocate of "persuasion" and "gentleness" as the sole power to be employed by religion, he cannot possibly regret the cessation of the old theocracy in which religious trespasses were punishable as lese majesty. He must have rather welcomed the transmutation of Judaism into a mere "religion." History, then, was to him not merely a process of deterioration but also a road to progress. Living at a time when, as he had put it in the Preface,[46] the "delusion" as to the rightness of religious coercion was gradually vanishing, he could exhort his brethren to thank the "God of mercy" for having brought about a change of heart with respect to the concept of religious power. Despite his deistically inspired catastrophic view of religious history—which contrasted anyway with his professed belief in the constancy of the moral and religious level of humanity in all ages[47]—he was wide open to the reality of progress. As a Jew profoundly sensitive to the long history of his people and familiar with its variegated aspects, he could not but acknowledge the evil as well as the good that historical changes had brought in their train.

45. Pp. 102, 120, 128; 132.
46. GS, III, 202.
47. See Jerusalem, pp. 95–97; Commentary, 95, 32–96, 2; 96, 8–97, 15.

In one particular respect did the catastrophic view of religious history dominate his outlook. He seized upon it as a rationale for the special destiny of the Jewish people. He accepted the Deistic notion—which was shared by the rabbinic tradition—that original monotheism had degenerated into idolatries and superstitions, and he used it to good purpose. Israel, he said, was chosen as a priestly nation to safeguard the true religion, to preserve "sound and unadulterated ideas"[48] about God and thereby stem and reverse the process of corruption. Although Mendelssohn's view somewhat oscillates between the assumption of an original monotheism and the evolutionist theory (introduced by Hume and Voltaire) which places paganism at the beginning,[49] the traditional notion is the one that prevails in *Jerusalem*. It enables him to interpret the election of Israel—an idea much ridiculed in radical Deism—as a divine act calculated to benefit the whole of humanity. This interpretation implies that the "covenant"[50] between God and Israel remains in force throughout history and that the "ceremonial law" by which the Jewish people is distinguished from all other nations is obligatory for the Jew until the end of days when, as the Prophets foretold, the true faith will be universally accepted. Mendelssohn makes this point very forcefully in the final part of Section II where he takes a stand against those who (like the "Searcher"), were trying to persuade the Jews that the time was ripe for a union of faiths in which the distinctive characteristics of Judaism were to be submerged in an enlightened form of Christianity. Following this call, Mendelssohn points out, would be tantamount to deserting the vocation for which the Jewish people had been created. He adds a number of further considerations. Metaphysically speaking, it is diversity, not uniformity, that seems to be the law of nature; weighing the issue in terms of practicality, agreement in the understanding of religious dogma is

48. *Jerusalem,* p. 118.
49. See Julius Guttmann, "Mendelssohn's *Jerusalem* . . . ," in Jospe, ed., *Studies,* p. 370.
50. *Jerusalem,* pp. 98, 127.

a hopeless proposition in view of the subtlety of the subject; and, most important of all, insistence on a so-called union of faiths as a precondition of civil admission is a flagrant violation of the principle of toleration. It betrays a relapse into the barbaric ages, a barely concealed threat to liberty of conscience. With this last argument Mendelssohn returns to the principal theme of Section I and, as if to link the two parts of *Jerusalem* together, he repeats here at the end the phrase used at the beginning which describes liberty of conscience as mankind's "noblest treasure." Yet pride of place belongs to the religious argument: The Jewish people cannot and will not relinquish its destiny as the guardian of true monotheism. It was this argument which he stressed in an intimate letter to his friend Herz Homberg.[51]

There is some piquancy in the fact that, as we have seen, starting out from the Deistic concept of the decline of rational faith in history Mendelssohn arrived at an understanding of the special purpose and historic function of the Jewish people. This notion of a particular destiny of Israel is recognized by him as the *raison d'être* of the Sinaitic revelation. This revelation, he points out, adds nothing to the sum total of natural religion insofar as truths are concerned. It consists solely in a legislation prescribing a way of life in which the eternal truths of reason and the peculiar destiny of Israel as keeper of these truths find concrete and intense expression. This concept of a revelation which reveals no supernatural truths, but only precepts for action in conformity with truths of reason, may be said to form the central doctrine of Section II. It implies that there is no conflict between reason and revelation. The eternal verities of reason are confirmed by revelation and validated as the essence of Judaism. The *novum* of revelation is of a practical nature, is *Halakhah*, ordinances for conduct, not mysteries of the faith.

In thus formulating his view of reason and revelation, religious truths and revealed law, Mendelssohn reflects, in a way, the traditional distinction between Halakhah and Haggadah, Halakhah

51. *JubA* XIII, 134.

and credal matters (*emunot ve-de'ot*), Halakhah and Kabbalah.
His view of revealed legislation as the *specificum* of Judaism
would seem to be in tune with the accepted notion of Halakhah
as the terra firma of the religious tradition. There is also a large
area of agreement between his assertion of the rationality of Jewish beliefs and the traditional assumption—articulated in medieval
and Renaissance Jewish polemic against the Christian dogma—
that Judaism teaches nothing contrary to reason. Wherein Mendelssohn differs from the inherited Jewish position is the limita-
tion he puts upon the content of the doctrinal element in Judaism
by restricting it to the truths of natural religion. In his view the
Jewish religion merely spells out what human reason can discover
by its own unaided effort and can recognize as the truth everywhere and at all times. This is obviously different from the traditional claim that there is nothing in Judaism that *violates* human
reason. Mendelssohn's criterion of acceptability would seem to exclude whole areas of religious belief (e.g., rabbinic eschatology,
kabbalistic theosophy, and the like) which lie outside natural religion. Occasionally, he qualifies his general view by referring to
the truths of reason as the "essentials" of Judaism,[52] thereby implicitly allowing for the possibility that in addition to the verities
of natural religion Judaism developed also ideas of less than central significance that might claim acceptance. There is further evidence to the effect that his view of what constitutes legitimate
Jewish beliefs and insights was not severely confined to the elements of natural religion. He makes it clear that he regards the
Torah as a treasury of profound religious truths which are concealed when glanced at superficially but which yield their "beauty"
to the ardent and persistent student.[53] This particular remark—
which is reminiscent of a Zoharic simile[54]—is a far cry from the assertion that the truths of natural religion lie open to unspoiled
common sense and are within the grasp of common and even

52. *JubA* VII, 10, 95.
53. *Jerusalem*, p. 99.
54. See Commentary, 99, 12–35.

primitive people.[55] The wealth of religious ideas found in the Bible was, after all, an object of lifelong intensive study by Mendelssohn himself. His awareness of what was enshrined in the beliefs of Judaism defied the narrow bounds of natural religion, and his equation of the two spheres must be taken with a grain of salt. It implied, probably, no more than his conviction that in ancient Judaism religious beliefs were totally identical with reason.

What compelled Mendelssohn to exclude religious truths from the realm of revelation and to limit the Sinaitic covenant to the proclamation of laws can be fully explained only against the background of the Deistic debate that characterizes the seventeenth and eighteenth centuries. Deism was a coat of many colors, and this is not the place to relate Mendelssohn to its various hues and shades. It is relevant, however, to recall that he shares the fundamental outlook of such works as John Toland's *Christianity not Mysterious* (London, 1696) and Matthew Tindal's *Christianity as Old as the Creation* (London, 1730), which were averse to recognizing mysteries of the faith. Toland's book figures in his library list and there are indications that he was acquainted—and impressed—also with Tindal's work, as well as with John Locke's *The Reasonableness of Christianity* (London, 1695). He must have felt that if a case could have been made out—even though mistakenly, in his view—for a purely rational Christianity, the chances for successfully doing so for Judaism were infinitely better. He was particularly struck, it seems, by the argument (found in Locke and Tindal) that the knowledge of eternal truths by which salvation is attained cannot be of such a nature as to require a divine act of revelation. For, in Locke's words, "what shall become of all the rest of mankind, who having never heard of the promise or news of a Savior, not a word of a Messiah to be sent, or that was come, have had no thought or belief concerning him?"[56] Mendelssohn makes the same point even more forcefully in *Jerusalem*,

55. *Jerusalem*, pp. 94f.; *JubA* III. 2, 198; VII, 74f.
56. John Locke, *The Reasonableness of Christianity as delivered in the Scriptures*, § 162.

having expressed it on more than one previous occasion.[57] Since
a revelation, his version of the argument runs, can address only a
particular group of people at a particular time and in a particular
language, it is, by its very nature, an exclusive act limited to priv-
ileged recipients and, by virtue of its exclusiveness, it must be
considered unbefitting the justice of God and his equal love for
all men. It is the moral aspect of the matter that weighs with
Mendelssohn. How deeply he felt about it can be best gauged
from the letter he wrote to Rabbi Jacob Emden on this subject.[58]
The conclusion he drew amounted to an all-out denial of any revelation of truths necessary for man's eternal felicity. Hence Judaism could not be a repository of truths revealed. Its doctrinal beliefs must stem from natural religion. They must be such as are
accessible to all mankind. As we saw, this proviso did not rule out
the possibility of deepening and amplifying the truths grounded
in universal human reason and thereby arriving at specifically
Jewish beliefs. What was excluded was the notion (current in
Kabbalah) that there had been an Adamitic and, subsequently, a
Mosaic revelation of esoteric truths unfathomable by reason alone.
It is the mystical domain that Mendelssohn sought to banish from
Judaism. In this endeavor he was heir to a respectable rationalist
trend within the Jewish tradition itself.[59]

What greatly aided Mendelssohn in defining the Sinaitic revelation as a purely legislative act was Spinoza's *Tractatus Theologico-
politicus* (1670). Although he does not mention this work, traces of
its influence upon him abound in *Jerusalem*.[60] The *Tractatus* was
a powerful attempt to understand the Bible from the viewpoint of
the radical Enlightenment and to use this understanding as a po-

57. P. 94; see Commentary, 94, 13–21.
58. See Commentary quoted in preceding note.
59. Outstanding representatives of this antimystical trend were Moses
Maimonides, Elijah del Medigo, and Leone Modena.
60. Cf. Commentary, 97, 16–98, 35; 102, 34–103, 7; 128, 18–19; 29–31;
129, 2–6; 133, 3–14. It was Julius Guttmann who (1931) first drew attention
to some of Mendelssohn's borrowings from Spinoza; see his essay "Mendelssohn's *Jerusalem* . . . ," in Jospe, ed., *Studies*, pp. 361–86.

litical instrument. The way Spinoza did it was far more thorough-
going and incisive than Hobbes's. As a former Marrano brought
up under rabbinic tutelage in Amsterdam, he was infinitely more
familiar with the Bible (and postbiblical Hebrew literature) than
Hobbes was. Mendelssohn, whose brand of Enlightenment was of
the moderate, conciliatory sort,[61] had to take issue, and somehow
come to terms, with Spinoza's view of Judaism, which could not
be simply ignored. The—in his eyes tragic—figure of Spinoza had
always intrigued him and he had tried to interpret his pantheism
in a way calculated to take the sting out of it.[62] What he adopted
from the *Tractatus* was the thesis that the Sinaitic revelation was
solely concerned with legislation, not with metaphysical truths
nor with natural religion (the "dogmas of universal faith"). What
he rejected was the purely political interpretation of the Mosaic
law. In his view, the revelation of the divine commandments was
not designed merely to establish a Jewish commonwealth, as Spinoza had suggested. Nor did he regard obedience to the laws as
nothing more than a means conducive to temporal felicity, the
well-being of the state and its citizens. He explicitly linked the
fulfillment of the revealed law to both the temporal and eternal
felicity of the Jewish people, and he was able to do so because he
considered the laws to be intimately related to the eternal verities
of reason. They were symbolic embodiments of those truths as
well as of certain historical truths which testified to the providence of God. There was, in other words, a metaphysical horizon
to Halakhah. Not in the way, to be sure, in which Kabbalah interpreted the reasons of the commandments (*ṭaʿamey ha-miṣwot*)
as reflections of the divine essence and as vehicles of man's participation in the divine process itself but, in a far simpler way, as
constant reminders of universal truths of reason or of the particular historical experiences of the Jewish people in which divine
providence had manifested itself. Despite these reservations, on

61. See Altmann, *Die trostvolle Aufklärung*, p. 11f.
62. See ibid., pp. 28–49 ("Moses Mendelssohn on Leibniz and Spinoza").

Mendelssohn's part, about Spinoza's view, there remains, however, a basic identity of outlook insofar as the structural division between truths and legislation, natural religion and revealed law is concerned. Like Spinoza, Mendelssohn does not attribute to revelation as such anything beyond the giving of the law.

An important corollary of this fundamental identity of views is the characterization, by both, of the Mosaic legislation as a unique, inimitable "theocracy." Although Mendelssohn prefers to discard this term—it had acquired a pejorative connotation—he does, in fact, subscribe to the notion it implies and he has no hesitation in using some of the most striking examples adduced in the *Tractatus* in order to substantiate the term.[63] It is this particular character of the Mosaic dispensation (which had been emphasized also by Hobbes and Locke) that supplies him with the perspective from which to answer the "Searcher's" challenge: The Mosaic constitution is not an "ecclesiastical" power system but a politico-religious one, a theocracy in its purest sense, a *civitas Dei*, as we might say, in which the element of power derives not from religion as such but from religion as wedded to the state, God being the Sovereign.

The point at which Mendelssohn parts company with Spinoza concerns the question as to the validity of the Mosaic law after the cessation of the Jewish commonwealth. For Spinoza, who accords the law only political significance, the collapse of the state meant the end of its legal force. For Mendelssohn, who sees in the law an embodiment of eternal truths, its validity stands unimpaired insofar as it legislates on matters concerned with the personal life of the Jew independent of land and state. Mendelssohn makes this point with particular regard to the ceremonial law, the body of commandments that Spinoza had declared to be "indifferent" in themselves—that is, unrelated to reason and morality—and made obligatory only by the Mosaic state legislation. Mendelssohn disagrees. Far from being "indifferent," they are in his opinion replete with an inner meaning, related as they are to

63. See Commentary, 128, 18–19; 29–31; 129, 2–6.

eternal and historical truths. Moreover, they retain their validity, he holds, also, and perhaps primarily, because they represent the particularizing elements of Jewish existence. Hence they are of vital importance as long as the need for Jewish distinctiveness persists. In a magnificent gesture of defiance, Mendelssohn declares his readiness to forgo the benefits of civil admission in case the price demanded for it were the renunciation of religious distinctiveness. No more striking testimony to his unbending Jewish loyalty could be imagined than this proud utterance.

<h1 style="text-align:center">III</h1>

The reception which *Jerusalem* met among Mendelssohn's German contemporaries was, with few exceptions, far from friendly.[64] The prevailing sentiment even among those critics who expressed admiration for the author was open or ill-concealed annoyance with his outspoken *confessio judaica*. Some saw in it an attack on Christianity. Section I invited many misgivings because of its reasoning against ecclesiastical power. What the "Searcher" (Cranz) thought about the answer given to his challenge he revealed only after Mendelssohn's death. His "Churchly and Heretical Almanac" (1787) contains an obituary in which he wrote: "In his *Jerusalem* [Mendelssohn] pleased me as little as he did many thousands of enlightened Christians and Jews. I cannot help suspecting that reasons of a political nature prevented him from stating his true opinion."[65] Mendelssohn himself hinted at the less than sympathetic manner in which his book had been received in a letter to Homberg written on June 14, 1783:

Jerusalem is a booklet of a special kind about which I would very much like to hear your opinion. This much is sure, its character is of a sort which neither orthodox nor heterodox people of both nations [Jews and Christians] expected. For all expected religious squabble, whereas I, following my bad habit, look at every step for speculative matter that can be tied in and in so doing I let the club drop. This displeases most readers. But who does write for most readers?

64. For a detailed account see *JubA* VIII, pp. lix–lxxxviii.
65. See *JubA* VIII, p. lx, where the full text is given.

Out of the many echoes, good and bad, a few samples may be offered here. A glowing tribute came from Kant who, in a letter to Mendelssohn, hailed the book as "the harbinger of a great, though slowly emerging, reform which will benefit not only your nation but others as well." He singled out for praise Mendelssohn's interpretation of Judaism as a religion consonant with liberty of conscience and he expressed the hope that the Christian churches would likewise endeavor to rid themselves of those features of the faith which troubled the conscience because they connected eternal salvation with belief in supposedly historical events. Kant was a radical Deist who strove to liberate religion from its historical elements, and he obviously projected his own ideas upon Mendelssohn.[66] His often-quoted laudatory letter should therefore be read with this fact in mind.

Mendelssohn was extremely happy with Kant's tribute and with two more, which came from Christian Garve, a widely respected philosopher of the Enlightenment, and Johann Gottfried Herder, the poet and trailblazer of Romanticism. It did not matter to him that Garve disputed the correctness of his theory of contracts and that Herder's praise was tinged with reservations. He valued the cordiality of their reaction. Herder disagreed with Mendelssohn's denial of ecclesiastical rights to power and property but he couched his opposition in amiable terms: "To be sure, in the heavenly, or future Jerusalem no one will doubt your theory," which clearly implied that in the present world the doctrine had no *locus standi*. This criticism appears again and again in reviews and books. Theologians generally felt that Mendelssohn had overstated his case and that he had done so because he had failed to differentiate between religion and church. While it was true that religion needed no coercive power and no property, the church as a corporate society did require them. This point was made most effectively in Johann Friedrich Zöllner's *On Moses Mendelssohn's Jerusalem* (Berlin, 1784). The author, a member of the Berlin Consistory and an admirer of Mendelssohn, undertook the task of

66. See also Commentary, 87, 4–14; 133, 14–28.

closely examining the premises of natural law on which the theory under question was based, and he found them wanting. Yet his was by no means the last word. Not only did Mendelssohn object but his position was defended by the illustrious jurist Höpfner. Ultimately, the conflict boiled down to a divergence of opinion between the old and the new school in natural law. Mendelssohn and Höpfner followed the Pufendorf-Wolff tradition, while Zöllner inclined toward the Thomasius school. Hufeland, another prominent jurist of the Thomasius school, was likewise a critic of Mendelssohn. He too found fault with the whole theory of imperfect rights and duties on which Mendelssohn's theses rested. Rather unfairly, he suggested that Mendelssohn's interpretation of natural law principles was devised in such a way as to yield the desired results. Höpfner, though taking Mendelssohn's side vis-à-vis Zöllner, questioned another thesis of his, the one which limits the legality of coercive rights instituted by the state to duties of humanity which are noncoercible in the state of nature. By this curb on positive legislation Mendelssohn had intended to safeguard the liberty of conscience.

The most severe but also most brilliant opposition to *Jerusalem* came from Johann Georg Hamann, the "Magus of the North," who seized the opportunity of delivering a well-aimed blow not merely to Mendelssohn, for whom he had a great deal of affection, but to the whole school of the Berlin Enlightenment of which he was a sworn enemy. His *Golgatha and Sheblimini!* (Berlin, 1784)[67] sprang from a deep aversion to what he considered shallow reasoning bereft of a sense of revelation through language and the inner eye of faith. Hamann, who was close to Herder, Jacobi, and Lavater, had contempt for natural law, which, he claimed, facilitated the legitimization of absolutism in government, a point of view that has been confirmed by contemporary historians.[68]

67. For an account of this book see *JubA* VIII, p. lxxiif. An excellent text edition with two sets of commentary is Lothar Schreiner's (Gütersloh, 1956).

68. See Diethelm Klippel, *Politische Freiheit und Freiheitsrechte im deutschen Naturrecht des 18. Jahrhunderts* (Paderborn, 1976), pp. 46f., 63f., and passim.

The secularization of hallowed concepts, the replacement of the biblical covenant idea by the theorem of the social contract, the recourse to the right of self-preservation as the source of legality; all this was anathema to him. He accused Mendelssohn of having betrayed his native heritage, the faith of his fathers, by aligning himself with the secular notions of natural law which were "empty shells" and "fruits of a pitiful sophistry." He charged Mendelssohn with Hobbesian tendencies, as allegedly evidenced by his definition of a "right" (*jus*). In the end, he even characterized Mendelssohn's basic attitude as "atticism" akin to "atheism." His merciless dissection and indictment of *Jerusalem* proceeds, to all intents and purposes, from a stance of (nonorthodox) fideism totally divorced from the Enlightenment frame of mind. The cryptic style and the partly apocalyptic imagery employed in his work are the very antithesis of Mendelssohn's lucid and graceful presentation. There is, therefore, no possibility of debate, only a clash of two worlds. Hamann's attack (to which no reply was given) is of value, however, because it puts in sharp relief the road Mendelssohn had taken.[69] Hamann's occasional flashes of insight allow us to perceive more clearly that Mendelssohn was leading the way to a nontheological, nonmystical version of Judaism such as came to dominate nineteenth- and early twentieth-century Jewish society. What Hamann flatly ignored was the fact that *Jerusalem*, for all its rationalist outlook, still retains firm roots in the Jewish tradition and an unshakable loyalty to its values; and that the plea for liberty of conscience and civic equality, which is at the heart of the work as a whole, was meant to secure for the Jewish people a fair share in the modern world which was about to dawn.

69. Cf. Fritz Bamberger, "Die geistige Gestalt Moses Mendelssohns," in *MGWJ*, LXXIII (n.s. XXXVII) (1929), 81–92, where an attempt is made to illumine Mendelssohn's personality by comparison with Hamann. The question how Mendelssohn arrived at his view of Judaism as a compound of separate parts is treated from a biographical angle in Bamberger's essay "Mendelssohn's Concept of Judaism," in Jospe, ed., *Studies*, pp. 343–60.

IV

The present edition of *Jerusalem* contains not only a new translation but also a rather extensive commentary, the need for which should be patent to all who have grappled with the text and were puzzled by the difficulty of comprehending it fully. The explicit references in which it abounds need to be identified and put in historical perspective. There is also a host of hidden references which call for clarification. *Jerusalem* is a book replete with learning—especially in natural and ecclesiastical law—and steeped in an exceedingly great variety of literature. Those who merely glance at it superficially may deceive themselves into believing that they have taken the measure of the book. Those who are serious in undertaking its study will realize that there is far more to it than meets the eye. It is for this kind of reader that the commentary is intended. It represents a revised and abridged version of my commentary—in German—in Volume VIII of the Mendelssohn Jubilee Edition which contains, *inter alia,* the text of *Jerusalem* (1783) and a more elaborate introduction than the one offered here.[70] I want to thank Mr. Günther Holzboog, publisher of the Jubilee Edition, for kindly permitting me to reproduce here the introduction and the commentary in a form suited to an Anglo-American readership.

ALEXANDER ALTMANN

70. *Moses Mendelssohn Gesammelte Schriften Jubiläumsausgabe,* edited by Alexander Altmann et al., Vol. VIII (Writings on Judaism II), ed. Alexander Altmann (Stuttgard-Bad Cannstatt, 1983).

MENDELSSOHN'S JERUSALEM

Jerusalem

oder

über religiöse Macht

und

Judentum.

Von

Moses Mendelssohn.

Mit allergnädigsten Freyheiten.

Berlin,
bey Friedrich Maurer, 1783.

Title page of the first edition.

SECTION I

STATE and religion—civil and ecclesiastical constitution—secular and churchly authority—how to oppose these pillars of social life to one another so that they are in balance and do not, instead, become burdens on social life, or weigh down its foundations more than they help to uphold it—this is one of the most difficult tasks of politics. For centuries, men have strived to solve it, and here and there enjoyed perhaps greater success in settling it practically than in resolving it in theory. Some thought it proper to separate these different relations of societal man into moral entities, and to assign to each a separate province, specific rights, duties, powers, and properties. But the extent of these different provinces and the boundaries dividing them have not yet been accurately fixed. Sometimes one sees the church move the boundary stone deep into the territory of the state; sometimes the state permits itself encroachments which, according to accepted standards, seem equally violent. Immeasurable evils have hitherto arisen, and still threaten to arise, from the dissension between these moral entities. When they take the field against each other, mankind is the victim of their discord; when they are in agreement, the noblest treasure of human felicity is lost; for they seldom agree but for the purpose of banishing from their realms a third moral entity, *liberty of conscience*, which knows how to derive some advantage from their disunity.

Despotism has the advantage of being consistent. However burdensome its demands may be to common sense, they are, nevertheless, coherent and systematic. It has a definite answer to every question. You need not trouble yourself any more about limits; for he who has everything no longer asks, "how much?" The same holds true for ecclesiastical government, according to Roman Catholic principles. It deals fully with every circumstance, and is, as it were, all of a piece. Grant it all its demands; you will at least know where you stand. Your structure is completely built, and perfect calm reigns in all its parts. To be sure, only that dreadful calm which, as Montesquieu says, prevails during the evening in a fortress which is to be taken by storm during the night. Yet he who considers tranquillity in doctrine and life to be felicity will find it nowhere better secured to him than under a Roman Catholic despot; or rather, since even in this case power is still too much divided, under the despotic rule of the church itself.

But as soon as liberty dares to move anything in this systematic structure, ruin immediately threatens on all sides; and in the end, one no longer knows what will remain standing. Hence the extraordinary confusion, the civil as well as ecclesiastical disturbances, during the early years of the Reformation, and the striking embarrassment on the part of the teachers and reformers themselves whenever they had occasion to settle the question of "how far?" in matters of right. Not only was it difficult, in practice, to keep the great multitude within proper bounds, once it was released from its fetters, but even in theory, one finds the writings of those times full of vague and wavering ideas whenever the definition of ecclesiastical power is discussed. The despotism of the Roman church was abolished—but what other form was to be introduced in its place? Even now, in our more enlightened times, the textbooks of ecclesiastical law could not be rid of this vagueness. The clergy will not or cannot give up all claims to a *constitution,* yet no one really knows in what it should consist. One wishes to settle doctrinal differences, without recognizing a Supreme Judge. One still continues to refer to an independent church, without knowing where it is to be found. One advances a claim to power and rights, yet one cannot state who should exercise them.

Thomas Hobbes lived at a time when fanaticism, combined with a disorderly sense of liberty, no longer knew any bounds and was ready to bring royal authority under its foot and subvert the entire constitution of the realm (as it eventually did). Weary of civil strife and by nature inclined toward a quiet, speculative life, he regarded tranquillity and safety, no matter how they were obtained, as the greatest felicity; and these, he thought, were to be found only in the unity and indivisibility of the highest power in the state. He believed, therefore, that the public welfare would be best served if everything, even our judgment of right and wrong, were made subject to the supreme power of the civil authority. In order to do so more legitimately, he assumed that man is *entitled* by nature to everything it has endowed him with the *ability* to obtain. The state of nature is a state of tumult, a *war of all against all,* in which everyone *may* do what he *can* do; everything one has the power to do is right. This unfortunate condition lasted until men agreed to put an end to their misery, to renounce right and might, as far as public safety was concerned, and to place both in the hands of an established authority. Henceforth, whatever that authority ordered was right.

Hobbes either had no taste for civil liberty or wished to see it destroyed rather than have it thus abused. But in order to retain for himself the liberty of thought, of which he made more use than anyone else, he resorted to a subtle twist. According to his system, all *right* is grounded in *power,* and all *obligation* in *fear.* Since God is infinitely superior in power to any civil authority, the right of God is also infinitely superior to the right of the latter. Consequently, the fear of God obliges us to perform duties which must not yield to any fear of the civil authority. This, however, applies only to *inward religion,* which was the philosopher's sole concern. The outward [mode of] *worship* he subjected entirely to the dictates of the civil authority; every innovation in church matters without its sanction is not only high treason, but blasphemy as well. The collisions which are bound to ensue between inward and outward worship he sought to remove by means of the subtlest distinctions; and although many gaps still remain, making the weakness of the accord quite evident, one cannot help admiring the ingenuity with which he sought to render his system coherent.

There is, at bottom, a great deal of truth in all Hobbes's assertions. The absurd consequences to which they lead follow solely from the exaggeration with which he propounded them, whether out of a love of paradox or in compliance with the needs of his time. Moreover, in his day the concepts of natural law were, in part, still not sufficiently enlightened. In matters of moral philosophy Hobbes has the same merit as Spinoza has in metaphysics. His ingenious errors have occasioned inquiry. The ideas of *right* and *duty*, of *power* and *obligation*, have been better developed; one has learned to distinguish more correctly between physical and moral ability, between might and right. These distinctions have become so intimately fused with our language that, nowadays, the refutation of Hobbes's system seems to be a matter of common sense, and to be accomplished, as it were, by language itself. This is a distinctive feature of all moral truths. As soon as they are brought to light, they become so much a part of the spoken language and so connected with man's everyday notions that they become evident even to ordinary minds; and now we wonder how man could ever have stumbled on so level a road. But we fail to consider the pains it cost to clear this path through the wilderness.

Hobbes himself must have been aware, in more ways than one, of the inadmissible results which necessarily followed from his exaggerated propositions. If men are not bound by nature to any duty, they do not even have a duty to keep their contracts. If there is, in the state of nature, no binding obligation other than that based upon fear and powerlessness, contracts will remain valid only as long as they are supported by fear and powerlessness. Thus, men, by their contracts, will not have come any step closer to their security, and will still find themselves in the primitive state of universal warfare. But if contracts are to remain valid, man must by nature, without contracts and agreements, lack the moral ability to act against a compact into which he has voluntarily entered; that is, he must not be permitted to do so, even if he can; he must not have the *moral* faculty, even though he may have the *physical. Might* and *right* are, therefore, different things; and in the state of nature, too, they were heterogeneous ideas. Moreover, Hobbes prescribes to the highest authority in the state strict laws not to command anything which would be contrary to its subjects' welfare. For although that authority is not accountable to any man, it does owe an account to the Supreme Judge; and even though, according to his principles, it is not bound by the fear of any *human power,* it is still bound by the fear of the *Omnipotent,* who has made his will in this respect sufficiently known. Hobbes is very explicit on this point, and is, in fact, less indulgent to the gods of the earth than his system would lead one to expect. Yet this very fear of the Omnipotent, which should bind kings and princes to certain duties toward their subjects, can also become a source of obligation for every individual in the state of nature. And so we would once again have a *solemn* law of nature, even though Hobbes does not want to admit it. In this fashion, in our day, every student of natural law can gain a triumph over Thomas Hobbes, to whom, at bottom, he nevertheless owes this triumph.

Locke, who lived during the same period of deep confusion, sought to protect the liberty of conscience in another manner. In his letters *concerning toleration* he proceeds from the basic definition: *A state is a society of men who unite for the purpose of collectively promoting their temporal welfare.* From this it follows, quite naturally, that the state is not to concern itself at all with the citizens' convictions regarding their eternal felicity, but is to tolerate everyone who conducts himself well as a citizen, that is, who does not interfere with the temporal felicity of his fellow citizens. The state as such is not to take notice of differences of religion, for religion as such has no necessary influence on temporal matters, and is linked to them solely through the arbitrary measures of men.

Very well! If the dispute allowed itself to be settled by a verbal definition, I would know of none that is more convenient; and if by this means one could have talked the agitated minds of his time out of their intolerance, it would not have been necessary for the good Locke himself to go into exile as often as he did. But what prevents us, they ask, from seeking to promote collectively our eternal welfare as well? And indeed, what reason do we have to restrict the purpose of society solely to the *temporal?* If men *can* promote their eternal felicity by public measures, it should be their natural duty to *do* so, their rational obligation to join forces for this purpose and to enter into social relations. If, however, this be the case, and the state as such be preoccupied solely with the temporal, a question arises: To whom are we to entrust the care for the eternal? To the church? Now we are, once again, back at our starting point. State and church—concern for the temporal and concern for the eternal—civil and ecclesiastical authority. The former relates to the latter as the importance of the temporal does to that of the eternal. The state is, therefore, subordinate to religion, and must give way whenever a collision arises. Now resist, whoever can, Cardinal Bellarmine and the frightful concatenation of his arguments [to the effect] that the head of the church, on behalf of the eternal, ought to be in command over everything temporal, and therefore possesses, at least indirectly,* sovereign authority over all goods and minds in the world; that all secular realms are indirectly subject to the dominion of the spiritual monarch, and must take their orders from him if they have to alter their form of government, depose their kings and appoint others in their place, because very often the eternal

---

* Bellarmine himself was nearly declared a heretic by Pope Sixtus V for ascribing to him only indirect power over temporal matters of kings and princes. His work was placed on the Index of the Inquisition.

welfare of the state cannot be maintained in any other way—and so forth according to the maxims of his order, which Bellarmine propounds with so much ingenuity in his work *De Romano pontifice*. All the objections raised in voluminous works against the cardinal's sophisms seem ineffective as soon as the state completely abandons the care for eternity.

On the other hand, it is, in the strictest sense, neither in keeping with the truth nor advantageous to man's welfare to sever the temporal so neatly from the eternal. At bottom, man will never partake of eternity; his eternality is merely an *incessant temporality*. His temporality never ends; it is, therefore, an essential part of his permanency and inseparable from it. One confuses ideas if one opposes his temporal welfare to his eternal felicity. And this confusion of ideas is not without practical consequences. It shifts the borders of the sphere in which man can act in accordance with his capacities, and strains his powers beyond the goal which Providence has so wisely set for him. "On the dark path," if I may be allowed to quote my own words,* "on the dark path man has to walk here, he is granted just as much light as he needs for the next steps he has to take. More would only blind him, and any lateral light would only confuse him." It is necessary for man to be reminded constantly that with this life all does not end for him; that there stands before him an endless future, for which his life here below is a preparation, just as in all of creation every present is a preparation for the future. This life, say the rabbis, is a vestibule in which one must comport oneself in the manner in which one wishes to appear in the inner chamber. But you must also beware of establishing any further opposition between this life and the future, and of leading men to think that their true welfare in this life is not one and the same as their eternal felicity in the future; that it is one thing to care for their temporal, and another to care for their eternal well-being, and it is possible to preserve one while neglecting the other. Delusions of this kind

* See *Notes to Abbt's Friendly Correspondence*, p. 28.

shift the viewpoint and the horizon of the weak-sighted man who
has to walk along a narrow path; he is in danger of becoming
dizzy and of stumbling on a level road. Thus many a man does
not dare to enjoy the benefits bestowed by Providence in the here
and now for fear of losing an equal portion in the hereafter, and
many a man has become a bad citizen on earth in the hope of
thereby becoming a better citizen of heaven.

I have sought, through the following considerations, to clarify
for my own benefit the ideas of state and religion, of their limits
and their influence on each other as well as upon [the state of]
felicity in civil life. As soon as man recognizes that outside of
society he can fulfill his duties toward himself and toward the author of his existence as poorly as he can fulfill his duties toward
his neighbor, and, hence, can no longer remain in his solitary condition without a sense of wretchedness, he is obliged to leave that
condition and to enter into society with those in a like situation in
order to satisfy their needs through mutual aid and to promote their
common good by common measures. Their common good, however,
includes the present as well as the future, the spiritual as well as
the earthly. One is inseparable from the other. Unless we fulfill
our obligations, we can expect felicity neither here nor there,
neither on earth nor in heaven. Now, two things belong to the true
fulfillment of our duties: *action* and *conviction*. Action accom-
plishes what duty demands, and conviction causes that action to
proceed from the proper source, that is, from pure motives.

Hence actions and convictions belong to the perfection of man,
and society should, as far as possible, take care of both by collective efforts, that is, it should direct the actions of its members toward the common good, and cause convictions which lead to these
actions. The one is the *government,* the other the *education* of societal man. To both man is led by *reasons;* to actions by *reasons
that motivate the will,* and to convictions by *reasons that persuade
by their truth.* Society should therefore establish both through public institutions in such a way that they will be in accord with the
common good.

The reasons which lead men to rational actions and convictions rest partly on the relations of men to each other, partly on the relations of men to their Creator and Keeper. The former are the province of the *state*, the latter that of *religion*. Insofar as men's actions and convictions can be made to serve the common weal through reasons arising from their relations to each other, they are a matter for the civil constitution; but insofar as the relations between man and God can be seen as their source, they belong to the *church*, the *synagogue*, or the *mosque*. In a good many textbooks of the so-called ecclesiastical law one reads serious inquiries as to whether Jews, heretics, and heterodox believers can also have a church. In view of the immeasurable privileges which the church so-called is in the habit of arrogating to itself, the question is not as absurd as it must appear to an unbiased reader. To me, however, as it can be easily imagined, the difference of nomenclature is of no consequence. Public institutions for the formation [*Bildung*] of man that concern his relations with God I call *church;* those that concern his relations with man I call *state*. By the formation of man I understand the effort to arrange both actions and convictions in such a way that they will be in accord with his felicity; that they will *educate* and *govern* men.

Blessed be the state which succeeds in governing the nation by education itself; that is, by infusing it with such morals and convictions as will of themselves tend to produce actions conducive to the common weal, and need not be constantly urged on by the spur of the law. In social life, man must renounce certain of his rights for the common good or as one may say, he must very often sacrifice his own advantage to benevolence. He will be happy if this sacrifice is made on his own prompting and when he realizes, in each instance, that he acted solely for the sake of benevolence. *Benevolence*, in reality, makes us happier than *selfishness;* but we must, while exercising it, be aware that it springs from ourselves and is the display of our powers. Not, as some sophists interpret it, because everything in man proceeds from self-love; but because benevolence is no longer benevolence, and has neither value nor merit if it does not flow from the free impulse of the benevolent individual.

This will perhaps enable us to give a satisfactory answer to the well-known question: *Which form of government is the best?* This question has hitherto received contradictory answers, all of them having the same appearance of truth. It is, in reality, too vague a question, almost as vague as a similar one in medicine: *Which food is the most wholesome?* Every complexion, every climate, every age, sex, and mode of life, etc., requires a different answer. The same is true with regard to our politico-philosophical problem. For every people, at every level of culture at which it finds itself, a different form of government will be the best. Certain despotically ruled nations would be extremely miserable if they were left to govern themselves, as miserable as certain free-spirited republicans if they were subjected to the rule of a monarch. Indeed, many a nation will alter its form of government as often as changes take place in its culture, way of life, and convictions, and, in the course of centuries, will pass through the whole cycle of forms of government, in all their shades and combinations, from anarchy to despotism; yet it will always be found to have chosen the form of government which was best for it under existing circumstances.

Under all circumstances and conditions, however, I consider the infallible measure of the excellence of a form of government to lie in the degree to which it achieves its purposes by morals and convictions; in the degree, therefore, to which government is by education itself. In other words, in the degree to which the citizen is given the opportunity to understand vividly (*anschauend*) that he has to renounce some of his rights only for the common good; that he has to sacrifice some of his own advantage only for the sake of benevolence; and that he therefore gains as much, on the one hand, through a display of benevolence as he loses, on the other, by sacrifice. Indeed, that by means of sacrifice itself he greatly adds to his inner felicity, since it enhances the merit and the worth of the benevolent act and therefore also the true perfection of the benevolent individual. It is, for example, not advisable for the state to assume all the duties of love for our fellow man down to the *distribution of alms,* and to transform them into public institutions. Man is conscious of his own worth when he performs charitable acts, when he vividly (*anschauend*) perceives how he alleviates the distress of his fellow man by his gift; when he gives because he *wants* to give. But if he gives because he *must,* he feels only his fetters.

Hence, one of the state's principal efforts must be to govern men through morals and convictions. Now, there is no other way of improving the convictions, and thereby the morals, of men than through *persuasion.* Laws do not alter convictions; arbitrary punishments and rewards produce no principles, refine no morals. Fear and hope are no criteria of truth. Knowledge, reasoning, and persuasion alone can bring forth principles which, with the help of *authority* and *example,* can pass into *morals.* And it is here that religion should come to the aid of the state, and the church should become a pillar of civil felicity. It is the business of the church to convince people, in the most emphatic manner, of the truth of noble principles and convictions; to show them that duties toward men are also duties toward God, the violation of which is in itself the greatest misery; that serving the state is true service of God; that charity is his most sacred will; and that true knowledge of the Creator cannot leave behind in the soul any hatred for men. To teach this is the business, duty, and vocation of religion; to preach it, the business and duty of its ministers. How, then, could it ever have occurred to men to permit religion to teach and its ministers to preach exactly the opposite?

But if the character of a nation, the level of culture to which it has ascended, the increase in population which has accompanied the nation's prosperity, the greater complexity of relations and connections, excessive luxury, and other causes make it impossible to govern the nation by convictions alone, the state will have to resort to public measures, coercive laws, punishments of crime, and rewards of merit. If a citizen is unwilling to defend the fatherland from an inner sense of duty, let him be tempted by rewards or compelled by force. If men no longer have any sense of the intrinsic value of justice, if they no longer realize that honesty in trade and traffic is true felicity, let injustice be chastised and fraud be punished. Admittedly, in this manner the state attains the ultimate aim of society only by half. External motivations do not make a man happy, even though they have an effect on him. The man who avoids deception because he loves honesty is happier than one who is merely afraid of the arbitrary punishments the state linked with fraud. But to his fellow man it does not matter what motives cause the wrong to remain undone, or by what means his rights and property are safeguarded. The fatherland is defended, regardless of whether the citizens fight for it out of love or out of fear of positive punishment, even though the defenders themselves will be happy in the former and unhappy in the latter case. If the *inner felicity of society* cannot be entirely preserved, let at least *outward peace and security* be obtained, if need be, through *coercion.*

The state will therefore be content, if need be, with mechanical deeds, with works without spirit, with conformity of action without conformity in thought. Even the man who does not believe in laws must obey them, once they have received official sanction. The state may grant the individual citizen the right to pass judgment on the laws, but not the right to act in accordance with his judgment. This right he had to renounce as a member of society, for without this renunciation civil society is a chimera. Not so with religion! It knows no act without conviction, no work without spirit, no conformity in deed without conformity in the mind. Religious actions without religious thoughts are mere puppetry, not service of God. They themselves must therefore proceed from the spirit, and can neither be purchased by reward nor compelled by punishment. But religion withdraws its support also from civil actions, insofar as they are not produced by conviction, but by force. Nor can the state expect any further help from religion, once it can act only by means of rewards and punishments; for insofar as this is the case, man's duties toward God no longer enter into consideration, and the relations between man and his Creator are without effect. The only aid religion can render to the state consists in *teaching and consoling;* that is, in imparting to the citizens, through its divine doctrines, such convictions as are conducive to the public weal, and in uplifting with its otherworldly consolations the poor wretch who has been condemned to death as a sacrifice for the common good.

Here we already see an essential difference between state and religion. The state gives orders and coerces, religion teaches and persuades. The state prescribes *laws,* religion *commandments.* The state has *physical power* and uses it when necessary; the power of religion is *love* and *beneficence.* The one abandons the disobedient and expels him; the other receives him in its bosom and seeks to instruct, or at least to console him, even during the last moments of his earthly life, and not entirely in vain. In one word: civil society, viewed as a moral person, can have the *right of coercion,* and, in fact, has actually obtained this right through the social contract. Religious society lays no claim to the *right of coercion,* and cannot obtain it by any possible contract. The *state* possesses *perfect,* the *church* only *imperfect* rights. In order to place this in a proper light, I may be allowed to ascend to first principles and to examine more closely

> *the origin of the rights of coercion and*
> *the validity of contracts among men.*

I court the danger of becoming too speculative for some readers. Yet everyone is free to skip what does not suit his taste. To the friends of natural law it may not be disagreeable to see how I sought to define for myself its first principles.

The *authority [Befugnis]* (the moral capacity) to make use of a thing as a means for promoting one's felicity is called a *right.* This capacity is called moral if it is consistent with the laws of wisdom and goodness, and the things which can serve as means of attaining felicity are called *goods.* Man has, therefore, a right to certain goods or means toward felicity, insofar as this right does not contradict the laws of wisdom and goodness.

Whatever must be done in accordance with the laws of wisdom and goodness, or the opposite of which would be contrary to the laws of wisdom or goodness, is called *morally necessary*. The moral necessity (obligation) to do, or omit doing something is a *duty*.

The laws of wisdom and goodness cannot contradict each other. If, therefore, I have a right to do something, my fellow man cannot have the right to prevent me from doing it; otherwise, the very same action would be morally possible and morally impossible at the same time. To every right, therefore, there corresponds a duty; to the right to act, there corresponds the duty to suffer [the action], to the right to demand, the duty to perform; etc.*

Wisdom combined with goodness is called *justice*. The law of justice on which a right is founded is either of such a nature that all the conditions under which the predicate belongs to the subject are invested in the holder of the right, or they are not. In the first case, it is a *perfect,* in the second an *imperfect right*. That is to say, with an imperfect right, a part of the conditions under which the right applies is dependent on the knowledge and conscience of the person who bears the duty. In the first instance, therefore, he is *perfectly* bound to perform the duty which corresponds to the other person's right; in the second instance, he is bound only *imperfectly*. There are *perfect* and *imperfect duties* as well as *rights*. The first are called compulsory rights and com-

---

* One may object that, in time of war, a soldier has the right to kill an enemy, without the latter being obligated to submit to being killed.

However, the soldier has this right not as a man, but as a member or as a mercenary of the state engaged in war. For the state is either actually offended, or pretends to be offended, and [it claims] that it can obtain satisfaction only by the use of force. The battle therefore is not really between man and man, but between state and state, and, obviously, only one of the two warring states has right on its side. The offender is certainly obligated by the duty to give satisfaction to the offended, and to suffer everything without which the latter cannot regain his injured rights.

pulsory duties; the others, however, are called *claims* (*petitions*) and *duties of conscience*. The first are *external*, the others only *internal*. Compulsory rights may be *exacted* by force, but petitions may be *denied*. Omission of compulsory duties is an offense, an injustice; omission of duties of conscience, however, is merely *unfairness*.

The goods to which a man has an exclusive right are (1) his own capacities; (2) whatever he produces by means of those capacities or advances by his care, that is, cultivates, tends, protects, etc. (the products of his industry); (3) goods of nature, which he has connected with the products of his industry in such a way that they cannot be separated from them without being destroyed and which he has consequently appropriated. These goods constitute his *natural property*. Even in the state of nature, before any contract whatsoever was enacted among men, they were excluded from the original *joint ownership of goods*. For men originally possess in common only those goods which are produced by nature, without man's industry and care. *Not all property is merely conventional*.

Man cannot be happy without *beneficence*, not without *passive*, but also not without *active*, beneficence. He cannot become perfect except through mutual assistance, through an exchange of service and reciprocal service, through active and passive connection with his fellow man.

If, therefore, a man possesses goods or owns certain means of attaining felicity which he can spare, that is, which are not necessarily required for maintaining his *existence* but serve the *improvement of his existence,* he is obligated to employ a part of them for the benefit of his fellow man, that is, for *benevolence*. For the *improvement of one's existence* is inseparable from *benevolence*.

But for similar reasons, he, too, has a right to the benevolence of his fellow man. He may expect and lay claim to the assistance of others by means of the goods which they can spare in order to help him attain his perfection. Only let it always be remembered what we mean by the word *goods;* viz., all of man's *internal* and *external* capacities, insofar as they can become the means of achieving felicity for him or for others. Therefore everything that man possesses in the state of nature in the way of industry, capacity, and powers, everything which he can call *his own,* is devoted partly to his *own use* (his own benefit), partly to *benevolence.*

However, since man's capacity is limited and therefore exhaustible, it may occasionally happen that the same capacity or goods cannot simultaneously serve me and my neighbor. Nor can I employ the same capacity or goods for the benefit of all my fellow men, or at all times, or under all circumstances. And since I am obliged to make the best possible use of my powers, everything depends on a choice, and on the more precise determination as to *how much* of what is mine should I devote to *benevolence?* For whose benefit? At what time and under what circumstances?

Who is to make these decisions? Who shall settle the cases of collision? Not my neighbor, for he is not aware of all the grounds on which the conflict of duties must be decided. Besides, everyone else would have the same right, and if, as would most likely happen, each of my fellow men were to decide to his own advantage, the predicament would not be resolved.

Hence, in the state of nature, to me, and to me alone, appertains the right to decide *whether, to what extent, when, for whose benefit,* and under what conditions I am obliged to exercise beneficence. In the state of nature I cannot be made to exercise beneficence by compulsory means at any time. My duty to be beneficent is only a *duty of conscience,* concerning which, externally, I do not have to render an account to anyone, just as my right to the beneficence of others is only a right to petition, which may be refused. In the state of nature, all of men's *positive* duties toward each other are only *imperfect* duties, just as their positive rights against one another are only imperfect rights, and not duties which can be exacted or rights that can be enforced. Only the duties and rights of omission are perfect in the state of nature. I am perfectly obliged not to *injure* anyone, and I have a perfect right to prevent anyone from *injuring* me. To injure, however, means, as is well known, *to act against the perfect right of another person.*

One might, indeed, imagine that the duty to provide indemnification is a positive duty incumbent upon man even in the state of nature. If I have done injury to my neighbor, I am externally obligated, without any contract, and solely by the laws of natural justice, to make restitution to him for the injury inflicted, and he may compel me by force to do so.

However, even though indemnification is indeed a positive act, the obligation to provide it is derived, in reality, from the duty of omission: *Do not offend!* For the injury which I have inflicted upon my neighbor must be regarded as an *ongoing offense,* as long as its effects are not undone. I act, therefore, strictly speaking, contrary to a negative duty, as long as I omit the indemnity; for I continue to offend. Therefore, the duty to provide indemnification constitutes no exception to the rule that in the state of nature man is *independent,* that is, under no positive obligation to anyone. No one has a compulsory right to prescribe to me how much of my powers I should employ for the good of others and upon whom the benefit of my labors should be conferred. It must be left solely to my discretion to determine the rule by which I am to settle cases of collision.

Nor is the natural relationship between parents and children opposed to this universal law of nature. It can readily be conceived that in a state of nature the only people who are independent are those who can be confidently expected to be capable of making rational decisions in cases of collision. Therefore, before they reach the age when they can be confidently expected to be capable of using their reason, children have no claim to independence, and must let others decide how and for what purposes they are to employ their powers and capacities. The parents, on their part, must train their children, step by step, in the *art of making rational decisions in cases of collision,* and gradually allow them, as their reason grows stronger, to make free and independent use of their powers.

Now it is true that even in the state of nature parents are *exter-*

nally obligated to do certain things for the benefit of their children. These things, one might suppose, represent a positive duty which can be enforced, without any contract, in accordance with the eternal laws of wisdom and goodness. But it seems to me that the right to compel the education of children belongs, in the state of nature, solely to the parents themselves, vis-à-vis each other, but not to any third party, who might wish to look after the children's interest and force their parents to educate them. No one, in the state of nature, has the authority to coerce parents to educate their children. But that the parents themselves have the right to compel each other to do so, follows from the agreement which they are presumed to have made, in fact, if not in words.

Whoever helps to beget a being capable of felicity is obligated, by the laws of nature, to promote its felicity, as long as it is not yet able to provide for its own advancement. This is the natural duty of education which is, to be sure, only a duty of conscience. Still, by the act itself, the parents have agreed to assist each other in this respect, that is, to discharge together their duty of conscience. In a word: the parents, through the very act of cohabitation, have entered into a state of matrimony. They have made a tacit contract to render capable of felicity, that is, *to educate,* the being, destined for felicity, for whose coming into the world they are jointly responsible.

All the duties and rights of the state of matrimony flow quite naturally from this principle. It is not necessary to adopt, as the teachers of jurisprudence are in the habit of doing, a double principle, in order to derive from it all the duties of marriage and the household. The duty to educate follows from the agreement to beget children; and the obligation to set up a common household follows from the common duty of education. Marriage, therefore, is, in reality, nothing other than an agreement between two persons of different sexes to bring children into the world; and upon this agreement rests the entire system of their mutual duties and rights.* For in what follows it will be shown that men, by

* When individuals of different religions enter into a state of matrimony, the principles according to which they will conduct their household and edu-

cate their children are agreed upon in the marriage contract. But what if the husband or wife changes his or her principles after marriage and converts to another religion? Does this give the other party the right to press for a divorce? In a small treatise (*Das Forschen nach Licht und Recht,* Berlin, Friedrich Maurer, 1782), which purports to have been written in Vienna and which I shall have occasion to refer to more extensively in the second section, it is stated that just such a case is now pending there. A Jew who converted to the Christian religion is said to have expressed his desire to retain his wife who has remained Jewish, and legal proceedings are said to have been initiated. The aforementioned author decides according to the system of liberty: "One rightly supposes," he says, "that a difference of religion cannot be recognized as a valid cause for divorce. According to the principles of the wise Joseph, difference of opinion in churchly matters cannot stand in the way of social ties."

Very rash, I should think. I hope an emperor who is as just as he is wise will also lend his ear to the counterarguments, and will not permit the system of liberty to be misused to inflict oppression and violence. If marriage is merely a civil contract (and it cannot be anything else between a Jew and a Jewess, even according to Catholic principles), the wording and the conditions of the contract must be interpreted and explained in accordance with the intentions of the contracting parties, and not those of the legislator or judge. If, according to the principles of the contracting parties, it can be maintained with certainty that they must have understood certain words in this and no other way, and that, had they been asked, they would have explained them in this and in no other way, then this morally certain explanation, which is taken to be a tacit and implied condition of the contract, must be as valid in law as if it had been explicitly agreed upon.

Now since both partners still professed the Jewish religion, at least outwardly, when they entered into the contract, it is obvious that they had no other intention but to conduct their household according to Jewish rules of life and to educate their children according to Jewish principles. It is at least certain that the partner who took her religion seriously could have assumed nothing else; and had she been, at that time, apprehensive of a change of this kind, and had such a condition come up for discussion, she certainly would not have expressed herself in any other way. She knew and expected nothing other than to take her place in a household governed by ancestral rules of life and to bear children whom she would be able to educate according to the principles of her fathers. If the difference is important to this person, if it is a matter of record that the difference of religion must have been important to her, at the time the contract was entered into, the contract must be interpreted according to her notions and convictions. Even if the entire state were to have different views on this matter, it would have no influence on the meaning of the contract. The husband has changed his principles and adopted another religion. If the wife is now forced to enter into a household which is contrary to her conscience and to educate her children according to principles which are not her own; in a word, if she is compelled to accept and have agreement, leave the state of nature and enter into the state of society. Consequently, the duty of parents to educate their children, even though it can, in some respects, be called a compulsory duty, is no exception to the previously mentioned *law of nature:* that man, in the state of nature, is independent, and that to him alone belongs the right to settle cases of collision between [his] *own use* and *benevolence.*

This right constitutes man's *natural liberty,* which makes up a great portion of his felicity. Independence, therefore, is included among his *proper goods,* which he is entitled to employ as a means of attaining felicity. Whoever disturbs him in the use of this right *offends him* and commits an external act of injustice. Man, in the state of nature, is the master of all that is *his,* of the free use of his powers and capacities, of the free use of whatever

---

forced upon her conditions of a marriage contract to which she never agreed, she would obviously suffer an injustice and, by a pretense of liberty of conscience, one would obviously allow oneself to be misled into the most absurd coercion of conscience. The conditions of the contract can now no longer be fulfilled. The husband, who has changed principles, is, if not *in dolo,* at least *in culpa,* [responsible for the fact] that this is the case. Must the wife submit to coercion of conscience because the husband wants to have liberty of conscience? When did she agree or when could she have agreed to that? Should not her conscience also be free, and should not the party that caused the change answer also for its consequences, indemnify the other party, and reinstate her, as far as possible, in her former status? Nothing, it seems to me, could be simpler, and the matter speaks for itself. No one ought to be compelled to accept conditions of a contract to which he could not have agreed without violating his own principles.

With respect to the education of their children, both parties have an equal right. If we had impartial educational institutions, it would be necessary, in such disputed cases, to educate the children impartially, until they reached the age of reason and were able to choose for themselves. But as long as such institutions have not been established, as long as our educational institutions are still connected with a positive religion, it is evident that the prerogative to educate the children belongs to the party that has remained true to the principles formerly common to both, and has not changed them. This, too, follows quite naturally from the aforementioned principles; and it is violent presumption and religious oppression if the opposite occurs anywhere. An emperor as just and wise as Joseph will surely not permit such violent abuse of the power of the church in his states.

he has produced by exercising them (that is, the fruits of his industry) or of whatever he has inseparably connected with the fruits of his industry. It depends on him alone *how much, when,* and for the benefit of *which* of his fellow men he will dispense with some of the goods which he can spare. All his fellow men have only an imperfect right to his surplus goods, a right to *petition;* and he, the absolute master, has a *duty of conscience* to devote a part of his goods to *benevolence.* Indeed, he is even obligated at times to sacrifice [what he has set aside for] his *own use* to benevolence, insofar as the practice of benevolence renders man happier than selfishness. But this sacrifice must proceed from his own will and his own free impulse. All this seems to be settled beyond any doubt. But I will go a step farther.

Once this independent man has passed a judgment, that judgment must be valid. If, in the state of nature, I have decided *to whom, when,* and *how much* I wish to relinquish of what belongs to me; if I have sufficiently declared this, my free decision, and my neighbor, for whose benefit this declaration was made, has received the property, the action must have *force* and *effect,* if my right is to mean anything at all. If my declaration is ineffective and leaves matters as they were; if it does not produce, in regard to a right, the changes which I had resolved on, my supposed right to make such a declaration contains an obvious contradiction. Therefore, my decision must have an effect—it must change the condition of the right. The property in question must cease to be *mine* and actually have become that of my neighbor. My neighbor's previously imperfect right must have become, through this transaction, a perfect right, just as my formerly perfect right must have been transformed into an imperfect right. Otherwise my decision would be null and void. Consequently, after the transaction has been completed, I can no longer claim the relinquished property without acting unjustly. If I do so, I offend; I act in opposition to the perfect right of my neighbor.

This holds true of material, *movable* goods that can be passed from hand to hand, as well as of *immovable* or even *spiritual* goods, the right to which can be ceded and received only by a sufficient *declaration of will.* In reality, everything depends solely upon this declaration of will, and even the actual transfer of movable goods is valid only insofar as it is taken to be a sign of a sufficient declaration of will. The mere transfer, viewed by itself, neither gives nor takes away a right, whenever this intent is not connected with it. If I put something in my neighbor's hand, I have not yet, on that account, *delivered* it to him; if I take something belonging to him into my hand, I have not yet, by that action, rightfully *received* it, unless I indicate that the act is done with this intent. Since, however, the transfer itself is only valid as a sign, other significant signs may be substituted for it in cases in which the actual delivery of goods does not take place. It is, therefore, possible to cede and relinquish to others one's right to immovable or even intangible goods by means of sufficiently intelligible signs.

In this manner, property can pass from person to person. Whatever I have made my own by my industry becomes, through cession, the property of another, and I cannot take it back from him without committing an *injustice.*

And now we need take but one more step, and the validity of contracts will be placed on a sure footing. The right to decide cases of collision is in itself, as was shown above, an *intangible* [literally, incorporeal] good of the independent man, insofar as it can become a means of attaining felicity. In the state of nature, every man has a perfect right, and his neighbor has an imperfect right, to the enjoyment of this means toward felicity. Since, however, the use of this right is, at least in many cases, not absolutely necessary for self-preservation, it is a *dispensable* good, one which, as we have shown, can be ceded and relinquished to someone else through a sufficient declaration of will. An act by which this is done is called a *promise,* and if the *acceptance* by the second party is added to it, that is, if the other party sufficiently indicates its consent to this transfer of rights, a *contract* comes into being. Thus, a contract is nothing but the *cession,* by the one party, and the *acceptance*, by the other party, of the right to decide cases of collision involving certain goods which the promising party can spare.

Such a contract must be kept, according to what has been shown above. The right to decide, which previously formed a part of my goods, that is, which was my own, has become, through this cession, the good of my neighbor, his property, and I cannot take it away from him again without committing an offense. The claim which he, as well as everyone else, could make to the use of my independence, insofar as it is not necessary for my self-preservation, has been transformed by this act into a perfect right, which he is entitled to make effective by force. This consequence is indisputable, if my right to decide is to have force and effect.*

I will now leave my speculative considerations and return to my former track. But first I must lay down the conditions under which a contract is valid and must be kept, in accordance with the principles outlined above.

1. Caius possesses a property (some means toward felicity: the use of his natural abilities themselves, or the right to the fruits of his industry and to the goods of nature connected with them, or whatever else has become his by right, whether it be something tangible or intangible, such as privileges, liberties and the like).

2. This property, however, is not indispensable to his *existence*

---

* To this very plausible analysis of ideas I have been led by my very worthy friend, *Assistenzrath* Klein, the philosophical jurist, with whom I have had the pleasure of discussing this matter. It seems to me that this theory of contracts is both simple and fruitful. Ferguson, in his *Moral Philosophy*, and his excellent translator find the necessity of keeping promises in the expectation aroused in our fellow man, and in the immorality of deception. But from this, it seems, there results only a duty of conscience. Whatever part of my goods I was formerly conscience-bound to relinquish for the benefit of my fellow men in general, I am now conscience-bound to grant to this individual in particular because of the *expectations* I have aroused in him. But what has transformed this *duty of conscience* into a *compulsory duty?* It seems to me that in order to explain this it is indispensable to have recourse to the above-mentioned principles of cession in general, and the rights of deciding in cases of collision in particular.

and *can*, therefore, be employed for the sake of *benevolence*, that is, for the use of others.

3. Sempronius has an *imperfect right* to this property. He can, like everyone else, *petition*, but not *compel*, Caius that this property should *now* be used for his benefit. The right to decide belongs to Caius, is his, and may not be taken away from him by force.

4. Caius, however, makes use of his perfect right, decides in favor of Sempronius, and makes this decision known by sufficient signs; that is, Caius *makes a promise.*

5. *Sempronius accepts*, and likewise indicates his consent in a significant manner.

Thus, Caius's declaration takes effect and comes into force; that is, the very property which was formerly the property of Caius, which belonged to him, has become, through this act, the property of Sempronius. Caius's perfect right has turned into an imperfect right, just as Sempronius's imperfect right has been transformed into a perfect, compulsory one.

Caius must keep his legally binding promise; if he refuses, Sempronius can use force to compel him to do so.

It is by agreements of this kind that man leaves the state of nature and enters into the state of social relations. His own nature impels him to enter into associations of various kinds in order to transform his fluctuating rights and duties into something definite. Only the savage, like the beast, clings to the enjoyment of the present moment. Civilized man lives for the future as well, and wants to be able to count on something certain also in the next moment. Even the urge to procreate, if it is not to be merely a brute instinct, compels man, as we have seen above, to enter into a social contract, to which we find something analogous even among many animals.

Let us now apply this theory of rights, duties, and contracts to the difference between state and church, from which we started. Both state and church have as their object actions as well as convictions, the former insofar as they are based on the relations be-

tween man and nature, the latter insofar as they are based on the
relations between nature and God. Men need each other; they
hope for, promise, expect from, and render to each other services
and reciprocal services. The mixture of abundance and want,
power and need, selfishness and benevolence given them by nature impels them to enter into a social connection in order to obtain a wider field of action for their capacities and needs. Every
individual is obliged to use a part of his capacities and of the
rights acquired through them for the benefit of the society of
which he is a member. But which part? When? And to what
purpose?

Viewed in itself, all this ought to be determined solely by the
person who is to perform [the act of benevolence]. But men may
also think it proper to renounce this right of independence by
means of a *social contract* and to transform these imperfect duties
into perfect ones by the enactment of *positive laws,* that is, men
may agree upon these specifics and determine how much of his
rights every member may be compelled to use for the benefit of
society. The state, or whoever represents the state, is viewed as a
moral person who has the power to dispose of these rights. The
state, therefore, has rights and prerogatives with regard to the
property and actions of men. It can give and take, prescribe and
prohibit according to law; and since it is also concerned with actions as such, it may *punish* and *reward.* The duty toward my
neighbor is externally satisfied if I render him his due, irrespective of whether my action be enforced or voluntary. If the state
cannot achieve its ends by means of *interior* motives, and thereby
take care of me too, it at least operates by *external* ones, and helps
my neighbor to what is *his.*

Not so the church! It is founded on the relationship between
God and man. God is not a being who needs our benevolence, requires our assistance, or claims any of our rights for his own use,
or whose rights can ever clash or be confused with ours. These
erroneous notions must have resulted from the, in many respects,
inconvenient division of duties into those toward God and those

toward man. The parallel has been drawn too far. Toward God—
toward man—one thought. Just as from a sense of duty toward our
neighbor we sacrifice and relinquish something of our own, so we
should do likewise from a sense of duty toward God. Men require
service; so does God. The duty toward myself may come into conflict and collision with the duty toward my neighbor; likewise, the
duty toward myself may clash with the duty toward God.

Nobody will expressly agree with these absurd propositions if
they are put before him in plain language, yet everyone has more
or less imbibed them, as it were, and infected his blood with them.
From this source flow all the unjust presumptions which the so-
called ministers of religion have at all times permitted themselves
to make in the name of the church. All the violence and persecution which they have perpetrated, all the discord and strife, mu-
tiny and sedition which they have plotted, and all the evils which
from time immemorial have been perpetrated under the cloak of
religion by its fiercest enemies, hypocrisy and misanthropy, are
purely and simply the fruits of this pitiful sophistry, of an illusory
conflict between God and man, the rights of the Deity and the
rights of men.

In the system of human duties, those toward God form, in reality, no special division. Rather, all of men's duties are obligations
toward God. Some of them concern ourselves, others our fellow
men. We ought, from love of God, to love ourselves in a rational
manner, to love his creatures; just as we are bound, from a rational love of ourselves, to love our fellow men.

The system of our duties rests on a twofold principle: the relation between man and nature, and the relation between creature
and Creator. The former is moral philosophy, the latter, *religion,*
and to the man who is convinced of the truth that the relations
obtaining in nature are but expressions of the divine will, both
principles will coincide. To him the moral teachings of reason will
be sacred, just as religion is. Nor does religion, or the relations between God and man, demand any other duties; it only gives those
same duties and obligations a more exalted *sanction.* God does not

need our assistance. He desires no *service* from us,* no sacrifice of our rights for his benefit, no renunciation of our independence for his advantage. His rights can never come into conflict and confusion with ours. He wants only what is best for us, what is best for every single individual; and this must, evidently, be self-consistent, and cannot contradict itself.

All these commonplaces are so trite that sound common sense wonders how people could ever have been of a different mind. And yet from time immemorial men have acted in opposition to these self-evident principles. Happy will they be if in the year 2240 they cease to act against them.

The immediate conclusion to be drawn from these maxims is evidently, as it seems to me, that the church has no right to goods and property, no claim to contributions and renunciations; that its prerogatives can never conflict with ours; and that, hence, there can never be a case of collision [of duty] between the church and its citizens. But this being the case, there can be no contract between the church and the citizens, for all contracts presuppose cases of collision which are to be decided. Where no imperfect rights exist, no collisions of claims arise; and where no decision is required between one set of claims and another, a contract would be an absurdity.

It follows that no human contract whatsoever can give the church a right to goods and property, because by its very nature, the church cannot advance any claim upon any of these, or have an imperfect right to them. It can, therefore, never acquire a compulsory right, nor can any compulsory duty toward it ever be imposed on its members. The only rights possessed by the church are to admonish, to instruct, to fortify, and to comfort; and the duties

* The words "service," "honor," etc. have an entirely different meaning when used in reference to God from the sense they bear when they are used in reference to man. Divine service is not a service which I render to God. The honor of God is not an honor which I do God. In order to preserve the words, one changed their meaning. But the common man still clings to the meaning to which he is accustomed and still adheres to his usual mode of speaking, which has given rise to much confusion in religious matters.

of the citizens toward the church are an *attentive ear* and a *willing heart*.* Nor has the church any right to reward or to punish actions. Civil actions are the concern of the state; specifically religious actions, by their very nature, permit neither coercion nor bribery. They either flow from the free impulse of the soul, or they are an empty show and contrary to the true spirit of religion.

But if the church has no property, who is to pay the teachers of religion? Who is to remunerate the preachers of the fear of God? Religion and pay—teaching virtue and salary—preaching the fear of God and remuneration. These notions seem to shun one another. What influence can the teacher of wisdom and virtue hope to have when he teaches for pay and is for sale to the highest bidder? What impression can the preacher of the fear of God expect to make when he seeks remuneration? *Behold, I have taught you laws and ordinances, as the Eternal, my God* [commanded] *me* (Deut. 4:5). According to the rabbis' interpretation [the words] *as . . . my God . . . me* signify: *Just as He taught me without* [exacting] *payment, so do I teach you* [gratis], *and so should you teach* those in your care. Payment and remuneration are so contrary to the nature of this exalted occupation, so incompatible with the way of life which it demands, that the slightest proclivity toward gain and profit seem to degrade the profession. The desire for wealth, which we readily condone in any other profession, appears to us to be avarice and greed in this one, or it actually does degenerate very soon into avarice and greed among the men who dedicate themselves to this noble work, because it is so contrary to the nature of their calling. The most they can be granted is compensation for their loss of time; ascertaining the amount and dispensing it is the business of the state, not of the church. What concern has the church with things that are for sale, fixed by contract and paid for? Time constitutes a part of our property, and

---

* The Psalmist sings:

> Sacrifice and offering Thou didst not desire,
> Mine ears hast Thou opened. (Ps. 40:7)

the man who uses it for the common good may hope for compensation from the public purse. The church does not remunerate; religion buys nothing, pays nothing, and allots no wages.

These are, in my opinion, the boundaries between state and church, insofar as they have an influence upon the actions of men. In respect to convictions, state and church come somewhat closer to each other; for here the state has no other means of acting effectively than the church has. Both must teach, instruct, encourage, motivate. But neither may reward or punish, compel or bribe; for the state, too, cannot have acquired by means of any contract the slightest compulsory right over our convictions. In general, men's convictions pay no heed to benevolence, and are not amenable to any coercion. I cannot renounce any of my convictions, as a conviction, out of love for my neighbor; nor can I cede and relinquish to him, out of benevolence, any part of my own power of judgment. I am likewise in no position to arrogate to myself or in any way acquire a right over my neighbor's convictions. The right to our own convictions is inalienable, and cannot pass from person to person; for it neither gives nor takes away any claim to property, goods and liberty.

Hence, the smallest privilege which you publicly grant to those who share your religion and convictions is to be called an *indirect bribe*, and the smallest liberty you withhold from dissidents an *indirect punishment*. They have, at bottom, the same effect as a direct reward for agreement, and a direct punishment for opposition. It is a paltry delusion when the distinction between *reward* and *privilege*, between *punishment* and *restriction*, is so much insisted upon in some text books of ecclesiastical law. To the linguist, such a notation may be useful, but to the poor wretch who must do without his rights as a man because he cannot say: *I believe*, when he does not believe, who will not be a Moslem with his lips and a Christian at heart, this distinction brings only a sorry consolation. And what are the limits of privilege, on the one hand, and of restriction, on the other? With a moderate gift for dialectics, one amplifies these concepts and goes on extending them until they become civil felicity, on the one hand, and oppression, exile, and misery on the other.*

Fear and hope act upon men's *appetitive urge*, rational arguments on their *cognitive faculty*. You lay hold of the wrong means when you seek to induce men, through fear and hope, to accept or reject certain propositions. Indeed, even if this is not altogether your object, you still impede your better intentions if you do not try to keep fear and hope out of view as far as possible. You bribe and deceive your own heart, or your heart has deceived you, if you believe that examining the truth is feasible and that freedom of inquiry remains inviolate, when status and dignity await the inquirer if he arrives at one conclusion, and contempt and indigence if he arrives at another. Notions of good and evil are instruments for [directing] the *will*, those of truth and untruth for [directing] the *intellect*. Whoever wants to act upon the intellect must first of all lay aside the former instruments; otherwise he is in danger of proceeding contrary to his own intention. He may smooth over where he should cut right through, and fix where he should demolish.

What form of government is therefore advisable for the church? None! Who is to be the arbiter if disputes arise over religious matters? He to whom God has given the ability to convince others. For what can be the use of a government where there is nothing to govern? What use are authorities where no one is to be a subject? What good is a judiciary where there are no rights and claims to be adjudicated? Neither state nor church is authorized to judge in religious matters; for the members of society could not have granted that right to them by any contract whatsoever. The state, to be sure, is to see to it from afar that no doctrines are propagated which are inconsistent with the public welfare; doctrines

* Some time ago, in an otherwise rather tolerant state, a board composed of learned and distinguished men made certain dissidents pay double the regular fee for approbation. When they were called to account for this action by the authorities, they excused themselves by saying that, surely, dissidents were everywhere *deterioris conditionis* in civil life. The strange thing is that the increase in fees has remained unchanged to this day.

which, like atheism and Epicureanism, undermine the foundation on which the felicity of social life is based. Let Plutarch and Bayle inquire ever so much whether a state might not be better off with atheism than with superstition. Let them count and compare ever so much the afflictions which have hitherto befallen and still threaten to befall the human race from these sources of misery. At bottom, this is nothing else than inquiring whether a slow fever is more fatal than a sudden one. No one would wish either upon his friends. Hence, every civil society would do well to let neither of them, neither fanaticism nor atheism, take root and spread. The body politic becomes sick and miserable, whether it is worn down by cancer or consumed by fever.

But it is only from a distance that the state should take notice of this, and only with wise moderation should it favor even those doctrines upon which its true felicity is based. It should not interfere directly in any dispute or wish to decide it through the use of its authority. For it evidently acts contrary to its own purpose when it directly forbids inquiry, or allows disputes to be decided in any other manner than by rational arguments. Nor need it trouble itself with all the principles which a dominant or merely tolerated faith (*Dogmatik*) may adopt or reject. It is a question only of those fundamental principles on which all religions agree, and without which felicity is but a dream, and virtue itself ceases to be virtue. Without God, providence, and a future life, love of our fellow man is but an innate weakness, and benevolence is little more than a foppery into which we seek to lure one another so that the simpleton will toil while the clever man enjoys himself and has a good laugh at the other's expense.

It will hardly be necessary to touch upon the further question of whether it is permissible to have teachers and priests affirm under oath that they subscribe to certain doctrines of the faith. To affirm what doctrines should this be done? The fundamental articles of all religions, of which we have already spoken, cannot be confirmed by any oath. You must take the swearer's word that he accepts them; otherwise, his oath is an empty sound, words, which he tosses into the air at no greater cost to himself than is required by a simple assurance. For all trust in oaths, and the entire esteem accorded to them, rest, to be sure, solely on these fundamental doctrines of morality. But if it be particular articles of this or that religion to which I am to swear, or which I am to abjure; if it be principles without which virtue and prosperity can well endure among men, even if, in the opinion of the state or the persons who represent the state, they are ever so necessary for my eternal salvation—then I would ask: what right does the state have to pry into men's souls and to force them to make avowals which can bring neither comfort nor profit to society? This [right] could not have been conceded to it, for all the conditions of a contract enumerated above are absent here. The matter in question does not concern any of my dispensable goods, which I am to relinquish to my neighbor; it does not concern any object of benevolence, and cases of collision to be decided do not occur here. But how can the state arrogate to itself an authority which cannot be conceded by any contract, which cannot pass from one person to another and be transferred by any declaration of intent? Into the bargain, let us, however, inquire whether an oath concerning belief or disbelief is a real concept at all—whether men's opinions, their agreement or disagreement in respect to rational propositions are altogether matters on which they can be sworn.

Oaths give rise to no new duties. The most solemn invocation of God to be a witness of the truth neither gives nor takes away a right which did not already exist without it, nor does it impose on the man who invokes God any obligation which was not incumbent upon him even without an oath. Oaths merely serve to awaken man's conscience, if by chance it has fallen asleep, and to draw his attention to what the will of the judge of the world has already demanded of him. Oaths, therefore, are, properly speaking, designed neither for the man of conscience nor for the confirmed good-for-nothing. The former must know anyhow—must, without oaths and imprecations, be deeply imbued with the truth, that God is a witness not only of man's every word and assertion, but of all his thoughts and most secret sentiments, and that He does not let the transgression of his most holy will go unpunished. And the confirmed, unconscionable villain?

> "He fears not God,
> who spares not man."

Oaths are therefore only for the ordinary, middling sort of man, or, at bottom, for every one of us, insofar as we all must, in many a case, be numbered among this class. They are for weak, irresolute, and vacillating men, men who have principles, but do not always abide by them; men who are lazy and indolent with regard to the good which they do know and understand, men who give in to their moods in order to indulge some weakness, procrastinate, extenuate, look for excuses and, in most cases, think they have found them. They want to remain true to their intent, but lack the firmness to do so. It is these people whose will must be steeled and whose conscience must be roused. The man who at this moment denies a fact in court may perhaps still have someone else's property in his possession, yet without being so resolutely wicked as to want to be unjust. He may have used up the property, or let it pass out of his hands, and may now only want to gain time by his denial. And so, perhaps, the good inclination which contends within him for justice is put off from day to day until it is tired out and succumbs. One must therefore hasten to his assistance and, first of all, transform the case that is liable to procrastination into an action that takes place now when the present moment is decisive, and excuses can no longer be resorted to; and then we must summon, in addition, all the solemnity, and gather up all the force and emphasis, with which the recollection of God, the all-righteous avenger and retributor, can act upon the mind.

This is the purpose of an oath. And from this, it seems to me, it is obvious that men can be made to take oaths only about things which affect their external senses, things of which they are able to maintain the truth with the conviction which the evidence of the external senses carries with it, and concerning which they can

say: This I *heard, saw, said, received, gave,* or *did not hear,* etc.
But we are putting their conscience to a cruel torture when we
question them about things which are solely a matter of the *internal sense.* Do you believe? Are you convinced? Persuaded? Do
you think so? In case there still remains any doubt in some corner
of your mind or heart, let us know it or God will avenge the
abuse of his name. For Heaven's sake, spare the tender and honest innocent! Even if he had to state a proposition from the first
book of Euclid, he would, at that moment, hesitate and suffer in-
expressible torment.

The perceptions of the internal sense are in themselves rarely
so palpable that the mind is able to retain them securely and to
give them expression as often as it may be desired. They will slip
away from it at times, just when it thinks it has taken hold of
them. I may feel sure of something right now, but a moment later,
some slight doubt of its certainty may sneak or steal its way into
a corner of my soul and lurk there, without my being aware of
its presence. Many things for which I would suffer martyrdom today may perhaps appear problematic to me tomorrow. If, in addition, I must also put these internal perceptions into words and
signs, or swear to words and signs which other men lay before
me, the uncertainty will be still greater. My neighbor and I cannot possibly connect the very same words with the very same internal sensations, for we cannot compare them, liken them to one
another and correct them without again resorting to words. We
cannot illustrate the words by things, but must again have recourse to signs and words, and finally, to metaphors; because,
with the help of this artifice, we reduce, as it were, the concepts
of the internal sense to external sensory perceptions. But, given
this fact, how much confusion and indistinctiveness are bound to
remain in the signification of words, and how greatly must the
ideas differ which different men, in different ages and centuries,
connect with the same external signs and words!

Dear reader, whoever you may be, do not accuse me of skepticism or of employing some evil ruse in order to turn you into a

skeptic. I am perhaps one of those who are the farthest removed
from that disease of the soul, and who most ardently wish to be
able to cure all their fellow men of it. But precisely because I
have so often performed this cure on myself, and tried it on others, I have become aware of how difficult it is, and what little
hope one has of success. With my best friend, whom I believed
to be ever so much in accord with me, I very often failed to come
to terms about certain truths of philosophy and religion. After a
long dispute and altercation, it would sometimes emerge that we
had each connected different ideas with the same words. Not in-
frequently, we thought alike, yet expressed ourselves differently;
but just as often we believed ourselves to be in agreement when
we were still very far apart in our thoughts. And yet neither of
us was unpracticed in thinking; we were both used to dealing
with abstract ideas, and it seemed to both of us that we were ear-
nestly seeking the truth for its own sake rather than for the sake
of scoring a point. Nevertheless, our ideas had to rub against each
other for a long time before they could be made to fit themselves
to one another, and before we could say with any assurance:
Here we agree! Oh! I should not like to have for a friend anyone
who has had this experience in his lifetime, and can still be intol-
erant, and can still hate his neighbor because he does not think or
express himself on religious matters in the same way as he does;
for he has divested himself of all humanity.

And you, my fellow men! You take a man with whom you have,
perhaps, never discussed such matters, and put before him the
subtlest propositions of metaphysics and religion, clothed, as they
were, centuries ago, in words, in so-called symbols; you make him
affirm by the holiest of names, that he means by these words precisely what you mean; and that both you and he mean the very
same thing as the one who wrote them down centuries ago. You
make him affirm that he subscribes to these propositions with all
his heart and harbors no doubt concerning any of them. With
this sworn agreement you then connect office and honor, power
and influence—enticements which are quite capable of removing

many a contradiction, and suppressing many a doubt. And if it turns out in the end that the man's convictions are not what he pretended they were, you accuse him of the most heinous of all crimes; you charge him with perjury, and you let happen what must happen in the case of such an outrage. Now, putting it mildly, is there not an equal measure of guilt on both sides?

"Indeed," say the most fair-minded among you, "we do not make anyone swear to his faith. We allow the conscience its liberty. It is only when we appoint a fellow citizen to a certain office that we make him swear that he accepts this office, which is entrusted to him on the condition of conformity, not without conformity. This is a contract which we conclude with him. Should doubts afterwards arise which cancel this conformity, he is surely free to be true to his conscience and to resign the office. Is there any liberty of conscience or are there any rights of man which permit him to violate a contract?"

Very well then! To this semblance of justice I will not oppose all the arguments which can be opposed to it in accordance with the self-evident principles mentioned above. What is the use of unnecessary repetitions? But for humanity's sake, consider the results which this procedure has thus far produced among the most civilized people. Count all the men who occupy your academic chairs and pulpits, and have their doubts about many a proposition to which they swore when they assumed office; take all the bishops who sit in the House of Lords, all the truly great men who hold high office in England and can no longer accept the Thirty-nine Articles, to which they have sworn, as unconditionally as they did when they were first set before them. Count them, and then still say that civil liberty cannot be granted to my oppressed nation because so many of its members think little of an oath! Alas! God keep my heart free from misanthropic thoughts! These sad reflections could easily allow them to get the better of me.

No! Out of respect for mankind I am rather persuaded that all these men do not recognize as perjury what is laid at their door under this name. Sound reason, perhaps, tells them that no one, neither the state nor the church, had a right to make them swear in matters of faith; that neither state nor the church had a right to connect office, honors, and dignity with the belief in certain propositions and the willingness to swear to them, or to make the belief in certain propositions the condition on which these benefits were to be conferred. Such a condition, they think, is in itself null and void, since it serves no one's interest, since no man's rights and possessions are harmed if it is broken.* If, therefore, a wrong was committed—and it cannot be denied by them that this is the case—it happened at the time when the promised advantages tempted them to take so inadmissible an oath. Now, however, it is impossible to remedy this evil; least of all can it be remedied by their resigning the office obtained in this way. At that time, they made use of God's most holy name in a manner, admittedly, inexcusable in his eyes, in order to obtain permissible earthly advantages. But what was done cannot be undone by now renouncing the fruits they derived from it. Indeed, the confusion, scandal and other bad results which would be likely to follow from the resignation of their office, accompanied by a public confession of their deviation, could only augment the evil. Hence their fellow men as well as they themselves and their kith and kin would do far better to let the matter rest and to continue rendering state and church the services for which Providence has bestowed upon them the inclination and ability. It is this inclination and ability that constitutes their vocation for public service, and not their convictions about eternal truths and rational propositions which, at bottom, concern only themselves and none of their fellow men. Even though some men are too scrupulous to owe their fortune to such fine-spun excuses, one still should

* That is to say, a condition is valid and binds the contract if a possibility is conceivable in which it can have an influence on deciding cases of collision. Opinions, however, can be linked with external advantages only by an erroneous conscience, and I doubt whether they can ever constitute a legally valid condition.

not totally condemn those who are weak enough to resort to them. I would, at any rate, charge men of their caliber not with perjury, but with human weakness.

To conclude this section I will recapitulate the results to which my reflections have led me.

State and church have for their object the promotion, by means of public measures, of human felicity in this life and in the future life.

Both act upon men's *convictions* and *actions*, on principles and their application; the state, by means of reasons based on the relations between man and man, or between man and nature, and the church, the religion of the state, by means of reasons based on the relations between man and God. The state treats man as the *immortal son of the earth;* religion treats him as the *image of his Creator.*

Principles are free. Convictions, by their very nature, permit no coercion or bribery. They belong in the realm of man's cognitive faculty and must be decided by the criterion of truth or untruth. Good and evil act upon his capacity of approval and disapproval. Fear and hope guide his impulses. Reward and punishment direct his will, spur his energy, encourage, entice, or deter him.

But if principles are to make man happy, he must not be scared or wheedled into adopting them. Only the judgment reached by his powers of intellect can be accepted as valid. To let ideas of good and evil interfere with his deliberations is to permit the matter to be decided by an unauthorized judge.

Hence, neither church nor state has a right to subject men's principles and convictions to any coercion whatsoever. Neither church nor state is authorized to connect privileges and rights, claims on persons and title to things, with principles and convictions, and to weaken through outside interference the influence of the power of truth upon the cognitive faculty.

Not even the social contract could grant such a right to either state or church. For a contract concerning things which, by their very nature, are *inalienable,* is intrinsically invalid, and cancels itself.

Not even the most sacred oath can change, in this respect, the nature of things. Oaths do not engender new duties; they are merely solemn confirmations of that to which we are in any case obligated by nature or through a contract. Where no duty exists, an oath is a vain invocation of God, which may be blasphemous, but can in itself create no obligation.

Moreover, men can swear only to what they know by the evidence of their external senses, to what they saw, heard, touched. Perceptions of the internal senses are not the object of confirmation by oath.

Hence, all adjurations and abjurations in reference to principles and doctrinal opinions are inadmissible; and if a man has taken such an oath, it obligates him to nothing but regret for having acted in a culpably thoughtless manner. If I swear this minute to an opinion, I am nevertheless free to disavow it a moment later. The misdeed of taking a *vain oath* has been committed, even if I retain the opinion; and I do not commit *perjury* if I repudiate it.

It must not be forgotten that, according to my principles, the state is not authorized to connect income, offices of honor, and privilege with certain doctrinal opinions. With regard to the teaching profession, it is the duty of the state to appoint instructors who are able to teach wisdom and virtue, and to promulgate those useful truths upon which the felicity of human society directly rests. All particulars must be left to the best of the teacher's knowledge; otherwise, endless confusion and collisions of duties will arise which, in the end, will frequently lead even the virtuous into hypocrisy and unscrupulousness. No offense against the dictates of reason remains unavenged.

But what if the harm has already been done? Suppose the state appoints and pays a teacher for propounding certain fixed doctrinal opinions. The man later discovers that these doctrines are unfounded. What is he to do? How must he act in order to extricate his foot from the trap into which an erroneous conscience made him step?

Three different ways are open to him here. He locks up the truth in his heart and continues to teach untruth, against his better judgment; he resigns from his position without giving his reason for doing so; or, finally, he openly testifies to the truth, and leaves it to the state to determine what is to become of his position and salary, or whatever else he is to suffer on account of his invincible love of truth.

None of these ways, it seems to me, is to be absolutely rejected under all circumstances. I can conceive of a state of mind in which it is pardonable before the tribunal of the all-righteous Judge if one continues to mix into his otherwise salutary exposition of truths beneficial to the public some untruth that, perhaps, on account of an erroneous conscience, has been sanctioned by the state. I would, at any rate, be careful not to accuse, on this account, an otherwise honest teacher of hypocrisy or Jesuitry, unless I were thoroughly acquainted with his circumstances and state of mind—so thoroughly as perhaps no man ever can be with his neighbor's state of mind. Whoever boasts of having never spoken on such matters differently from what he thought, has either never thought at all, or perhaps, at this very moment, finds it advantageous to strut about with an untruth which his own heart contradicts.

In reference, therefore, to convictions and principles, religion and state are on the same footing: both must avoid any semblance of coercion or bribery, and confine themselves to teaching, admonishing, persuading, and reprimanding. It is different with *actions*. The relations between man and man require actions as such; the relations between God and man require them only insofar as they lead to convictions. An action beneficial to the public does not cease to be beneficial, even if it is brought about by coercion, whereas a religious action is religious only to the degree to which it is performed voluntarily and with proper intent.

The state can therefore compel actions beneficial to the public; it can reward and punish, distribute offices and honors, disgrace and banishment, in order to stir men to actions whose intrinsic value will not impress itself forcefully enough on their minds. It is for this reason that the most perfect right as well as the ability

to do these things *could have been, and had to be,* granted to the
state through the social contract. Hence the state is a moral person, which possesses its own goods and prerogatives, and may
dispose of them as it pleases.

Divine religion is far from all this. It bears the same relation
toward actions as toward convictions, for it commands actions
only as tokens of convictions. It is a moral person, but its rights
imply no coercion. It does not prod men with an iron rod; it
guides them with bands of love. It draws no avenging sword, dispenses no temporal goods, assumes no right to any earthly possessions, and claims no external power over the mind. Its weapons
are reason and persuasion; its strength is the divine power of
truth. The punishments it threatens, just like the rewards it promises, are the *effects of love*—salutary and beneficial for the very
person who has to endure them. By these signs I recognize thee,
daughter of Divinity! Religion! who alone, in truth, grantest bliss
on earth even as in heaven.

Excommunication and the right to banish, which the state may
occasionally permit itself to exercise, are diametrically opposed to
the spirit of religion. To banish, to exclude, to turn away the
brother who wishes to take part in my edification and lift up his
heart to God in beneficial union together with me! If religion permits itself no arbitrary punishments, it should least of all allow
this torture of the soul which, alas, is felt only by a person who
truly has religion. Think of all the unfortunate ones who from time
immemorial were supposed to have been improved by excommunication and damnation. Reader! To whatever visible church,
synagogue, or mosque you may belong! See if you do not find more
true religion among the host of the excommunicated than among
the far greater host of those who excommunicated them. Now, excommunication either has civil consequences or does not have them.
If it does produce civil misery, its burden falls only on the high-
minded man who believes that he owes this sacrifice to divine
truth. He who has no religion must be mad if he exposes himself
to the least danger for the sake of an imaginary truth. If, however,

its consequences are but of a spiritual nature, as some people wish to persuade themselves, they, again, afflict only the man who is still susceptible to this kind of feeling. The irreligious man laughs at such things and remains impenitent.

But how is it possible to separate excommunication from all civil consequences? To grant the church disciplinary power, as I have said elsewhere and, I think, with justice—to grant the church disciplinary power without injuring civil felicity, is like the answer of the most supreme Judge to the prosecutor: *Let him be in your hands; but spare his life!* Break the barrel, as the commentators add, but don't let the wine run out! For what ecclesiastical excommunication or ban is without any civil consequences, without any influence, at least, upon the civil reputation, upon the good name, of the expelled and upon the trust placed in him by his fellow citizens, without which no one can pursue his occupation and be useful to his fellow men, that is, be civilly happy?

Some people still appeal to the law of nature. Every society, they say, has the right of exclusion. Why should not also a religious society have it?

But I reply: this is precisely where a religious society constitutes an exception. By virtue of a higher law, no society can exercise a right which is diametrically opposed to the primary purpose of the society itself. To exclude a dissident, says a worthy clergyman of this city, to expel a dissident from the church is like forbidding a sick person to enter a pharmacy. In fact, the most essential purpose of religious society is *mutual edification.* By the magic power of sympathy one wishes to transfer truth from the mind to the heart; to vivify, by participation with others, the concepts of reason, which at times are lifeless, into soaring sensations. When the heart clings too strongly to sensual pleasures to listen to the voice of reason, when it is on the verge of ensnaring reason itself, then let it be seized here with a tremor of pious enthusiasm, kindled by the fire of devotion, and acquainted with joys of a higher order which outweigh even in this life the joys of the senses. And would you turn away from the door the sick man who is most in need of this medicine, who needs it all the more, the less he feels the necessity, and in his delirium imagines that he is healthy? Should it not rather be your first concern to restore to him this feeling and to call back to life that part of his soul which is, as it were, threatened with gangrene? But instead of doing this, you refuse him all assistance, and let the helpless fellow die a moral death, from which, perhaps, you might have rescued him?

A certain Athenian philosopher acted in a much nobler manner and more in accordance with the purposes of his school. An Epicurean came away from his banquet, his senses clouded by the night's debauchery, and his head wreathed with roses. He stepped into the lecture-hall of the Stoics, in order to indulge, at the hour of dawn, the last pleasure of an enervated voluptuary—the pleasure of scoffing. The philosopher left him undisturbed, redoubled the fire of his eloquence against the seductions of debauchery, and described with irresistible force the felicity of virtue. The disciple of Epicurus listened, grew attentive, cast down his eyes, tore the wreaths from his head, and became himself an adherent of the Stoa.

SECTION II

THE ESSENTIAL point of this contention—a contention that flatly contradicts an otherwise universally held principle—I already attempted to set forth on a previous occasion. Mr. Dohm's excellent work *On the Civil Improvement of the Jews* led to the inquiry: *To what extent should a naturalized colony be permitted to retain its own jurisdiction in ecclesiastical and civil matters in general and the right of excommunication and expulsion in particular?* Legal power of the church—the right of excommunication—if a colony is to have these, it must have been enfeoffed with them, as it were, by the state or by the mother church. Someone who possesses this right by virtue of the social contract must have ceded or relinquished a part of it to the colony, insofar as it concerns the latter. But what if no one can possess such a right? What if neither the state nor the mother church herself can claim any right to use coercion in religious matters? If according to the principles of sound reason, the divinity of which we must all acknowledge, neither state nor church would be authorized to assume any right in matters of faith other than the right to teach, any power other than the power to persuade, any discipline other than the discipline of reason and principles? If this can be proved and made clear to common sense, no explicit contract, much less usage or prescription, will be powerful enough to maintain a right that runs counter to it; all ecclesiastical coercion will be unlawful, all external power in religious matters will be violent usurpation; and if this is so, the mother church may not and cannot bestow a right which does not belong to it, nor give away a power which it unjustly arrogated to itself. It may be that this abuse, through some common prejudice or other, has become so widespread and so deeply rooted in the minds of men that it would not be feasible or advisable to abolish it all at once, without wise preparation. But in that case, it is at least our duty to oppose it from afar, and, first of all, to set up a dam against its further expansion. If we cannot eradicate an evil completely, we must at least cut off its roots.

This was the result of my reflections, and I dared to submit my thoughts to the judgment of the public,* even though I could not at that time state my reasons as fully as has been done in the preceding section.

I have the good fortune to live in a state in which these ideas of mine are neither new nor particularly striking. The wise monarch by whom it is ruled has, from the beginning of his reign, made it his constant purpose to put mankind in possession of its full rights in matters of faith. He is the first among the monarchs of this century who has never lost sight of the total import of the wise maxim, *"Men were created for each other. Instruct your neighbor, or tolerate him!"** He certainly left intact, with wise

---

* In the Preface to Menasseh ben Israel's *Defense of the Jews.*

** These are the words of my late friend, Mr. Iselin, in one of his last papers in *Ephemerides of Mankind.* The memory of this truly wise man should be unforgettable to every one of his contemporaries who esteems virtue and truth. It is, therefore, all the more incomprehensible to me how I could have overlooked him when mentioning the beneficent men who first sought to propagate the principles of unlimited tolerance in Germany. It was he who taught them to their fullest extent, indeed earlier and in a clearer voice than anyone else in our language. It is with pleasure that I quote here a passage from [his] review of my *Preface to Rabbi Menasseh* in *Ephemerides* (No. 10, October 1782, p. 429), where this subject is referred to, in order to do justice, after his death, to a man who was so just to everyone in his lifetime: "The editor

moderation, the privileges of external religion he found installed. It will, perhaps, still take centuries of culture and preparation before men understand that privileges on account of religion are neither lawful nor, actually, useful and that it would therefore be a veritable boon totally to abolish all civil discrimination on account of religion. Nevertheless, under the rule of this wise man the nation has become so much accustomed to tolerance and for-

---

of *Ephemerides of Mankind* agrees entirely also with what Mr. Mendelssohn says about the legislative rights of the authorities concerning the opinions held by the citizens and about the agreements which individuals may enter into among themselves with regard to such opinions. And he adopted this way of thinking not only since Mr. Dohm and Mr. Lessing wrote, but he already professed it more than thirty years ago. By the same token, he also acknowledged long ago that what one calls religious tolerance is not a favor, but a duty on the part of the government. No one could have expressed himself more clearly than he did when he wrote in the following manner (*Dreams of a Friend of Mankind*, Vol. II, pp. 12 and 13): 'If, therefore, one or more religions are introduced into his states, a wise and just sovereign will not permit himself to infringe upon their rights to the advantage of his own. Every church, every association, which has divine worship for its aim is a society to which the sovereign owes protection and justice. To deny this to them, even for the sake of favoring the best religion, would be contrary to the spirit of true piety.'

"With respect to civil rights, the members of all religions are equal, with the sole exception of those whose opinions run counter to the principles of human and civil duties. Such a religion cannot lay claim to any rights in the state. Those who have the misfortune of being attached to it can expect tolerance only as long as they do not disturb the social order by unjust and harmful acts. If they perform such acts, they must be punished, *not for their opinions but for their deeds.*" What is said, however, in the preceding passage (p. 423) concerning some erroneous opinion about middlemen in commerce—an opinion allegedly ascribed by me, without justification, to the editor of *Ephemerides*—stands in need of correction. It was not Mr. Iselin, but another, otherwise judicious, writer who had published a paper in *Ephemerides,* in which he asserted the harmfulness of middlemen, a view that was, in fact, refuted by the editor [Mr. Iselin].

The remarks made in the same article against my coreligionists, I pass over in silence. This is not the place to defend the latter, and I leave this business to Mr. Dohm, who can do it with less partiality. Besides, one quite easily forgives the prejudice of a citizen of Basel against a people which he could have had an opportunity of knowing only from its vagrant section or from the *Observations d'un Alsacien.*

bearance in matters of faith that coercion, excommunication and the right of expulsion have, at least, ceased to be popular concepts.

But what must bring true joy to the heart of every honest man is the earnestness and the zeal with which several worthy members of the local clergy endeavor to spread these principles of reason, or rather of the true fear of God, among the people. Indeed, some of them have not hesitated to give full approval to the arguments advanced by me against the universally adored idol of ecclesiastical law and to applaud their conclusions in public. How lofty must be the notions these men have of their vocation if they show such readiness to disregard all secondary considerations! What noble confidence they must place in the power of truth, if they dare to set it squarely on its own pedestal, without any other prop! Even though otherwise we should differ ever so much in our principles, I could not help but express my wholehearted admiration and respect for them on account of these sublime convictions.

Some other readers and reviewers behaved quite strangely in this matter. They did not indeed dispute my arguments but, on the contrary, allowed them to stand. No one attempted to show the slightest connection between doctrinal opinions and rights. No one discovered a flaw in the conclusion that my assent or failure to assent to certain *eternal truths* gives me no right over things, no authority to dispose of goods and minds according to my own pleasure. Yet, nevertheless, they were startled by the immediate conclusions of my arguments as if by an unexpected apparition. What? So there is no ecclesiastical law at all? So everything that so many authors and, perhaps, we ourselves, have written, read, heard and argued about ecclesiastical law is devoid of any foundation? This, it seemed to them, was going too far; but there must be some hidden flaw in the conclusion, if the result is not necessarily to be true.

In the *Göttingische Anzeigen,* the reviewer quotes my assertion that there exists no right to persons and things which is connected with doctrinal opinions, and that all the contracts and agreements in the world cannot make such a right possible; and he then adds, "all this is new and harsh. First principles are negated, and all dispute comes to an end."

Indeed, it is a question of first principles which one refuses to recognize. But should there be an end to all dispute on account of this? Must one never doubt principles? If so, men of the Pythagorean school could dispute forever how their teacher happened to come by his golden hip, and no one would dare to ask: Did Pythagoras actually have a golden hip?

Every game has its laws, every contest its rules, according to which the umpire decides. If you want to win the stake or carry away the prize, you must submit to the principles. But whoever wishes to reflect on the theory of games may certainly examine the fundamentals. Just as in a court of law. A criminal court judge who had to try a murderer induced him to confess his crime. But the wicked fellow maintained that he knew no reason why it should not be just as permissible to murder a man as to kill an animal, for his own advantage. To this fiend the judge could justly reply: "You deny the basic principles, lad! With you all dispute is at an end. But you will at least comprehend that we, too, are permitted, for our own advantage, to rid the earth of such a monster." Yet the priest charged with preparing him for death ought not to have answered him in this manner. He was obligated to engage him in discussion about the principles themselves and to remove his doubts, if he entertained them in earnest. It is no different in the arts and sciences. Each one of them presupposes certain fundamental concepts, of which it gives no further account. Nevertheless, there is not a single point in the entire sum of human knowledge that is to be placed beyond question, not one iota that may not be subjected to investigation. If my doubt lies beyond the limits of *this* tribunal, I must be referred to another. Somewhere I must be heard and directed along the right path.

The case which the reviewer cites as an example, in order to refute me, completely misses the mark. "Let us," he says, "apply them (the denied principles) to a particular case. The Jewish community in Berlin appoints a person who is to circumcise its male children according to the laws of its religion. This person receives, by agreement, certain rights to such and such an income, to a particular rank in the community, etc. After a while, he has doubts concerning the doctrine or law of circumcision; he refuses to fulfill the contract. Does he still retain the rights he acquired by contract? The same applies everywhere."

And in what sense "everywhere"? I will admit the possibility of the case which, it is to be hoped, will never occur.* What is this example—adduced as it is ad hominem—supposed to prove? Surely not that, according to reason, rights over persons and goods are connected with doctrinal opinions, and are based on them? Or that positive laws and contracts can render such a right possible? According to the reviewer's own statement, it is chiefly a question of these two points, neither of which is found in the case he invented. For the circumciser would enjoy his income and rank not because he approves of the doctrinal opinion, but because of the operation he performs in place of the fathers of the families. Now, if his conscience prevents him from continuing this labor, he will, of course, have to give up the reward previously stipulated. But what does this have in common with the privileges granted to a person because he assents to one or another doctrine or because he accepts or rejects this or that eternal truth?

The only case which might bear some resemblance to this fictitious example is the one in which the state employs and remunerates teachers who are supposed to propagate certain doctrines in

* Among the Jews, one receives neither a remuneration nor a specific rank in the community for the office of circumcision. On the contrary, whoever possesses the [requisite] skill performs this meritorious act with pleasure. Indeed, the father, who, properly speaking, is obliged to perform the duty of circumcising his son, usually has to choose among several competitors who apply for it. The only reward which the circumciser can expect for his performance consists in his being seated at the head of the table at the festive meal following the circumcision, and in his saying the blessing after the meal— According to my seemingly new and harsh theory, all religious offices ought to be filled in like manner.

such and such a manner, but who later feel conscience-bound to depart from the doctrines prescribed to them. In the preceding section I dealt at length with this case which so often has occasioned loud and heated disputes, and I sought to discuss it in accordance with my principles. But it seems to me to accord just as little with the paradigm mentioned. One may recall the distinction I made between actions which are demanded as actions and those that merely signify convictions. A foreskin is cut off: the circumciser may think and believe whatever he pleases of the practice itself, just as a creditor who obtained satisfaction through the courts is repaid, no matter what the debtor may think of his obligation to pay. But how can one apply the same standard to a teacher of religious truths, whose teachings can certainly bring but small profit if mind and heart do not agree with them, if they do not flow from inner conviction? In the passage cited I already indicated that I would not dare to prescribe to a hard-pressed teacher who finds himself in such a predicament how to behave as an honest man, or to reproach him if he acted otherwise, and that, in my opinion, everything depends on the time, the circumstances, and the state in which he finds himself. Who can in this matter adversely judge the conscientiousness of his neighbor? Who can force him to use a criterion which he may not consider appropriate for such a critical decision?

However, this investigation does not lie entirely in my path, and has little in common with the two questions on which everything depends, and which I shall repeat here once more:

1. Are there, according to the laws of reason, rights over persons and things that are connected with doctrinal opinions, and are acquired by giving assent to them?

2. Can contracts and agreements produce *perfect* rights, engender compulsory duties, where, in the absence of any contract, imperfect rights and duties are not already in existence?

One of these propositions must be shown to follow from natural law, if I am to be found guilty of error. The fact that one finds my assertion new and harsh is of no consequence, as long as it does not contradict the truth. I still do not know of any author who has touched upon these questions and examined them as they apply to ecclesiastical power and the right of excommunication. They all start from the point of view that there is a *jus circa sacra;* only everyone fashions it in his own way, and enfeoffs with it sometimes an invisible person, sometimes this or that visible person. Even Hobbes, who ventured to move in this respect farther than anyone else from the established concepts, could not completely disengage himself from this idea. He concedes such a right, and only searches for the person to whom it may be entrusted with the least harm. All believe that the meteor is visible and only strive to fix its altitude by different systems. It would not be an unheard-of occurrence if an unprejudiced person, looking straight at the place in the sky where it was supposed to appear, were to convince himself, with the aid of much weaker capacities, of the truth that no such meteor could be seen.

I come now to a far more important objection that has been raised against me, and which has chiefly caused me to write this work. Once more, without refuting my arguments, one has opposed to them the sacred authority of the Mosaic religion which I profess. What are the laws of Moses but a system of religious government, of the power and right of religion? "Reason may agree," says an anonymous author* in reference to this subject, "that all ecclesiastical law and the power of an ecclesiastical court by which opinions are enforced or constrained is absurd; that no case can be conceived in which such a law is well-founded; and that art can create nothing for which nature has not produced the seed. But as reasonable as everything you say on this subject may be," he apostrophizes me, "it directly contradicts the faith of your fathers in the strict sense, and the principles of the [Jewish] church, which are not simply assumed by the commentators, but are expressly laid down in the Books of Moses themselves. According to common sense, there can be no worship

* *The Searching for Light and Right in a Letter to Mr. M. Mendelssohn,* Berlin, 1782.

without conviction, and every act of worship resulting from coercion ceases to be one. The observance of divine commandments from fear of the punishment attached to them is slavery, which, according to purified concepts, can never be pleasing to God. Yet it is true that Moses connects coercion and positive punishment with the nonobservance of duties related to the worship of God. His statutory ecclesiastical law decrees the punishment of stoning and death for the sabbath-breaker, the blasphemer of the divine name, and others who depart from his laws." "The whole ecclesiastical system of Moses," he says elsewhere, "did not consist only of teaching and instruction in duties but was at the same time connected with the strictest ecclesiastical laws. The arm of the church was provided with the sword of the curse. Cursed be he, it is written, who does not obey all the words of this law to do them, etc. And this curse was in the hands of the first ministers of the church." "Ecclesiastical law armed with power has always been one of the principal cornerstones of the Jewish religion itself, and a primary article in the credal system of your fathers. How, then, can you, my dear Mr. Mendelssohn, remain an adherent of the faith of your fathers and shake the entire structure by removing its cornerstones, when you contest the ecclesiastical law that has been given through Moses and purports to be founded on divine revelation?"

This objection cuts me to the heart. I must admit that the notions given here of Judaism, except for some indiscretion in the terms used, are taken to be correct even by many of my coreligionists. Now if this were the truth, and I were convinced of it, I would, indeed, shamefully retract my propositions and bring reason into captivity under the yoke of—but no! Why should I dissimulate? Authority can humble but not instruct; it can suppress reason but not put it in fetters. Were it true that the word of God so manifestly contradicted my reason, the most I could do would be to impose silence upon my reason. But my unrefuted arguments would, nevertheless, reappear in the most secret recesses of my heart, be transformed into disquieting doubts, and the doubts would resolve themselves into childlike prayers, into fervent supplications for illumination. I would call out with the Psalmist:

> Lord, send me Thy light, Thy truth,
> that they may guide and bring me
> unto Thy holy mountain, unto Thy dwelling place!

It is, in any event, harsh and offensive to impute to me—as do the anonymous *Searcher for Light and Right* and Mr. Mörschel, the non-anonymous author of a postscript to the work of the "Searcher"—the odious intention of overthrowing the religion I profess and of renouncing it surreptitiously, as it were, though not expressly. Imputative inferences like these ought to be banished forever from the intercourse of learned men. Not everyone who holds a certain opinion is prepared to accept, at the same time, all the consequences flowing from it, even if they are ever so correctly deduced. Imputations of this kind are hateful and lead only to bitterness and strife, by which truth rarely gains anything.

Indeed, the Searcher goes so far as to address me in the following manner: "Is it possible that the remarkable step you have now taken could actually be a step toward the fulfillment of the wishes which Lavater formerly addressed to you? After that appeal, you must undoubtedly have reflected further on the subject of Christianity and, with the impartiality of an incorruptible searcher after truth, weighed more exactly the value of the Christian systems of religion which lie before your eyes in manifold forms and modifications. Perhaps you have now come closer to the faith of the Christians, having torn yourself from the servitude of iron churchly bonds, and having commenced teaching the liberal system of a more rational worship of God, which constitutes the true character of the Christian religion, thanks to which we have escaped coercion and burdensome ceremonies, and thanks to which we no longer link the true worship of God either to Samaria or Jerusalem, but see the essence of religion, in the words of our teacher, wherever the true adorers of God pray in spirit and in truth."

This suggestion is advanced with sufficient solemnity and pathos. But, my dear sir, shall I take this step without first deliberating whether it will indeed extricate me from the confusion in which you think I find myself? If it be true that the cornerstones of my house are dislodged, and the structure threatens to collapse, do I act wisely if I remove my belongings from the lower to the upper floor for safety? Am I more secure there? Now Christianity, as you know, is built upon Judaism, and if the latter falls, it must necessarily collapse with it into *one* heap of ruins. You say that my conclusions undermine the foundation of Judaism, and you offer me the safety of your upper floor; must I not suppose that you mock me? Surely, the Christian who is in earnest about *light and truth* will not challenge the Jew to a fight when there seems to be a contradiction between truth and truth, between Scripture and reason. He will rather join him in an effort to discover the groundlessness of the contradiction. For this is their common concern. Whatever else they have to settle between themselves may be postponed to a later time. For the present, they must join forces to avert the danger, and either discover the paralogism or show that it is only a seeming contradiction that has frightened them.

I could, in this way, avoid the trap, without engaging in any further discussion with the Searcher. But what advantage would I derive from such a subterfuge? His associate, Mr. Mörschel, without knowing me personally, has seen all too deeply into my game. As he avers, he "discovered in the rebuked preface slight indications which lead him to conclude that I am as far removed from the religion into which I was born as from the one which he received from his fathers." To substantiate his assumption, after referring to p. IV, 1. 21 (where I mention together, in one line, pagans, Jews, Moslems, and adherents of natural religion, and ask for tolerance for all of them), p. V, 1. 8 (in which I speak again of tolerance for naturalists), and finally p. XXXVII, 1. 13

(where I speak of *eternal truths* which religion should teach), he literally quotes the following passage: "Reason's house of worship needs no locked doors. It does not have to guard anything inside, nor does it have to prevent anyone from entering. Whoever wishes to be a quiet observer, or to participate, is most welcome to the devout in his hour of edification." One sees that, in Mr. Mörschel's opinion, no adherent of revelation would plead so openly for toleration of naturalists, or speak so loudly of *eternal truths* which religion should teach, and that a true Christian or Jew should hesitate before he calls his house of prayer "reason's house of devotion."

I certainly do not know what could have led him to these ideas; yet they contain the entire ground of his assumption and induce him, as he says, not to invite me "to profess the religion he professes or to refute it if I am unable to join it, but to entreat me, in the name of all who have the cause of truth at heart, to express myself clearly and distinctly with respect to what must always be the most important thing for man." His intention, he assures me, is certainly not to convert me; nor does he wish to be the cause of objections against the religion from which he expects contentment in this life and unlimited felicity thereafter. Nevertheless, he would very much like—What do I know of what the dear man does not want and nevertheless still wants? In the first place, therefore, in order to calm the kindhearted author of this letter [let me state]: I have never publicly contested the Christian religion, nor shall I ever engage in dispute with its true adherents. And lest one should again accuse me of having wished by this declaration to intimate, as it were, that I have in my hands triumphant weapons with which to combat this faith, if I were so inclined; that the Jews possess secret information, hidden documents which throw a different light on the facts than the one in which the Christians present them or other such pretenses, the likes of which one considered us capable of inventing or actually imputed to us—in order to remove any suspicion of this kind once and for all, I hereby testify before the eyes of the public that I

at least have nothing new to advance against the faith of the
Christians; that, as far as I know, we are not acquainted with any
other accounts of the historical facts, and can present no other
documents than those which are universally known; that I, therefore, for my part, have nothing to advance that has not already
been stated and repeated countless times by Jews and naturalists,
and to which the opposite party has not replied time and again.
It seems to me that in the course of so many centuries, and particularly in our own, which is so fond of writing, enough has been
said and resaid in this matter. Since the parties have nothing new
to adduce, it is high time to close the books. Let him who has eyes
see, let him who has reason examine, and live according to his
conviction. What is the use of champions standing by the road-
side and offering battle to every passerby? Too much talk about a
matter does not render it any clearer, but rather obscures whatever faint light of truth there is. Take any proposition you please
and talk, write or argue about it—for or against it, often and long
enough—and you can be sure that it will continue to lose more
and more of whatever clearness it may once have possessed. Too
much detail obstructs the view of the whole. Mr. Mörschel has,
therefore, nothing to fear. Through me he shall certainly not become the cause of objections against a religion from which so
many of my fellow men expect contentment in this life and unlimited felicity thereafter.

I must, however, also do justice to his searching eye. What he
saw was, in part, not wrong. It is true that *I recognize no eternal
truths other than those that are not merely comprehensible to
human reason but can also be demonstrated and verified by human powers.* Yet Mr. Mörschel is misled by an incorrect conception of Judaism when he supposes that I cannot maintain this
without departing from the religion of my fathers. On the contrary, I consider this an essential point of the Jewish religion and
believe that this doctrine constitutes a characteristic difference
between it and the Christian one. To say it briefly: I believe that
Judaism knows of no revealed religion in the sense in which

Christians understand this term. The Israelites possess a divine *legislation*—laws, commandments, ordinances, rules of life, instruction in the will of God as to how they should conduct themselves in order to attain temporal and eternal felicity. Propositions and prescriptions of this kind were revealed to them by Moses in a miraculous and supernatural manner, but no doctrinal opinions, no saving truths, no universal propositions of reason. These the Eternal reveals to us and to all other men, at all times, through *nature* and *thing*, but never through *word* and *script*.

I fear that this may be astonishing, and again seem new and harsh to some readers. Invariably, little attention has been paid to this difference; one has taken *supernatural legislation* for a *supernatural revelation of religion*, and spoken of Judaism as if it were simply an earlier revelation of religious propositions and doctrines necessary for man's salvation. I shall, therefore, have to explain myself more fully. In order to avoid being misunderstood, I must ascend to prior [fundamental] ideas so that my reader and I will set out from the same position and be able to proceed at the same pace.

One calls eternal truths those propositions which are not subject to time and remain the same in all eternity. They are either *necessary*, in themselves *immutable*, or *contingent*; that is, their permanence is based either on their *essence*—they are true in this and no other way because they are *conceivable* in this and no other way—or on their *reality*: they are universally true, they exist in this and no other way because they became *real* in this and no other way; because of all the possible [truths] of their kind they are the *best*, in this and no other way. In other words, necessary as well as contingent truths flow from a common source, the source of all truth: the former from the *intellect*, the latter from the *will* of God. The propositions of necessary truths are true because God *represents them to himself* in this and no other way; the contingent, because God approved them and considered them to be in conformity with his wisdom in this and no other way. Examples of the first kind are the propositions of pure mathematics and of the art of logic; examples of the second are the general propositions of physics and psychology, the laws of nature, according to which this universe, the world of bodies and the world of spirits, is governed. The former are immutable even for the Omnipotent, because God himself cannot render his infinite intellect changeable; the latter, however, are subject to the will of God and are immutable only insofar as it pleases his holy will, that is, insofar as they are in accord with his intentions. His omnipotence can introduce other laws in their place and can, as often as it may be useful, allow exceptions to occur.

Besides these eternal truths, there are also *temporal, historical truths;* things which occurred once and may never occur again; propositions which have become true at one point in time and space through a confluence of causes and effects, and which, therefore, can only be conceived as true in respect to that point in time and space. Of this kind are all the truths of history, taken in its broadest sense; things of remote ages, which once took place, and are reported to us, but which we ourselves can never observe.

Just as these classes of propositions and truths differ by nature, so, too, do they differ in respect to their means of persuasion, or in the manner in which men convince themselves and others of them. The doctrines of the first kind, or the necessary truths, are founded upon *reason,* that is, on an immutable coherence and essential connection of ideas, according to which they either presuppose or exclude one another. All mathematical and logical proofs are of this kind. They all show the possibility or impossibility of thinking certain ideas in association with others. Whoever wishes to instruct his fellow man in them must not commend them to his belief, but should force them, as it were, upon his reason. He should not cite authorities and invoke the credibility of men who maintained exactly the same thing, but dissect the ideas into their essential elements and present them to his pupil, one by one, until his internal sense perceives their junctures and connections. The instructions which we may give others is, in Socrates' apt phrase, but a kind of midwifery. We cannot put anything into their minds which is not actually contained there already; yet we can facilitate the effort it would cost to bring to light what was hidden, that is, to render the unperceived perceptible and evident.

Besides reason, the truths of the second class require *observation* as well. If we wish to know what laws the Creator has prescribed for his creation, and according to what general rules the changes in it take place, we must experience, observe, and test individual cases; that is, we must, in the first place, make use of the evidence of the senses; and next, determine by means of reason what many particular cases have in common. Here, we shall indeed be obliged to accept many things, on faith and authority, from others. Our life span is not sufficient for us to experience everything ourselves; and we must, in many cases, rely on credible fellow men; we must assume that their observations and the experiments they profess to have made are correct. But we trust them only insofar as we know and are convinced that the objects themselves still exist, and that the experiments and observations may be repeated and tested by ourselves or by others who have the opportunity and the ability to do so. Indeed, if the result is important and has a considerable influence on our own felicity, or on that of others, we are far less satisfied with the report of the most credible witnesses, who tell us of the observations and experiments; but we seek an opportunity to repeat them ourselves, and to become convinced of them by their own evidence. Thus, the Siamese, for instance, may by all means trust the reports of the Europeans that in their part of the world water becomes solid and bears heavy burdens at certain times. They may accept this on faith, and, at all events, present it in their physics text books as an established fact, on the assumption that the observation can always be repeated and verified. But should there be any danger of lives being lost, should they have to entrust themselves or their kith and kin to this solidified element, they would be far less satisfied with the testimony of others, and would seek to convince themselves of its truth by various experiences, observations, and experiments of their own.

Historical truths, however—those passages which, as it were, occur but once in the book of nature—must be explained by themselves, or remain incomprehensible; that is, they can only be perceived, by means of the senses, by those who were present at the time and place of their occurrence in nature. Everyone else must accept them on authority and testimony. Furthermore, those who live at another time must rely altogether on the credibility of the testimony, for the thing attested no longer exists. The object itself and the direct observation of it, to which they may wish to appeal, are no longer to be found in nature. The senses cannot convince them of the truth. In historical matters, the authority and credibility of the narrator constitute the only evidence. Without testimony we cannot be convinced of any historical truth. Without authority, the truth of history vanishes along with the event itself.

As often, therefore, as it accords with the intentions of God that men be convinced of any particular truth, his wisdom grants them the most appropriate means of arriving at it. In the case of a necessary truth, it grants them the requisite degree of reason. If a law of nature is to be made known to them, it gives them the spirit of observation; and if a historical truth is to be preserved for posterity, it confirms its historical certainty and places the narrator's credibility beyond all doubt. It seems to me that only where historical truths are concerned does it befit the supreme wisdom to instruct men in a human manner, that is, through words and writing, and to cause extraordinary things and miracles to occur in nature, whenever this is required to confirm authority and credibility. Eternal truths, on the other hand, insofar as they are useful for men's salvation and felicity, are taught by God in a manner more appropriate to the Deity; not by sounds or written characters, which are comprehensible here and there, to this or that individual, but through creation itself, and its internal relations, which are legible and comprehensible to all men. Nor does He confirm them by miracles, which effect only historical belief; but He awakens the mind, which He has created, and gives it an opportunity to observe the relations of things, to observe itself, and to become convinced of the truths which it is destined to understand here below.

I therefore do not believe that the powers of human reason are insufficient to persuade men of the eternal truths which are indispensable to human felicity, and that God had to reveal them in a supernatural manner. Those who hold this view detract from the omnipotence or the goodness of God, on the one hand, what they believe they are adding to his goodness on the other. He was, in their opinion, good enough to reveal to men those truths on which their felicity depends, but not omnipotent, or not good enough to grant them the powers to discover these truths themselves. Moreover, by this assertion one makes the necessity of a supernatural revelation more universal than revelation itself. If, therefore, mankind must be corrupt and miserable without revelation, why has the far greater part of mankind lived without *true revelation* from time immemorial? Why must the two Indies wait until it pleases the Europeans to send them a few comforters to bring them a message without which they can, according to this opinion, live neither virtuously nor happily? To bring them a message which, in their circumstances and state of knowledge, they can neither rightly comprehend nor properly utilize?

According to the concepts of true Judaism, all the inhabitants of the earth are destined to felicity; and the means of attaining it are as widespread as mankind itself, as charitably dispensed as the means of warding off hunger and other natural needs. Here men are left to brute nature, which inwardly feels its powers and uses them, without being able to express itself in words and speech except in the most defective manner and, as it were, stammeringly. In another place, they are aided by science and art, shining brightly through words, images, and metaphors, by which the perceptions of the inner sense are transformed into a clear knowledge of signs and established as such. As often as it was useful, Providence caused wise men to arise in every nation on earth, and granted them the gift of looking with a clearer eye into themselves as well as all around them to contemplate God's works and communicate their knowledge to others. But not at all times is this necessary or useful. Very often, as the Psalmist says, *the babbling of children and infants will suffice to confound the enemy.* The man who lives simply has not yet devised the objections which so greatly confuse the sophist. For him the word *nature,* the mere sound, has not yet become a being that seeks to supplant the Deity. He still knows but little of the difference between direct and indirect causality; and he hears and sees instead the all-vivifying power of the Deity everywhere—in every sunrise, in every rain that falls, in every flower that blossoms and in every lamb that grazes in the meadow and rejoices in its own existence. This mode of conceiving things has in it something defective, but it leads directly to the recognition of an invisible, omnipotent being, to whom we owe all the good which we enjoy. But as soon as an Epicurus or a Lucretius, a Helvétius or a Hume criticizes the inadequacy of this mode of conceiving things and (which is to be charged to human weakness) strays too far in the other direction, and wants to carry on a deceptive game with the word *nature,* Providence again raises up other men among the people who separate prejudice from truth, correct the exaggerations on both sides, and show that truth can endure even if prejudice is rejected. At bottom, the material is always the same,—there endowed with all the raw but vigorous juices which nature gives it, here with the refined good taste of art, easier to digest, but only for the weak. On balance, men's doings and the morality of their conduct can perhaps expect just as good results from the crude mode of conceiving things as from these refined and purified concepts. Many a people is destined by Providence to wander through this cycle of ideas, indeed, sometimes it must wander through it more than once; but the quantity and weight of its morality may, perhaps, remain, on balance, about the same during all these various epochs.

I, for my part, cannot conceive of the education of the human race as my late friend Lessing imagined it under the influence of I-don't-know-which historian of mankind. One pictures the collective entity of the human race as an individual person and believes that Providence sent it to school here on earth, in order to raise it from childhood to manhood. In reality, the human race is—if the metaphor is appropriate—in almost every century, child, adult, and old man at the same time, though in different places and regions of the world. Here in the cradle, it sucks the breast, or lives on cream and milk; there it stands in manly armor, consuming the meat of cattle; and, in another place, it leans on a cane, once again without teeth. Progress is for the individual man, who is destined by Providence to spend part of his eternity here on earth. Everyone goes through life in his own way. One man's path takes him through flowers and meadows, another's across desolate plains, or over steep mountains and past dangerous gorges. Yet they all proceed on their journey, making their way to the felicity for which they are destined. But it does not seem to me to have been the purpose of Providence that mankind as a whole advance steadily here below and perfect itself in the course of time. This, at least, is not so well settled nor by any means so necessary for the vindication of God's providence as one is in the habit of thinking.

That we should again and again resist all theory and hypotheses, and want to speak of facts, to hear nothing but of facts, and yet should have the least regard for facts precisely where they matter most! You want to divine what designs Providence has for mankind? Do not frame hypotheses; only look around you at what actually happens and, if you can survey history as a whole, at what has happened since the beginning of time. This is fact, this must have been part of the design; this must have been decreed or, at least, admitted by Wisdom's plan. Providence never misses its goal. Whatever actually happens must have been its design from the beginning, or part of it. Now, as far as the human race as a whole is concerned, you will find no steady progress in its development that brings it ever closer to perfection. Rather do we see the human race in its totality slightly oscillate; it never took a few steps forward without soon afterwards, and with redoubled speed, sliding back to its previous position. Most nations of the earth live for many centuries at the same stage of culture, in the same twilight, one which seems much too dim for our pampered eyes. Now and then, a dot blazes up in the midst of the great mass, becomes a glittering star, and traverses an orbit which now after a shorter, now after a longer period, brings it back again to its starting point, or not far from it. Individual man advances, but mankind continually fluctuates within fixed limits, while maintaining, on the whole, about the same degree of morality in all periods—the same amount of religion and irreligion, of virtue and vice, of felicity and misery; the same result, if one compares like with like; of all these goods and evils as much as is required for the passage of the individual man in order that he might be educated here below, and approach as closely as possible the perfection which is apportioned to him and for which he is destined.

I return to my previous remark. Judaism boasts of no *exclusive* revelation of eternal truths that are indispensable to salvation, of no revealed religion in the sense in which that term is usually understood. Revealed *religion* is one thing, revealed *legislation,* another. The voice which let itself be heard on Sinai on that great day did not proclaim, "I am the Eternal, your God, the necessary, independent being, omnipotent and omniscient, that recompenses men in a future life according to their deeds." This is the universal *religion of mankind,* not Judaism; and the universal *religion of mankind,* without which men are neither virtuous nor capable of felicity, was not to be revealed there. In reality, it could not have been revealed there, for who was to be convinced of these eternal doctrines of salvation by the voice of thunder and the sound of trumpets? Surely not the unthinking, brutelike man, whose own reflections had not yet led him to the existence of an invisible being that governs the visible. The miraculous voice would not have instilled any concepts in him and, therefore, would not have convinced him. Still less [would it have convinced] the sophist whose ears are buzzing with so many doubts and ruminations that he can no longer hear the voice of common sense. He demands *rational proofs,* not miracles. And even if the teacher of religion were to raise from the dust all the dead who ever trod the earth, in order to confirm thereby an *eternal truth,* the skeptic would say: The teacher has awakened many dead, yet I still know no more about eternal truth than I did before. I know now that someone can do, and pronounce, extraordinary things; but there may be several suchlike beings, who do not think it proper to reveal themselves just at this moment. And all this is still far removed from the infinitely sublime idea of a *unique, eternal Deity* that rules the entire universe according to its unlimited will, and discerns men's most secret thoughts in order to reward their deeds according to their merits, if not here, then in the hereafter.

Anyone who did not know this, who was not imbued with these truths indispensable to human felicity, and was not prepared to approach the holy mountain, could have been stunned and over-whelmed by the great and wonderful manifestations, but he could not have been made aware of what he had not known before. No! All this was presupposed; it was, perhaps, taught, explained, and placed beyond all doubt by human reasoning during the days of preparation. And now the divine voice proclaimed: *"I am the Eternal, your God, who brought you out of the land of Mizrayim, who delivered you from bondage, etc."* A historical truth, on which this people's legislation was to be founded, as well as laws, was to be revealed here—commandments and ordinances, not eternal religious truths. "I am the Eternal, your God, who made a covenant with your fathers, Abraham, Isaac, and Jacob, and swore to make of their seed a nation of my own. The time for the fulfillment of this promise has finally come. To this end, I redeemed you from Egyptian slavery with unheard-of miracles and signs. I am your Redeemer, your Sovereign and King; I also make a covenant with you, and give you laws by which you are to live and become a happy nation in the land that I shall give you." All these are historical truths which, by their very nature, rest on historical evidence, *must* be verified by authority, and *can* be confirmed by miracles.

Miracles and extraordinary signs are, according to Judaism, no proofs for or against eternal truths of reason. We are, therefore, instructed in Scripture itself not to listen to a prophet if he teaches or counsels things contrary to established truths, even if he confirms his mission by miracles; indeed, we are to condemn to death the performer of miracles if he tries to lead us astray into idolatry. For miracles can only verify testimonies, support authorities, and confirm the credibility of witnesses and those who transmit tradition. But no testimonies and authorities can upset any established truth of reason, or place a doubtful one beyond doubt and suspicion.

Although the divine book that we received through Moses is, strictly speaking, meant to be a book of laws containing ordinances, rules of life and prescriptions, it also includes, as is well known, an inexhaustible treasure of rational truths and religious doctrines which are so intimately connected with the laws that they form but one entity. All laws refer to, or are based upon, eternal truths of reason, or remind us of them, and rouse us to ponder them. Hence, our rabbis rightly say: the laws and doctrines are related to each other, like body and soul. I shall have occasion to say more about this below, and shall content myself here with presupposing it as a fact, of the truth of which anyone can convince himself if he peruses the laws of Moses for that purpose, even if only in translation. The experience of many centuries also teaches that this divine law book has become, for a large part of the human race, a source of insight from which it draws new ideas, or according to which it corrects old ones. The more you search in it, the more you will be astounded at the depths of insight which lie concealed in it. At first glance, to be sure, the truth presents itself therein in its simplest attire and, as it were, free of any pretensions. Yet the more closely you approach it, and the purer, the more innocent, the more loving and longing is the glance with which you look upon it, the more it will unfold before you its divine beauty, veiled lightly, in order not to be profaned by vulgar and unholy eyes. But all these excellent propositions are presented to the understanding, submitted to us for consideration, without being forced upon our belief. Among all the prescriptions and ordinances of the Mosaic law, there is not a single one which says: *You shall believe or not believe.* They all say: *You shall do or not do.* Faith is not commanded, for it accepts no other commands than those that come to it by way of conviction. All the commandments of the divine law are addressed to man's will, to his power to act. In fact, the word in the original language that is usually translated as *faith* actually means, in most cases, *trust, confidence,* and firm reliance on pledge and promise. *Abraham trusted in the Eternal and it was accounted to him for piety* (Gen. 15:6); *The Israelites saw and trusted in the Eternal and in Moses, his servant* (Ex. 14:31). Whenever it is a question of the eternal truths of reason, it does not say *believe,* but *understand* and *know. In order that you may know that the Eternal is the true God, and there is none beside Him* (Deut. 4:39). *Therefore, know and take it to heart that the Lord alone is God, in heaven above and on the earth below, and there is none else* (ibid.). *Hear, O Israel, the Eternal, our God, is a unique, eternal being!* (Deut. 6:4). Nowhere does it say: *Believe, O Israel, and you will be blessed; do not doubt, O Israel, or this or that punishment will befall you.* Commandment and prohibition, reward and punishment are only for actions, acts of commission and omission which are subject to a man's will and which are guided by ideas of good and evil and, therefore, also by hope and fear. Belief and doubt, assent and opposition, on the other hand, are not determined by our faculty of desire, by our wishes and longings, or by fear and hope, but by our knowledge of truth and untruth.

Hence, ancient Judaism has no symbolic books, no *articles of faith.* No one has to swear to symbols or subscribe, by oath, to certain articles of faith. Indeed, we have no conception at all of what are called *religious oaths;* and according to the spirit of true Judaism, we must hold them to be inadmissible. Maimonides was the first to conceive of the idea of reducing the religion of his fathers to a certain number of principles, in order that, as he explains, religion, like all other sciences, would have its fundamental conceptions, from which all the others are deduced. This merely accidental idea gave rise to the *thirteen articles* of the Jewish catechism, to which we owe the morning hymn *Yigdal*, as well as some good writings by Chasdai, Albo, and Abrabanel. These are all the results they have had up to now. Thank God, they have not yet been forged into shackles of faith. Chasdai disputes them and proposes changes; Albo limits their number and wants to recognize only three basic principles which correspond rather closely to those which Herbert of Cherbury, at a later date, proposed for the catechism; and still others, especially Luria and his disciples, the latter-day Kabbalists, do not wish to recognize any fixed number of fundamental doctrines, and say: In our teaching, everything is fundamental. Nevertheless, this debate was conducted as all controversies of this kind should be: with earnestness and zeal, but without animosity and bitterness. And although the thirteen articles of Maimonides have been accepted by the greater part of the nation, no one, as far as I know, has ever branded Albo a heretic because he wanted to reduce their number and lead them back to far more universal propositions of reason. In this respect, we have not yet disregarded the important dictum of our sages: *"Although this one loosens and the other binds, both teach the words of the living God."**

In truth, everything depends here also on the distinction between *believing* and *knowing*, between religious doctrines and religious commandments. To be sure, all human knowledge can be reduced to a few, fundamental concepts, which are laid down as the bases. The fewer these are, the more firmly the structure will stand. But laws cannot be abridged. In them everything is fundamental; and in this regard we may rightly say: to us, all words

---

* I have seen many a pedant quote this saying to prove that the rabbis do not believe in the principle of contradiction. I hope to live to see the day when all the peoples of the earth will admit this exception to the universal principle of contradiction: *"The fast day of the fourth and the fast day of the tenth month shall become days of joy and gladness if you but love peace and truth"* (Zechariah 8:19).

of Scripture, all of God's commandments and prohibitions are fundamental. Should you, nevertheless, want to obtain their quintessence, listen to how that great teacher of the nation, Hillel the Elder, who lived before the destruction of the second Temple, conducted himself in this matter. A heathen said: "Rabbi, teach me the entire law while I am standing on one foot!" Shammai, whom he had previously approached with the same unreasonable request, had dismissed him contemptuously; but Hillel, renowned for his imperturbable composure and gentleness, said: "Son, *love thy neighbor as thyself*. This is the text of the law; all the rest is commentary. Now go and study!"

I have sketched the basic outlines of ancient, original Judaism, such as I conceive it to be. Doctrines and laws, convictions and actions. The former were not connected to words or written characters which always remain the same, for all men and all times, amid all the revolutions of language, morals, manners, and conditions, words and characters which invariably present the same rigid forms, into which we cannot force our concepts without disfiguring them. They were entrusted to living, spiritual instruction, which can keep pace with all changes of time and circumstances, and can be varied and fashioned according to a pupil's needs, ability, and power of comprehension. One found the occasion for this paternal instruction in the written book of the law and in the ceremonial acts which the adherent of Judaism had to observe incessantly. It was, at first, expressly forbidden to write more about the law than God had caused Moses to record for the nation. "What has been transmitted orally," say the rabbis, "you are not permitted to put in writing." It was with much reluctance that the heads of the synagogue resolved in later periods to give the permission—which had become necessary—to write about the laws. They called this permission a destruction of the law and said, with the Psalmist, "There is a time when, for the sake of the Eternal, the law must be destroyed." According to the original constitution, however, it was not supposed to be like that. The ceremonial law itself is a kind of living script, rousing the mind and heart, full of meaning, never ceasing to inspire contemplation and to provide the occasion and opportunity for oral instruction. What a student himself did and saw being done from morning till night pointed to religious doctrines and convictions and spurred him on to follow his teacher, to watch him, to observe all his actions, and to obtain the instruction which he was capable of acquiring by means of his talents, and of which he had rendered himself worthy by his conduct. The diffusion of writings and books which, through the invention of the printing press, has been infinitely multiplied in our days, has entirely transformed man. The great upheaval in the whole system of human knowledge and convictions which it has produced has, indeed, had on the one hand advantageous consequences for the improvement of mankind, for which we cannot thank beneficent Providence enough. However, like every good which can come to man here below, it has also had, incidentally, many evil consequences, which are to be attributed partly to its abuse, and partly also to the necessary condition of human nature. We teach and instruct one another only through writings; we learn to know nature and man only from writings. We work and relax, edify and amuse ourselves through overmuch writing. The preacher does not converse with his congregation; he reads or declaims to it a written treatise. The professor reads his written lectures from the chair. Everything is dead letter; the spirit of living conversation has vanished. We express our love and anger in letters, quarrel and become reconciled in letters; all our personal relations are by correspondence; and when we get together, we know of no other entertainment than playing or *reading aloud.*

Hence, it has come to pass that man has almost lost his value for his fellow man. Intercourse with the wise man is not sought, for we find his wisdom in writings. All we do is encourage him to write, in case we should believe he has not yet published enough. Hoary age has lost its venerableness, for the beardless youth knows more from books than the old man knows from experience. Whether he understood correctly or incorrectly does not matter; it is enough that he knows it, bears it upon his lips, and

can talk about it more boldly than the honest old man who, perhaps, has the ideas rather than the words at his command. We no
longer understand how the prophet could have considered it so
shocking an evil for *a youth to be overbearing toward an old man,*
or how a certain Greek could prophesy the downfall of the state
because a mischievous youngster had made fun of an old man in a
public assembly. We do not need the man of experience; we only
need his writings. In a word, we are *literati, men of letters.* Our
whole being depends on letters; and we can scarcely comprehend
how a mortal man can educate and perfect himself without a
book.

This was not the case in the bygone days of ancient times.
Even though one cannot say that they were better, they were certainly different. One drew from different sources, one gathered
and preserved in different vessels; and one made one's own that
which had been preserved by completely different means. Man
was more necessary to man; teaching was more closely connected
with life, contemplation more intimately bound up with action.
The inexperienced man had to follow in the footsteps of the experienced, the student in those of his teacher; he had to seek his
company, to observe him and, as it were, sound him out, if he
wanted to satisfy his thirst for knowledge. In order to show more
clearly what kind of influence this circumstance had upon religion and morals, I must once again permit myself a digression
from my path, from which, however, I shall very soon retrace my
steps. My subject matter borders on so many others that I cannot
always keep to the same road, without deviating into byways.

It seems to me that the change that has occurred in different
periods of culture with regard to written characters has had, at all
times, a very important part in the revolutions of human knowledge in general, and in the various modifications of men's opinions and ideas about religious matters, in particular; and if it did
not produce them completely by itself, it at least cooperated in a
remarkable way with other secondary causes. Scarcely does a man
cease to be satisfied with the first impressions of the external

senses (and what *man* can long remain content with them?),
scarcely does he feel the urge implanted in his soul to form concepts out of these external impressions, when he becomes aware
of the necessity to attach them to perceptible signs, not only in
order to communicate them to others, but also to hold fast to
them himself, and to be able to consider them again as often as
necessary. The first steps toward the separation of general characteristics he *can*, and indeed *must*, take without making use of
signs, for even now all new abstract concepts must still be formed
without the help of signs and are only later designated by a name.
The common characteristic must first be separated by the power of
attention from the fabric with which it is interwoven and must be
rendered prominent. What facilitates this is, on the one hand, the
objective power of the impression which this characteristic is capable of making upon us, and, on the other hand, the subjective
interest we have in it. But this throwing into relief and consideration of the common characteristic costs the soul some effort. It
does not take long for the light which attention concentrated on
this point of the object to disappear again, and the object is lost
in the shadow of the whole mass with which it is united. The
soul is not capable of advancing much farther if this effort must
be continued for some time and has to be repeated too often. It has
begun to set things apart, but it cannot think. What is one to ad-
vise it to do? Wise Providence has placed within its [the soul's]
immediate reach a means which it can use at all times. It attaches,
either by a natural or an arbitrary association of ideas, the ab-
stracted characteristic to a perceptible sign which, as often as its
impression is renewed, at once recalls and illuminates this characteristic, pure and unalloyed. In this manner, as is well known,
originated the languages of men, which are composed of natural
and arbitrary signs, and without which man would be but little
distinguished from the irrational animals; for without the aid of
signs, man can scarcely remove himself one step from the sensual.

In the same way in which the first steps toward rational knowledge must have been taken, the sciences are still being expanded

and enriched by inventions; this is why the invention of a new scientific term is, at times, an event of great importance. The man who first invented the word *nature* does not seem to have made a very great discovery. Nevertheless, his contemporaries were indebted to him for enabling them to confound the conjurer who showed them an apparition in the air, and to tell him that his trick was nothing supernatural, but an *effect of nature*. Granted, they did not yet have any distinct notion of the properties of refracted light rays and how, by their means, an image can be produced in the air—and how far does our own knowledge of this subject extend today? Scarcely one step farther; for we are still but little instructed about the nature of light itself and about its internal component parts—still, they at least knew how to refer a particular phenomenon back to a universal law of nature, and were not compelled to attribute a special arbitrary cause to every trick. This is also true of the more recent discovery that air has weight. Even though we cannot explain weight itself, we are at least able to relate the observation that fluids will rise in airtight tubes to the universal law of gravity which, at first glance, should rather make them go down. We can render it intelligible how the general sinking, which we cannot explain, must have caused a rising in this case; and this, too, is a step farther in knowledge. Accordingly, one should not be in a hurry to declare every scientific term an empty sound, if it cannot be derived from prior elementary concepts. It should suffice if it only denotes a universal property of things in its true extent. The term *fuga vacui* would not have been objectionable had it not been more universal than the observation. One found that there are cases in which nature does not rush to fill a vacuum immediately. Therefore the term had to be rejected, not because it was empty but because it was incorrect. Thus, the terms *cohesion of bodies* and *general gravitation* still continue to be of great importance in the sciences, even though we still do not know how to derive them from prior fundamental concepts.

Before Baron von Haller discovered the law of *irritability*, many an observer will have noticed the phenomenon itself in the organic nature of living creatures. But it vanished in an instant, and did not sufficiently delineate itself from secondary phenomena to hold the observer's attention. Whenever he noticed it again, it was to him a single effect of nature, one which could not remind him of the multitude of cases in which he had noticed the same thing before. It was, therefore, lost again very soon, like those which had preceded it, and it left behind no distinct memory in the soul. Von Haller alone succeeded in detaching this circumstance from its context, in perceiving its universality and denoting it with a word; and now it has awakened our attention, and we know how to relate each particular case in which we notice something similar to a universal law of nature.

The designation of concepts is, therefore, doubly necessary; first, for ourselves, as a vessel, so to speak, in which to preserve them, and keep them near at hand for use; and, next, to enable us to communicate our thoughts to others. Now, in the latter respect, sounds or audible signs have a certain advantage; for, if we wish to communicate our thoughts to others, the concepts are already present in the soul, and we may, whenever necessary, produce the sounds by which they are denoted and made perceptible to our fellow men. But this is not the case with regard to ourselves. If, at another time, we wish to reawaken abstract concepts in our soul and to recall them to our mind by means of signs, these signs must present themselves of their own accord, and not wait until our will summons them, since they already presuppose the ideas we wish to recall. Visible signs provide this advantage because they are permanent, and need not always be reproduced in order to make an impression.

The first visible signs which men used to designate their abstract concepts were presumably the things themselves. Since everything in nature has a character of its own which distinguishes it from all other things, the sense impression which this thing makes upon us will draw our attention chiefly to this distinctive feature, will excite the idea of it, and can therefore serve very well to designate it. Thus, the lion may have become a sign of courage, the dog, of faithfulness, the peacock of proud beauty, and thus did the first physicians carry live snakes with them as a sign that they knew how to render the harmful harmless.

In the course of time, one may have found it more convenient to take images of the things, either in bodies or on surfaces, instead of the things themselves; later, for the sake of brevity, to make use of outlines, and next, to let a part of the outline stand for the whole, and at last, to compose out of heterogeneous parts a shapeless but *meaningful whole;* and this mode of designation is called *hieroglyphics.*

All this could have developed, as one sees, quite naturally; but the transition from hieroglyphics to our alphabetical script seems to have required a leap, and the leap seems to have required more than ordinary human powers.

The opinion of some that our alphabetical script consists merely of signs of sounds, and can be applied to things and concepts only by means of sounds, is, to be sure, completely without foundation. Admittedly, script reminds us, who have a more lively conception of audible signs, first of all of perceptible words. For us, therefore, the road from script to things leads across and through speech; but there is no reason why it should be necessarily so. To one born deaf, script is the immediate designation of things; and if he were to regain his hearing, written signs would, initially, no doubt, bring first to his mind the things immediately connected with them, and only then, by means of those very things, the sounds which correspond to them. The real difficulty presented, I imagine, by the transition to our script consisted in the fact that, without preparation and cause, one had to conceive a deliberate plan of designating, by means of a small number of elementary signs and their possible transpositions, a multitude of concepts which would seem neither to admit of being surveyed nor, at first glance, of being arranged in classes, and thereby encompassed.

Nevertheless, even here, the path of the understanding was not entirely without guidance. Since one very often had occasion to transform script into speech and speech into script, and thus to compare audible and visible signs, one must soon have noticed that the same sounds often recur in the spoken language, as do the same parts in different hieroglyphic images, though always in different combinations, by means of which they multiply their meaning. In the end, one must have realized that the sounds which man can produce and render perceptible are not as infinite in number as the things denoted by them, and that one could easily encompass the entire range of all perceptible sounds and divide it into classes. And thus, in the course of time, one could extend and continuously improve this division, which was at first incompletely attempted, and one could assign to each class a corresponding hieroglyphic character. Even under this assumption it still remains one of the most glorious discoveries of the human spirit; one sees at any rate how men may have been led, step by step, without any flight of inventiveness, to think of the immeasurable as measurable, and to divide, so to speak, the starry firmament into figures, and thus to assign to every star its place, without knowing their number. I believe that in the case of the audible signs it was easier to discover the trace which one only had to follow in order to perceive the figures under which the immeasurable host of human concepts can be accommodated; and from then on, it was no longer so difficult to apply the same rule to written characters, and to arrange them, too, and divide them into classes. I think, therefore, that a people born deaf would have needed greater inventive powers to pass from hieroglyphics to alphabetical writing; because in the case of written characters it is not so readily apparent that they have a comprehensible range and can be divided into classes.

I employ the word *classes* whenever it is a question of the elements of audible languages; for even today, in our living, developed languages, writing is far from being as variegated as speech, and the same written sign is read and pronounced differently in different combinations and positions. Yet it is evident that by the frequent use of writing we have made our spoken languages more

monotonous and, following the rules and requirements of written characters, more elementary. For this reason, the nations
which are unacquainted with writing have a far greater diversity
in their spoken language, and many of the sounds in these languages are so indeterminate that we are able to indicate them
by our written characters only very imperfectly. In the beginning, therefore, one had to take things in their totality, and to
designate a multitude of similar sounds by one and the same written character. As time went on, however, finer distinctions were
perceived, and more characters were adopted to designate them.
But that our alphabet was borrowed from some kind of hieroglyphic writing can still be discerned today in most of the shapes
and names of the letters of the Hebrew alphabet,* from which, as
history clearly shows, all other known ways of writing originated.
It was a Phoenician who instructed the Greeks in the art of writing.

All these different modifications of writing and modes of designation must also have had different effects on the progress and
improvement of concepts, opinions, and knowledge. In one respect, to their advantage. The observations, experiments, and reflections in astronomical, economic, moral, and religious matters
were multiplied, propagated, facilitated, and preserved for posterity. These are the cells in which the bees collect their honey,
and save it for their own enjoyment and that of others. However,
as always happens in things human, what wisdom builds up in
one place, folly readily seeks to tear down in another, usually employing the very same means and tools. Misunderstanding, on the
one hand, and misuse, on the other, transformed what should
have been an improvement of man's condition into corruption and
deterioration. What had been simplicity and ignorance now became seduction and error. On the one hand, misunderstanding:
the great multitude was either not at all or only half instructed in
the notions which were to be associated with these perceptible

---

* א ox   ב house   ג camel   ד door   ו hook   ז sword   כ fist,
spoon   ל stimulus   ן fish   ס support, base   ע eye   פ mouth   ק ape
ש teeth

signs. They saw the signs not as mere signs, but believed them to be the things themselves. As long as one still used the things themselves or their images and outlines, instead of signs, this error was easily made. For besides their signification, the things also had a reality of their own. The coin was, at the same time, a piece of merchandise which had its own use and utility; therefore, the ignorant person could easily misjudge and wrongly specify its value as a coin. Hieroglyphic script could, to be sure, partly correct this error, or at least did not foster it as much as the outlines did, for its images were composed of heterogeneous and ill-matched parts, misshapen and preposterous figures which had no existence of their own in nature and could, therefore, as one should think, not be taken for writing. But this enigmatic and strange character of the composition itself afforded superstition the material for all sorts of inventions and fables. On the other hand, hypocrisy and willful abuse were busy, and furnished it with tales which it was not clever enough to invent. Whoever had once acquired consequence and authority wished, if not to increase, at least to preserve them. Whoever had once given a satisfactory answer to a question never wanted to be remiss in his responses. There is no nonsense so absurd, no farce so farcical, that one will not resort to it, no fable so foolish that one will not seek to make a credulous person believe it, merely to be ready with a *because* for every *why?* The phrase *I do not know* becomes inexpressibly bitter once one has proclaimed oneself to be a pundit, if not a polymath, especially when station, office, and dignity seem to demand that we should know. Oh, how many a man's heart must palpitate when he is at the point of either losing consequence and authority or of becoming a traitor to truth; and how few there are who possess the sagacity of Socrates, always to answer, at first, *I know nothing*, even in case one knows a little more than his neighbor, in order to spare himself embarrassment, and to render humiliation easier beforehand, should such a confession become necessary.

At all events, one sees how this could have given rise to the

worship of animals and images, the worship of idols and human
beings, as well as fables and fairy tales, and though I do not claim
that this is the only source of mythology, I believe that it may
have contributed very much to the origin and propagation of all
these inanities. It will, in particular, help to explain a remark
which Professor Meiners has made somewhere in his writings. He
claims to have observed that among the original nations, that is,
among those that formed themselves and do not owe their culture
to any other nation, the worship of animals was, without exception, more in vogue than the worship of men and that, indeed, inanimate objects were deified and worshiped more readily than
were human beings. I assume the correctness of this remark, and
leave it to the philosophic historian to vouch for it. I shall try to
find an explanation!

If men designate the things themselves or their images and outlines as signs of ideas, they can find nothing more convenient and
significant to indicate moral qualities than the animals. The reasons for this are the same as those which my friend Lessing, in
his treatise on fables, ascribes to Aesop for choosing animals to
be the actors in his apologues. Every animal has its definite, distinctive character, and presents itself in this light at first glance,
since its features as a whole largely point to this peculiar mark of
distinction. One animal is agile, the other sharp-sighted; this one
is strong, that one, calm; this one is faithful and obedient to man,
that one is treacherous or loves liberty, etc. Indeed, even inanimate objects have something more defined in their exterior than
man has for man. At first glance, man reveals nothing, or rather,
everything. He possesses all these qualities; at least, he is not
completely lacking in any of them, and the greater or lesser degree he does not indicate at once on the surface. His distinctive
character, therefore, does not strike the eye, and he is the thing in
nature least suited to designate moral ideas and qualities.

Even today, the characters of the gods and heroes cannot be
better indicated in the plastic arts than by means of the animal
or inanimate images which are associated with them. If a Mi-

nerva and a Juno already differ in their features, they are far better distinguished by the animal characteristics that are given to
them. The poet, too, if he wishes to speak of moral qualities in
metaphors and allegories, usually has recourse to animals. Lion,
tiger, eagle, ox, fox, dog, bear, worm, dove—they all speak and
the meaning leaps to the eye. Therefore, at first one sought to indicate and render perceptible through suchlike signs the attributes of what was deemed most worthy of adoration. Since it was
necessary to attach those most abstract concepts to perceptible
things, and to such perceptible things as are the least ambiguous,
one presumably must have chosen animal images, or have composed certain figures out of several of them. And we have seen
how such an innocent thing, a mere mode of writing, can very
soon degenerate in the hands of man, and turn into idolatry. Naturally, therefore, all primitive idolatry will be more animal worship than worship of man. Men could not be used at all to designate divine attributes; and their deification must have proceeded
from an entirely different quarter. Heroes and conquerors, or
sages, lawgivers, and prophets, must have come over from a happier region of the world, one that had been educated earlier, and
[they must have] distinguished themselves so greatly through extraordinary talents, and shown themselves to be so exalted, that
one revered them as messengers of the Deity or as the Deity itself. That this was far more likely to happen among nations that
owed their culture not to themselves but to others is easy to conceive; for, as the common saying goes, a prophet seldom acquires
extraordinary authority in his own country. Mr. Meiners's remark
would accordingly be a sort of confirmation of my hypothesis that
the need for written characters was the first cause of idolatry.

In judging the religious ideas of a nation that is otherwise still
unknown, one must, for the same reason, take care not to regard
everything from one's own *parochial* point of view, lest one should
call idolatry what, in reality, is perhaps only *script*. Imagine a
second Omhya [Omai] who, knowing nothing of the secret art of
writing, and without being gradually accustomed to our ideas,

would be suddenly removed from his own part of the world to one of the most image-free temples of Europe—and to make the example more striking—to the *Temple of Providence*. He would find everything empty of images and ornaments; only there, on the white wall, [he would see] some black lines,* traced, perhaps, by chance. But no! All the members of the congregation look at these lines with reverence, fold their hands and direct their adoration to them. Now take him just as rapidly and just as suddenly back to Othaiti, and let him report to his curious fellow countrymen on the religious ideas of the Dessau *Philanthropin*. Will they not deride as well as pity the insipid superstition of their fellow men who have sunk so low as to show divine adoration to black lines on a white surface? Our own travelers may very often make similar mistakes when they report to us on the religion of distant peoples. They must acquaint themselves very intimately with the thoughts and opinions of a nation before they can say with certainty whether its images still have the character of script, or whether they have already degenerated into idolatry. In plundering the Temple, the conquerors of Jerusalem found the cherubim on the Ark of the Covenant, and took them for idols of the Jews. They saw everything with the eyes of barbarians, and from their point of view. In accordance with their own customs, they took an image of divine providence and prevailing grace for an image of the Deity, for the Deity itself, and delighted in their discovery. In the same way, at the present day, readers still laugh at the Indian philosophers who say that this universe is borne by elephants, and place the elephants upon a large turtle, and maintain that the latter is upheld by an enormous bear, and that the bear rests on an immense serpent. The good people have, perhaps, not thought of the question: What, then, does the immense serpent rest upon?

Now read for yourselves in the *Shasta* of the *Gentoos* the passage describing a symbol of this kind which probably gave rise to this legend. I take it from the second part of the *Reports from*

---

* The words: "God, all wise, all-powerful, all-good, rewarding the good."

Bengal and the Empire of Hindustan, by J. Z. Hollwell, who had received instruction in the holy books of the *Gentoos* and was able to see with the eyes of a native Brahmin. These are the words in the eighth section:

> *Modu* and *Kytu* (two monsters, *discord* and *rebellion*) had been overcome, and now the Eternal, having been invisible before, manifested himself and glory surrounded him on all sides.
> The Eternal spoke: Thou *Birma* (power of creation)! create and form all things of the new creation with the spirit which I shall breathe into thee.—And thou, *Bistnu* (power of preservation)! protect and preserve, according to my ordinance, the things and forms created.—And thou, *Sieb* (destruction, transformation)! change the things of the new creation and transform them with the power wherewith I shall invest thee.
> *Birma, Bistnu* and *Sieb* heard the words of the Eternal, bowed and expressed their obedience.
> At once Birma swam into the surface of *Johala* (abyss of the sea), and the children *Modu* and *Kytu* fled and vanished as he appeared.
> When through the spirit of *Birma* the motions of the abyss calmed down, *Bistnu* transformed himself into a mighty bear [read: boar] (symbol of strength, according to the Gentoos, because, relative to his size, he is the strongest animal), descended into the abyss of *Johala,* and on his tusks brought up *Murto* (the earth).—Then spontaneously there issued from him a mighty tortoise (symbol of stability, according to the Gentoos) and a mighty snake (their symbol of wisdom). And *Bistu* put the earth [read: the snake] erect upon the back of the tortoise, and placed *Murto* upon the head of the snake, etc.

All this one finds among them also depicted in images; and one sees how easily such symbols and hieroglyphics could mislead one into error.

As is well known, the history of mankind actually went through a period of many centuries, during which real idolatry became the dominant religion in nearly every part of the globe. The images lost their value as signs. The spirit of truth, which was to have been preserved in them, evaporated, and the empty vehicle that remained behind turned into a pernicious poison. The concepts of deity which still survived in the ethnic religions were so deformed by superstition, so corrupted by hypocrisy and priestcraft, that one had reason to wonder whether atheism might not be less detrimental to human felicity, whether godlessness itself, as it were, might not be less ungodly than such a religion. Men, animals, plants, the most hideous and despicable things in nature were worshiped and revered as deities, or rather feared as deities. For the official ethnic religions of those times had no idea of the Deity other than that of a dreadful being, superior in power to us dwellers on earth, easily provoked to anger and hard to appease. To the shame of the human intellect and heart, superstition knew how to combine the most incompatible ideas, permitting human sacrifice and animal worship to exist side by side. In the most magnificent temples, constructed and decorated according to all the rules of art, one looked, to the shame of reason, as Plutarch put it, for the deity worshipped there, and one found on the altar a hideous, long-tailed monkey; and to this monster blooming youths and maidens were slaughtered. So deeply had idolatry debased human nature! *One slaughtered men,* as the prophet put it in an emphatic antithesis, *one slaughtered men in order to offer them to the cattle that were worshiped.*

Here and there philosophers sometimes dared to oppose the universal depravity and to purify and enlighten concepts, openly or by secret devices. They sought to restore to the images their old meaning or to impart to them a new one, and thereby to reinfuse, as it were, the soul into the dead body. But in vain! Their rational explanations had no influence on the religion of the people. Eager as the uneducated man seems to be for explanations, he is equally dissatisfied when they are given to him in their true simplicity. What is comprehensible to him is soon looked upon as tedious and contemptible, and he constantly searches for new, mysterious, inexplicable things, which he takes to heart with redoubled pleasure. His avidity for knowledge always wants to be acute, but never satisfied. Hence, public instruction found no hearing among the populace; it rather met with the most obstinate resistance on the part of superstition and hypocrisy, and received its customary reward: contempt or hatred and persecution. The secret devices and measures by which the rights of truth should have been upheld, to some degree, took themselves, in part, the road of corruption, and became nurseries for all kinds of superstition, all kinds of vice, and all kinds of abominations.

A certain school of philosophers conceived the bold idea of removing men's abstract concepts from everything figurative and imagelike, and of attaching them to such written signs as could, by their nature, be taken for nothing else, to *numbers*. Since numbers in themselves represent nothing, and are not in natural relation with any sense impressions, one should suppose that they would not be liable to any misinterpretation; one must take them for arbitrary *written signs* of concepts, or else consider them unintelligible. Here, one should think, the rudest intellect could not confound signs with things, and every abuse would be prevented by this subtle device. To anyone who does not understand numbers they are empty figures. Those they do not enlighten they will, at least, not lead astray.

So the great founder of this school could have made himself believe. However, soon enough folly took its wonted course even in this school. Dissatisfied with what one found so intelligible, so comprehensible, one looked for a secret power in the numbers themselves; for an inexplicable reality, again, in the signs, by which their value as signs was again lost. One believed, or at least made others believe, that all the mysteries of nature and of the Deity were concealed in these numbers; one ascribed miraculous power to them, and wished to satisfy through them and by means of them not only men's curiosity and avidity for knowledge, but also all their vanity, their striving for high and unattainable things, their forwardness and greed, their avarice, and their madness. In a word, folly had once more frustrated wisdom's plans and, again, annihilated or even employed for its own use what wisdom had provided for a better purpose.

And now I am able to explain more clearly my surmise about the purpose of the ceremonial law in Judaism. The forefathers of our nation, Abraham, Isaac, and Jacob, remained faithful to the Eternal, and sought to preserve among their families and descendants pure concepts of religion, far removed from all idolatry. And now their descendants were chosen by Providence to be a *priestly* nation; that is, a nation which, through its establishment and constitution, through its laws, actions, vicissitudes, and changes was continually to call attention to sound and unadulterated ideas of God and his attributes. It was incessantly to teach, to proclaim, and to endeavor to preserve these ideas among the nations, by means of its mere existence, as it were. They lived under extreme pressure among barbarians and idolaters; and misery had made them nearly as insensitive to the truth as arrogance had made their oppressors. God liberated them from this state of slavery by extraordinary miracles; He became the Redeemer, Leader, King, Lawgiver, and Judge of this nation that He himself had fashioned, and He designed its entire constitution in a manner that accorded with the wise purposes of his providence. Weak and shortsighted is the eye of man! Who can say: I have entered into God's sanctuary, looked over the whole of his plan, and am able to determine the measure, goal, and limits of his purposes? But the modest searcher is permitted to form conjectures and to draw conclusions from the results, so long as he always remembers that he *can* but surmise.

We have seen how difficult it is to preserve the abstract ideas of religion among men by means of permanent signs. Images and hieroglyphics lead to superstition and idolatry, and our alphabetical script makes man too speculative. It displays the symbolic knowledge of things and their relations too openly on the surface; it spares us the effort of penetrating and searching, and creates too wide a division betwen doctrine and life. In order to remedy these defects the lawgiver of this nation gave the *ceremonial law*. Religious and moral teachings were to be connected with men's everyday activities. The law, to be sure, did not impel them to engage in reflection; it prescribed only actions, only doing and not doing. The great maxim of this constitution seems to have been:

Men must be impelled to perform actions and only induced to en-gage in reflection. Therefore, each of these prescribed actions, each practice, each ceremony had its meaning, its valid signifi-cance; each was closely related to the speculative knowledge of religion and the teachings of morality, and was an occasion for a man in search of truth to reflect on these sacred matters or to seek instruction from wise men. The truths useful for the felicity of the nation as well as of each of its individual members were to be utterly removed from all imagery; for this was the main pur-pose and the fundamental law of the constitution. They were to be connected with actions and practices, and these were to serve them in place of signs, without which they cannot be preserved. Man's actions are transitory; there is nothing lasting, nothing en-during about them that, like hieroglyphic script, could lead to idolatry through abuse or misunderstanding. But they also have the advantage over alphabetical signs of not isolating man, of not making him to be a solitary creature, poring over writings and books. They impel him rather to social intercourse, to imitation, and to oral, living instruction. For this reason, there were but a few written laws, and even these were not entirely comprehensi-ble without oral instruction and tradition; and it was forbidden to write more about them. But the unwritten laws, the oral tradition, the living instruction from man to man, from mouth to heart, were to explain, enlarge, limit, and define more precisely what, for wise intentions and with wise moderation, remained unde-termined in the written law. In everything a youth saw being done, in all public as well as private dealings, on all gates and on all doorposts, in whatever he turned his eyes or ears to, he found occasion for inquiring and reflecting, occasion to follow an older and wiser man at his every step, to observe his minutest actions and doings with childlike attentiveness and to imitate them with childlike docility, to inquire after the spirit and the purpose of those doings and to seek the instruction which his master con-sidered him capable of absorbing and prepared to receive. Thus teaching and life, wisdom and activity, speculation and sociability were most intimately connected; or rather, thus should it be, according to the initial plan and purpose of the lawgiver. But the ways of God are inscrutable! Here, too, within a short period, things took the road of corruption. It was not long before this brilliant circle, too, had been completed, and matters again returned to a point not far from the low level from which they had emerged as, alas! has been evident for many centuries.

Already in the first days after the lawgiving that had been so miraculous, the nation relapsed into the sinful delusion of the Egyptians, and clamored for an *image in the shape of an animal.* According to their own assertion, as it seems, not really to worship it as a deity; for with this the high priest and brother of the lawgiver would not have complied, even if his own life had been ever so much in danger. They spoke merely of a divine being which should lead them and take the place of Moses who, they believed, had deserted his post. Aaron could no longer resist the people's pressure; he molded them a calf, and in order to hold them fast to their resolution to revere as divine not that image, but the Eternal alone, he exclaimed: *Tomorrow shall be a feast in honor of the Eternal.* But on the feast-day, while dancing and banqueting, the mob uttered quite different words: *These are your gods, Israel, who brought you out of Egypt.* Now the fundamental law was transgressed; the bond of the nation was dissolved. Reasonable remonstrances rarely produce results with an excited mob, once disorder prevails; and one knows what hard measures the divine lawgiver had to decide upon in order to restore the rebellious rabble to obedience. It deserves, however, to be noticed and admired, that divine Providence knew how to turn to advantage this in itself unfortunate incident and how to use it for sublime purposes entirely worthy of Divinity.

I have already mentioned above that paganism had a more tolerable conception of the power of the Deity than of its goodness. The common man looks upon goodness and proneness to reconciliation as weakness. He envies everyone the least pre-eminence in power, wealth, beauty, honor, etc., but not pre-eminence in goodness. And how could he do this, since for the most part it depends only on himself to arrive at the degree of gentleness which he finds enviable? It requires some reflection if we are to comprehend that hatred and vindictiveness, envy and cruelty are, at bottom, nothing but *weakness* and merely the effects of fear. Fear, combined with accidental, uncertain superiority, is the mother of all these barbaric sentiments. Fear alone renders us cruel and implacable. He who is conscious with certainty of his superiority finds far greater felicity in indulgence and pardon.

Once this insight has been achieved, one can no longer hesitate to regard love as being at least as sublime a pre-eminence as power, to credit the Supreme Being, to whom all-power is ascribed, also with all-goodness, and to recognize the God of might also as the God of love. But how far removed was paganism from this refinement! You cannot find in all its theology, in all the poems and other testimonies of earlier times, any trace of its having attributed love and mercy toward the children of man to any of its deities. "Both the people," says Mr. Meiners,* speaking of the wisest Greek state, "both the people and most of their bravest generals and wisest statesmen surely considered the gods whom they worshiped as beings more powerful than men, but [also as beings] who had in common with them the same needs, passions, weaknesses, and even vices. To the Athenians as well as to the rest of the Greeks, all gods appeared to be so malicious that they imagined an extraordinary or long-lasting good fortune would draw upon itself the anger and disfavor of the gods and would be upset by their devices. Moreover, they considered these very same gods to be so irritable that they regarded all cases of misfortune as divine punishments inflicted upon them not because of a general depravity of morals, nor on account of individual great crimes, but because of trivial and, for the most part, involuntary cases of negligence in the performance of certain rites and ceremonies." In Homer himself, in that gentle and loving soul, the thought had not yet been kindled that the gods forgive out of

* *History of the Sciences in Greece and Rome,* vol. II, p. 27.

love, and that without benevolence they would not be happy in
their heavenly abode.

And now it may be seen how wisely the lawgiver of the Israelites made use of their horrible offense against the majesty [of
God] in order to acquaint the human race with so important a
doctrine, and to open up to it a source of consolation from which
we still draw refreshment of soul. What sublime and terrifying
preparation! The revolt had been subdued, the sinners had been
made to recognize their culpable offense, the nation was in dis-
may, and God's messenger, Moses himself, had almost lost heart:
"O Lord, as long as Thy displeasure is not allayed, let us not depart from here. For how shall it be known that I and Thy nation
have found favor in Thine eyes? Is it not when Thou goest with
us? Only then shall we, I and Thy nation, be distinguished from
all others on the face of the earth."

God: "In this, too, I shall comply with thy request; for thou hast
found grace in my eyes, and I have singled thee out by name as
the one favored by Me."

Moses: "Cheered as I am by these comforting words, I dare to
make a still bolder request! O Lord, let me behold Thy *Glory!*"

God: "I will let *all My goodness* pass before thee,* and through
the name of the Eternal, I shall let thee know in what manner I
am gracious to whom I am gracious and am merciful to whom I
am merciful. My Presence thou shalt see from behind; for My
face cannot be seen." Thereupon the Presence passed before
Moses, and a voice was heard: "*The Lord (who is, was and will
be) eternal being, all-powerful, all-merciful and all-gracious;
long-suffering, of great lovingkindness and truthfulness, who pre-
serveth His lovingkindness even to the thousandth generation;
who forgiveth transgression, sin and rebellion, yet alloweth nothing to go unpunished.*"** What man's feelings are so hardened that

* What a great thought! You want to behold all my Glory; I will let my
goodness pass before you. *You will see it from behind. From the front it is
not visible to mortal eyes.*
** Ex., ch.33, v.15ff. according to my translation, printed in Hebrew
characters.

he can read this with dry eyes? Whose heart is so inhuman that he can still hate his brother and remain unforgiving toward him?

It is true, the Eternal says that He *will allow nothing to go unpunished,* and it is well known that these words have given rise to all sorts of misunderstanding and misinterpretation. But if they are not to cancel completely what was said before, they lead directly to the great thought which our rabbis discovered in them—that *this, too, is a quality of divine love that for man nothing is allowed to go entirely unpunished.*

A venerable friend, with whom I once conversed upon religious matters, put the question to me *whether I would not wish to be assured by a direct revelation that I would not be miserable in the future.* We both agreed that I did not have to fear eternal punishment in hell, for God cannot let any of his creatures suffer unceasing misery. Nor can any creature, by his actions, deserve the punishment of being eternally miserable. That the punishment for sin must be proportionate to the offended majesty of God and, therefore, infinite—this hypothesis my friend had given up long ago, as many great men of his church had likewise done; and concerning this matter there was no more occasion for dispute. The concept of *duties toward God*—a mere half truth—has given rise to the equally unstable concept of an *offense against the majesty of God;* and this one, taken in its literal sense, has brought forth that inadmissible idea of the eternality of punishment in hell—an idea the abuse of which has made not many fewer men truly miserable in this life than it renders, in theory, unhappy in the next. My philosophic friend agreed with me that God created man for his, that is, man's felicity, and that He gave him laws for his, that is, man's felicity. If the slightest transgression of these laws were to be punished in proportion to the majesty of the lawgiver and, therefore, were to result in eternal misery, God would have given these laws to man for his perdition. Without these laws of so infinitely exalted a being, man would not have to become eternally miserable. Oh, if men could be less miserable without divine laws, who can doubt that God would have spared them the fire of his laws, since it must consume them so irretrievably? This being assumed, my friend's question became more precisely defined: *Whether I must not wish to be assured by a revelation that in the future life I should be exempt even from finite misery?*

No, I answered; this misery can be nothing other than a well-deserved chastisement; and, in God's paternal household, I shall gladly suffer the chastisement I deserve.

But what if the All-merciful wished to remit man's well-deserved punishment, too?

He will certainly do so as soon as the punishment is no longer indispensable for the improvement of man. I need no direct revelation to convince me of this. Whenever I transgress the laws of God, the moral evil [thereby engendered] makes me unhappy; and God's justice, that is, his all-wise love, seeks to guide me to moral improvement by means of physical misery. As soon as this physical misery, the punishment for sin, is no longer indispensable for my repentance [lit. change of mind], I am, without revelation, as certain that my Father will remit the punishment as I am certain of my own existence. And, in the opposite case, if this punishment is still useful for my moral improvement, I do not wish to be exempt from it in any way. In the state of this paternal ruler, the transgressor suffers no other punishment than the one he himself must wish to suffer were he to see its effects and consequences in their true light.

But, replied my friend, cannot God deem it proper to let a man suffer as an example to others; and is not exemption from this exemplary punishment to be desired?

No, I answered, in God's state no individual suffers merely for the benefit of others. If this should happen, this sacrifice for the benefit of others must confer a higher moral worth on the sufferer himself; it must also be important to him, for the sake of the interior increase of his perfection, to have promoted so much good by his suffering. And if this is the case, I cannot *fear* such a condition; nor can I *wish* for a revelation [assuring me] that I shall never be placed in this condition of magnanimous benevolence which brings felicity to my fellow creatures and myself. What I have to fear is sin itself. In case I have committed a sin, the divine

punishment is a benefit to me, an effect of his paternal all-merci-
fulness. As soon as it ceases to be a benefit to me, I am assured
that it will be remitted. Can I wish that my Father withdraw his
chastising hand from me before it has had the effect it was meant
to produce? If I request that God let a transgression of mine go
entirely unpunished, do I know what I am requesting? Oh, surely
this too is a quality of God's infinite love that He allows no transgression of man to go entirely unpunished. Surely

> All-power is God's alone;
> And love also is Thine, o Lord!
> When Thou renderest to everyone according to his deeds.
>
> Ps. 62:12–13.

That the doctrine of God's mercy was on this important occasion first made known to the nation through Moses, the Psalmist
attests in another place, where he quotes from the writings of
Moses the same words of which we are now speaking:

> He showed His ways to Moses,
> His doings to the Israelites;
> *All-merciful is the Lord, all-gracious,*
> *Long-suffering and of great goodness.*
> He will not always contend,
> Neither will He keep His anger forever.
> He dealeth not with us after our sins,
> Nor requiteth us according to our iniquities.
> As the heaven is high above the earth,
> So His love is toward them that revere Him.
> As far as morning is from evening,
> So far He removeth our transgressions from us.
> Even as fathers have compassion upon their children,
> So hath the Lord compassion upon them that revere Him.
> For He knoweth our frame;
> He remembereth that we are but dust, etc.*
>
> (Ps. 103)

---

* The contents of this entire psalm are altogether of the utmost importance.
Interested readers will do well to peruse it in its entirety with attention and
to compare it with the above remarks. It seems evident to me that it was
occasioned by this remarkable passage in Scripture and that it is but an out-
burst of fervent emotion, to which the poet was led by contemplation of this
extraordinary event. Therefore, at the beginning of the psalm he summons his

Now I can summarize briefly my conceptions of the Judaism of former times and bring them into a single focus. Judaism consisted, or, according to the intention of the founder, was to consist of:

1. Religious doctrines and propositions or *eternal truths* about God and his government and providence, without which man cannot be enlightened and happy. These are not forced upon the faith of the nation under the threat of eternal or temporal punishments, but, in accordance with the nature and evidence of eternal truths, recommended to rational acknowledgement. They did not have to be given by direct revelation, or made known through *word* and *script*, which are intelligible only *here* and *now*. The Supreme Being has revealed them to all rational creatures through *things* and *concepts* and inscribed them in the soul with a script that is legible and comprehensible at all times and in all places. For this reason our much-quoted poet sings:

> The heavens declare the majesty of God,
> And the firmament announceth the work of His hands;
> From one day this doctrine floweth into another;
> And night giveth instruction to night.
> *No teaching, no words,*
> *Without their voice being heard.*
> *Their choral resoundeth over all the earth,*
> *Their message goeth forth to the ends of the world,*
> *To the place where He hath set a tent for the sun, etc.*

Their effect is as universal as the beneficent influence of the sun, which, as it hurries through its orbit, sheds light and warmth over the whole globe. As the same poet explains still more clearly in another place:

> From sunrise to sundown
> The name of the Lord is praised.

---

soul to the most solemn thanksgiving for the divine promise of his grace and paternal mercy: *"Bless, my soul, the Lord!* Forget not all his *benefits!* He forgiveth all thine iniquities, He healeth all thy diseases. He redeemeth thy life from destruction, *He crowneth thee with love and mercy,"* etc.

Or, as the prophet says in the name of the Lord: *From the rising of the sun to its setting, My name is great among the heathens, and in every place frankincense is presented unto My name, even pure oblations, for My name is great among the heathens.*

2. Historical truths, or records of the vicissitudes of former ages, especially of the circumstances in the lives of the nation's forefathers; of their having come to know the true God, of their way of life before God; even of their transgressions and the paternal chastisement that followed them; of the covenant which God concluded with them; and of the promise, which He so often repeated to them, to make of their descendants, in the days to come, a nation consecrated to Him. These historical records contained the foundation for the national cohesion; and as historical truths they can, according to their nature, not be accepted in any other manner than on *faith*. Authority alone gives them the required evidence; these records were also confirmed to the nation by miracles, and supported by an authority which was sufficient to place the *faith* beyond all doubt and hesitancy.

3. Laws, precepts, commandments and rules of life, which were to be peculiar to this nation and through the observance of which it should arrive at national felicity, as well as personal felicity for each of its individual members. The lawgiver was God, that is to say, God not in his relation as Creator and Preserver of the universe, but God as Patron and Friend by covenant of their ancestors, as Liberator, Founder and Leader, as King and Head of this people; and He gave his laws the most solemn sanction, publicly and in a never heard-of, miraculous manner, by which they were imposed upon the nation and all their descendants as an unalterable duty and obligation.

These laws were *revealed,* that is, they were made known by God, through *words* and *script.* Yet only the most essential part of them was entrusted to letters; and without the unwritten explanations, delimitations, and more precise determinations, transmitted orally and propagated through oral, living instruction, even these written laws are mostly incomprehensible, or inevitably became so in the course of time. For no words or written signs preserve their meaning unchanged throughout a generation.

The written as well as the unwritten laws have directly, as *prescriptions for action* and rules of life, public and private felicity as their ultimate aim. But they are also, in large part, to be regarded as a kind of script, and they have significance and meaning as ceremonial laws. They guide the inquiring intelligence to divine truths, partly to eternal and partly to historical truths upon which the religion of this people was founded. The ceremonial law was the bond which was to connect action with contemplation, life with theory. The ceremonial law was to induce personal converse and social contact between school and teacher, inquirer and instructor, and to stimulate and encourage rivalry and emulation; and it actually fulfilled this mission in the early period, before the constitution degenerated and human folly again interfered to change, through misunderstanding and misdirection, the good into evil and the useful into the harmful.

In this original constitution, state and religion were not conjoined, but *one;* not connected, but identical. Man's relation to society and his relation to God coincided and could never come into conflict. God, the Creator and Preserver of the world, was at the same time the King and Regent of this nation; and his oneness is such as not to admit the least division or plurality in either the political or the metaphysical sense. Nor does this monarch have any needs. He demands nothing from the nation but what serves its own welfare and advances the felicity of the state; just as the state, for its part, could not demand anything that was opposed to the duties toward God, that was not rather commanded by God, the Lawgiver and Regent of the nation. Hence, in this nation, civil matters acquired a sacred and religious aspect, and every civil service was at the same time a true service of God. The community was a community of God, its affairs were God's; the public taxes were an offering to God; and everything down to the least police measure was part of the *divine service*. The Levites, who lived off the public revenue, received their livelihood from

God. They were to have no property in the land, *for God is their property*. He who must sojourn outside the land serves *foreign gods*. This [statement which occurs] in several places in Scripture cannot be taken in a literal sense. It actually means no more than that *he is subject to alien political laws which, unlike those of his own country, are not at the same time a part of the divine service.*

The same can be said of the crimes. Every sacrilege against the authority of God, as the lawgiver of the nation, was a crime against the Majesty, and therefore a crime of state. Whoever blasphemed God committed lese majesty; whoever sacrilegiously desecrated the Sabbath implicitly abrogated a fundamental law of civil society, for an essential part of the constitution was based on the establishment of this day. *"Let the Sabbath be an eternal covenant between Me and the children of Israel,"* said the Lord, *"a perpetual sign that in six days the Eternal, etc. . . ."* Under this constitution these crimes could and, indeed, had to be punished civilly, not as erroneous opinion, not as *unbelief*, but as *misdeeds*, as sacrilegious crimes aimed at abolishing or weakening the authority of the lawgiver and thereby undermining the state itself. Yet, nevertheless, with what leniency were even these capital crimes punished! With what superabundant indulgence for human weakness! According to an unwritten law, corporal and capital punishment could not be inflicted unless *the criminal had been warned by two unsuspected witnesses with the citation of the law and the threat of the prescribed punishment;* indeed, where corporal or capital punishment were concerned, the criminal had *to have acknowledged the punishment in express words, accepted it and committed the crime immediately afterwards in the presence of the same witnesses.* How rare must executions have been under such stipulations, and how many an opportunity must the judges have had of avoiding the sad necessity of pronouncing a sentence of death over their fellow creature and fellow image of God! *An executed man is*, according to the expression of Scripture, *a reproach to God.* How much the judges must have hesitated, investigated, and considered excuses before they signed a sentence of death! Indeed, as the rabbis say, any court competent to deal with capital offenses and concerned for its good name must see to it that in a period of *seventy* years not more than one person is sentenced to death.

This clearly shows how little one must be acquainted with the Mosaic law and the constitution of Judaism to believe that according to them *ecclesiastical right* and *ecclesiastical power* are authorized, or that temporal punishments are to be inflicted for unbelief or erring belief. *The Searcher for Light and Right,* as well as Mr. Mörschel, are therefore far removed from the truth when they believe I have abolished Judaism by my rational arguments against ecclesiastical right and ecclesiastical power. Truth cannot be in conflict with truth. What divine law commands, reason, which is no less divine, cannot abolish.

Not unbelief, not false doctrine and error, but sacrilegious offenses against the majesty of the lawgiver, impudent misdeeds against the fundamental laws of the state and the civil constitution were punished; and these were punished only when the sacrilege exceeded all bounds in its unruliness, and came close to rebellion; when the criminal was not afraid to have the law quoted to him by two fellow citizens, to be threatened with punishment and, indeed, to take the punishment upon himself and commit the crime in their presence. Here the religious villain becomes a sacrilegious desecrator of majesty, a state criminal. Moreover, as the rabbis expressly state, *with the destruction of the Temple, all corporal and capital punishments and, indeed, even monetary fines, insofar as they are only national, have ceased to be legal.* Perfectly in accordance with my principles, and inexplicable without them! The civil bonds of the nation were dissolved; religious offenses were no longer crimes against the state; and the religion, as religion, knows of no punishment, no other penalty than the one the remorseful sinner *voluntarily* imposes on himself. It knows of no coercion, uses only the staff [called] *gentleness,* and affects only mind and heart. Let one try to explain rationally, without my principles, this assertion of the rabbis!

But why, I hear many a reader ask, why this prolixity to tell us something that is very well known? Judaism was a hierocracy, an ecclesiastical government, a priestly state, a theocracy, if you will. We already know the presumptions which such a constitution permits itself.

By no means! All these technical terms cast the matter in a false light, which I must avoid. Invariably, all we want to do is to classify, to fit things into pigeonholes. Once we know in which pigeonhole a thing is to be placed, we are content, however incomplete the concept we have of it may otherwise be. But why do you seek a generic term for an individual thing, which has no genus, which refuses to be stacked with anything, which cannot be put under the same rubric with anything else? This constitution existed only once; call it the *Mosaic constitution,* by its proper name. It has disappeared, and only the Omniscient knows among what people and in what century something similar will again be seen.

Just as, according to Plato, there is an earthly and also a heavenly Eros, there is also, one might say, an earthly and a heavenly politics. Take a fickle adventurer, a conqueror of hearts, such as are met with in the streets of every metropolis, and speak to him of the *Song of Songs,* or of the love of erstwhile innocence in Paradise, as Milton describes it. He will believe that you are raving, or that you wish to rehearse your lesson as to how to overwhelm the heart of a prude by means of Platonic caresses. Just as little will a politician à la mode understand you if you speak to him of the simplicity and moral grandeur of that original constitution. As the former knows nothing of love but the satisfaction of base lasciviousness, the latter speaks, when statesmanship is the subject, only of power, the circulation of money, commerce, the balance of power and population; and religion is to him a means which the lawgiver uses to keep the unruly man in check, and the priest—to suck him dry and consume his marrow.

This false point of view, from which we are in the habit of regarding the true interest of human society, I had to remove from the eyes of my reader. For this reason, I have not called the object by any name, but sought to represent it with its properties and determinations. If we look at it directly, we shall see in true politics, as a philosopher said of the sun, a deity, where ordinary eyes see a stone.

I have said that the Mosaic constitution did not persist long in its erstwhile purity. Already in the days of the prophet Samuel, the edifice developed a fissure which widened more and more until the parts broke asunder completely. The nation asked for a visible king as its ruler, a king of flesh and blood, perhaps because the priesthood had already begun to abuse the authority which it had among the people, as Scripture reports about the sons of the High Priest, or perhaps because the splendor of a neighboring royal household dazzled the eyes. In any event, they demanded a *king such as all other peoples have.* The prophet, aggrieved by this, pointed out to them the nature of a human king, who had his own requirements and could enlarge them at will, and how difficult it was to satisfy an infirm mortal to whom one has transferred the rights of the Deity. In vain; the people persisted in their resolution, obtained their wish and experienced what the prophet had threatened them with. Now the constitution was undermined, the unity of interests abolished. State and religion were no longer the same, and a collision of duties was no longer impossible. Still, such a collision must have been a rare occurrence, as long as the king himself not only was of the nation, but also obeyed the laws of the land. But let one follow history through all sorts of vicissitudes and changes, through many good and bad, God-fearing and godless regimes, down to that sad period in which the founder of the Christian religion gave this cautious advice: *Render unto Caesar that which is Caesar's and unto God what is God's.* Manifest opposition, a collision of duties! The state was under foreign dominion, and received its orders from foreign gods, as it were, while the native religion still survived, retaining a part of its influence on civil life. Here is demand against demand, claim against claim. "To whom shall we give? Whom shall we obey?" Bear both burdens—went the advice—as well as you can; serve two masters with patience and devotion. Give to Caesar, and give to God too! To each his own, since the unity of interests is now destroyed!

And even today, no wiser advice than this can be given to the House of Jacob. Adapt yourselves to the morals and the constitution of the land to which you have been removed; but hold fast to the religion of your fathers too. Bear both burdens as well as you can! It is true that, on the one hand, the burden of civil life is made heavier for you on account of the religion to which you remain faithful, and, on the other hand, the climate and the times make the observance of your religious laws in some respects more irksome than they are. Nevertheless, persevere; remain unflinchingly at the post which Providence has assigned to you, and endure everything that happens to you as your lawgiver foretold long ago.

In fact, I cannot see how those born into the House of Jacob can in any conscientious manner disencumber themselves of the law. We are permitted to reflect on the law, to inquire into its spirit, and, here and there, where the lawgiver gave no reason, to surmise a reason which, *perhaps,* depended upon time, place, and circumstances, and which, *perhaps,* may be liable to change in accordance with time, place, and circumstances—if it pleases the Supreme Lawgiver to make known to us His will on this matter, to make it known in as clear a voice, in as public a manner, and as far beyond all doubt and ambiguity as He did when He gave the law itself. As long as this has not happened, as long as we can point to no such authentic exemption from the law, no sophistry of ours can free us from the strict obedience we owe to the law; and reverence for God draws a line between speculation and practice which no conscientious man may cross. I therefore repeat my earlier protestation: Weak and shortsighted is the eye of man! Who can say: I have entered into God's sanctuary, gauged the whole system of his designs, and am able to determine its measure, goal, and boundaries? I may surmise, but not pass judgment nor act according to my surmise. If in things human I may not dare to act contrary to the law on the mere strength of my own surmise and legal sophistry, without the authority of the lawgiver or cus-

todian of the law, how much less may I do so in matters divine?
Laws that depend on the possession of the Land [of Israel] and
institutions governing it carry their exemption with them. Without Temple and priesthood, and outside Judea there is no scope
for either sacrifices or laws of purification or contributions to the
priests, insofar as these depend on the possession of the Land. But
personal commandments, duties imposed upon a son of Israel,
without regard to the Temple service and landed property in
Palestine, must, as far as we can see, be observed strictly according to the words of the law, until it shall please the Most High to
set our conscience at rest and to make their abrogation known in
a clear voice and in a public manner.

This is obviously a case of "what God has joined together man
may not tear asunder." Even if one of us converts to the Christian
religion, I fail to see how it is possible for him to believe that he
thereby frees his conscience and rids himself of the yoke of the
law. Jesus of Nazareth was never heard to say that he had come
to release the House of Jacob from the law. Indeed, he said, in
express words, rather the opposite; and, what is still more, he
himself did the opposite. Jesus of Nazareth himself observed not
only the law of Moses but also the ordinances of the rabbis; and
whatever seems to contradict this in the speeches and acts ascribed
to him appears to do so only at first glance. Closely examined,
everything is in complete agreement not only with Scripture, but
also with the tradition. If he came to remedy entrenched hypocrisy
and sanctimoniousness, he surely would not have given the first
example of sanctimoniousness and authorized, by example, a law
which should be abrogated and abolished. Rather, the rabbinic
principle evidently shines forth from his entire conduct as well as
the conduct of his disciples in the early period. *He who is not
born into the law need not bind himself to the law; but he who is
born into the law must live according to the law, and die according to the law.* If his followers, in later times, thought differently
and believed they could release from the law also those Jews who
accepted their teaching, this surely happened without his authority.

And you, dear brothers and fellow men, who follow the teachings of Jesus, should you find fault with us for doing what the founder of your religion did himself, and confirmed by his authority? Should you believe that you cannot love us in return as brothers and unite with us as citizens as long as we are outwardly distinguished from you by the ceremonial law, do not eat with you, do not marry you, which, as far as we can see, the founder of your religion would neither have done himself nor permitted us to do? If this should be and remain your true conviction—which we cannot suppose of Christian-minded men—if civil union cannot be obtained under any other condition than our departing from the laws which we still consider binding on us, then we are sincerely sorry to find it necessary to declare that we must rather do without civil union; then that friend of mankind, Dohm, will have written in vain, and everything will remain in the melancholy condition in which it is now, or in which your love of mankind may think it proper to place it. It does not rest with us to yield on this matter; but it does rest with us, if we are honest, to love you, nevertheless, as brothers, and to beseech you as brothers to make our burdens as bearable as you can. Regard us, if not as brothers and fellow citizens, at least as fellow men and fellow inhabitants of the land. Show us ways and provide us with the means of becoming better men and better fellow inhabitants, and permit us to be partners in enjoying the rights of humanity as far as time and circumstances permit. We cannot, in good conscience, depart from the law, and what good will it do you to have fellow citizens without conscience?

"But, if so, how will the prophecy come true that someday *there will be only one shepherd and one flock?*"

Dear brothers, who have the best intentions toward mankind, do not allow yourselves to be deluded! In order to be under the care of this omnipresent shepherd the entire flock need neither graze in one pasture nor enter and leave the master's house through a single door. This is neither what the shepherd wants nor advantageous to the prosperity of the flock. Is it a case of mistaking ideas or deliberately seeking to confuse them? One puts it to you that a union of faiths is the shortest way to the brotherly love and brotherly tolerance which you kindhearted people so ardently desire. There are some who want to persuade you that if only all of us had one and the same faith we would no longer hate one another for reasons of faith, of the difference in opinion; that [in such a case] religious hatred and the spirit of persecution would be torn up by their roots and extirpated; that the scourge would be wrested from the hand of hypocrisy and the sword from the hand of fanaticism, and the happy days would arrive, of which it is said *the wolf shall dwell with the lamb, and the leopard beside the kid,* etc. The gentle souls who make this proposal are ready to go to work; they wish to meet as negotiators and make the humanitarian effort to bring about a compromise between the faiths, to bargain for truths as if they were rights, or merchandise for sale; they want to demand, offer, haggle, obtain by hook or by crook, surprise and outwit until the parties shake hands and the contract for the felicity of the human race can be written down. Many, indeed, who reject such an enterprise as chimerical and impracticable, nevertheless speak of the union of faiths as a very desirable state of affairs, and sadly pity the human race because this pinnacle of felicity cannot be reached by human powers. Beware, friends of men, of listening to such sentiments without the most careful scrutiny. They could be snares which fanaticism grown impotent wants to put in the way of liberty of conscience. You know that this foe of the good has many a shape and form: the lion's fury and the lamb's meekness, the dove's simplicity and the serpent's cunning; no quality is so foreign to it that it either possesses it not or knows not how to assume it in order to attain its bloodthirsty purposes. Since, through your beneficent efforts, it has been deprived of overt power, it puts on, perhaps, the mask of meekness in order to deceive you; it feigns brotherly love, effuses human tolerance, and secretly forges the fetters which it means to place on reason, so that it may hurl it back again unawares into the cesspool of barbarism, from which you have begun to pull it up.*

* Atheism, too, has its fanaticism, as sad experience teaches. True, it might

Do not believe this to be a merely imaginary fear, born of hypochondria. At bottom, a union of faiths, should it ever come about, could have but the most unfortunate consequences for reason and liberty of conscience. For supposing that people do come to terms with one another about the formula of faith to be introduced and established, that they devise symbols to which none of the religious parties now dominant in Europe could find any reason to object. What would thereby be accomplished? Shall we say that all of you would think just alike concerning religious truths? Whoever has but the slightest conception of the nature of the human mind cannot allow himself to be persuaded of this. The agreement, therefore, could lie only in the words, in the formula. It is for this purpose that the unifiers of faiths want to join forces; they wish to squeeze, here and there, something out of the concepts; to enlarge, here and there, the meshes of words, to render them so uncertain and broad that the concepts, regardless of their inner difference, may be forced into them just barely. In reality, everyone would then attach to the same words a different meaning of his own; and you would pride yourselves on having united men's faiths, on having brought the flock under a single shepherd? Oh, if this universal hypocrisy shall have any purpose whatsoever, I fear it would be intended as a first step again to confine within narrow bounds the now liberated spirit of man. The shy deer would then be sure enough to let itself be captured and bridled. Begin only by binding the faith to symbols, the opinion to words, as modestly and pliantly as you please; only es-

---

never become rabid unless compounded by *inner* atheism. But that *external,*
overt atheism can also become fanatical is as undeniable as it is difficult to
understand. As much as the atheist, if he wishes to be consistent, must always
act out of *selfishness,* and as little as it seems to accord with selfishness when
he seeks to propagate atheism and does not keep the secret to himself, one,
nevertheless, has seen him preach his doctrine with the most ardent enthusiasm, become enraged and, indeed, launch persecutions if his preaching did
not meet with a favorable reception. And zeal is frightful when it takes possession of an avowed atheist, when innocence falls into the hands of a tyrant
who fears all things but no God.

tablish, for once and for all, the articles: then woe to the unfortunate, who comes a day later, and who finds something to criticize even in these *modest, purified* words! He is a disturber of the peace. To the stake with him!

Brothers, if you care for true piety, let us not feign agreement where diversity is evidently the plan and purpose of Providence. None of us thinks and feels exactly like his fellow man; why then do we wish to deceive each other with delusive words? We already do this, unfortunately, in our daily intercourse, in our conversations, which are of no particular importance; why then also in matters that have to do with our temporal and eternal welfare, our whole destiny? Why should we make ourselves unrecognizable to each other in the most important concerns of our life by masquerading, since God has stamped everyone, not without reason, with his own facial features? Does this not amount to doing our very best to resist Providence, to frustrate, if it be possible, the purpose of creation? Is this not deliberately to contravene our calling, our destiny in this life and the next?—Rulers of the earth! If it be permitted to an insignificant fellow inhabitant thereof to lift up his voice to you: do not trust the counselors who wish to mislead you by smooth words to so harmful an undertaking. They are either blind themselves, and do not see the enemy of mankind lurking in ambush, or they seek to blind you. Our noblest treasure, the liberty to think, will be forfeited if you listen to them. For the sake of your felicity and ours, *a union of faiths is not tolerance;* it is diametrically opposed to true tolerance! For the sake of your felicity and ours, do not use your powerful authority to transform some *eternal truth,* without which civil felicity can exist, into a *law,* some *religious opinion,* which is a matter of indifference to the state, into an *ordinance of the land!* Pay heed to the [right] *conduct* of men; upon this bring to bear the tribunal of wise laws, and leave us *thought and speech* which the Father of us all assigned to us as an inalienable heritage and granted to us as an immutable right. Should, perhaps, the link between *right* and *opinion* be too prescriptive, and should the time not yet be

ripe for abolishing it completely without courting damage, try, at
least, to mitigate as much as you can its pernicious influence, and
to put wise limits to prejudice that has grown gray with age.* At
least pave the way for a happy posterity toward that height of culture, toward that universal tolerance of man for which reason still
sighs in vain! Reward and punish no doctrine, tempt and bribe
no one to adopt any religious opinion! Let everyone be permitted
to speak as he thinks, to invoke God after his own manner or that
of his fathers, and to seek eternal salvation where he thinks he
may find it, as long as he does not disturb public felicity and acts
honestly toward the civil laws, toward you and his fellow citizens.
Let no one in your states be a searcher of hearts and a judge of
thoughts; let no one assume a right that the Omniscient has re-
served to himself alone! If we render unto *Caesar* what is *Caesar's,* then do you yourselves render unto *God what is God's! Love
truth! Love peace!*

* Alas, we already hear the Congress in America striking up the old tune
and speaking of a *dominant religion.*

COMMENTARY

COMMENTARY

33, 1   The Draft has: "Church and state." Mendelssohn uses the terms "church" and "religion" interchangeably throughout the book, a procedure which was criticized by some reviewers on the grounds that it tended to obscure the character of the church as a corporate entity. Mendelssohn does in fact recognize the institutional character of the church (see his definition, p. 41), but he considers the rights and functions of the church to be ideally determined by the essence of religion.

33, 2–3   State and church are "pillars of social life" insofar as they answer to the needs of human society; see below, p. 40. The (modern) state has a purely secular character; it represents "secular authority" and no longer forms an organic unity with the church as was the case in the Christian state (*respublica christiana*) of former times. Mendelssohn considers the church too as an organ of society and as subject to the principles of reason and natural law. In so doing he follows the consensus of Protestant ecclesiastical lawyers of the 18th century (Territorialists as well as Collegialists) who regarded the church both legally and historically as a voluntary and equalitarian "association" (*societas; coetus*); see Schlaich, *Kollegialtheorie*, Index, s.v. *societas*.

33, 8–9   Mendelssohn implies that he will endeavor to answer the still unresolved question by a new theory of his own. As

he remarks below, the doctrines hitherto proposed are "full of
vague and wavering ideas" (p. 34) or untenable even if they
are consistent (pp. 35–40: critique of Hobbes and Locke).
What he sets out to undertake is an examination of "first principles" which until now had been considered unassailable (pp.
80–81; 83–84). In his polemical treatise *Golgatha and Sheblimini!* Johann Georg Hamann spoke of the author of "Jerusalem" as "the theorist," using this term in a pejorative sense
(see Hamann, *Werke,* III, 294; 303).

33, 9–23 The phrase echoes a passage in Israel G. Canz's *Disciplinae morales omnes,* §2472, which reads in English translation: "It is, then, a singular concern of the church that the
three indeed illustrious rights—those appertaining to the
church (*iura collegialia*), to the state (*iura majestatis*), and to
the conscience (*iura conscientiae*)—be tempered in such a way
that certain limits subsist between them and that the boundaries circumscribing them be in no manner infringed upon.
*For immeasurable evils (infinita mala) have arisen from the
abuse of these rights of a threefold nature*" (emphasis supplied). The last sentence is obviously the one paraphrased by
Mendelssohn in the sentence beginning "Immeasurable evils."
Similarly in the Draft (see Appendix): "Border disputes between these [rights] have caused immeasurable evils." Mendelssohn had excerpted a number of paragraphs from Canz's
work when collecting material for "Jerusalem."

Mendelssohn's reference to the "liberty of conscience" also
takes its cue from Canz; see §2468. The attempt to find a happy
medium between the pretensions of the state and episcopal
lust for power has been said to characterize Collegialism (of
which Canz was an eminent spokesman); see Schlaich, *loc.
cit.,* 134.

34, 11–12 Montesquieu, *De l'esprit des lois,* V, 14: "Comme le
principe du gouvernement despotique est la crainte, le but en
est la tranquillité; mais ce n'est point une paix, c'est le silence
de ces villes que l'ennemi est près d'occuper." For a discussion
of Montesquieu's view of despotism as a form of government
operating through the motive of fear, see Mendelssohn, *GS,*
IV.2, 290f. Mendelssohn agreed with F. H. Jacobi that a perfectly virtuous character had perhaps the best chance of form-

ing under despotic rule (*JubA* VI.1, 108; 237), his reason probably being that it was steeled through adversity. He labeled the Roman Catholic Church and the Roman Catholic state despotic because of the Inquisition and the state-abetted canon law concerning heretics (*Ketzerrecht*). The latter held sway in Germany until the Peace of Augsburg (1555); cf. Martin Heckel, *Staat und Kirche*, 56–67.

34, 17–30 It seems that by "the early years of the Reformation" Mendelssohn understands the 16th and the first half of the 17th century in which the activity of the "reformers" unfolded and was reflected in the work of the "teachers" (theologians and ecclesiastical lawyers). As for the "striking embarrassment" he mentions, this may refer, in the first place, to the prevalent indecision concerning the theory and practice of excommunication (*ius excommunicationis*). Its retention by Luther and Calvin amounted to the survival of an essentially papal institution, which was opposed, however, by Zwingli and others. A candid reference to this anomaly Mendelssohn could have found in J. L. Fleischer's *Einleitung zum geistlichen Rechte* ("Introduction to Ecclesiastical Law"); see Altmann, *Essays*, 176. Another source of "embarrassment" which he may have had in mind was the contradictory definitions of the churchly prerogatives of princes. Melanchthon's doctrine of *cura religionis*, though designating the prince as "custodian of the law" (*custos utriusque tabulae*), nevertheless confined his rights to the externals of churchly life; according to his view, only the church (or more precisely, the *ecclesia vera* of the truly faithful) was authorized to decide on internal matters such as appointing the clergy. On the other hand, the principle of *cuius regio, eius religio* vindicated full episcopal power to the prince, thereby acknowledging the historical role which the secular arm had played in securing the success of the Reformation. In J. H. Boehmer's *Jus ecclesiasticum Protestantium* it was stated that this principle (*axioma*) dated back to the early period of the Reformers, which meant that there had indeed been a clash of views that could be construed as an "embarrassment." In reality, the principle referred to was not introduced in the reformatory epoch (which was by no means inclined to compromise) but as late as in Joachim

Stephani's *Institutiones iuris canonici* (Frankfurt, 1599) where it expresses the episcopal theory of *persona duplex:* princely and episcopal power are combined in one person; see Johannes Heckel, *Cura religionis;* Martin Heckel, *Staat und Kirche,* 80.

34, 30–35, 3   Mendelssohn refers here to textbooks of ecclesiastical law that were written in the second half of the 17th and during the 18th century and reflected the influence of Samuel Pufendorf's *De habitu Religionis Christianae ad vitam civilem* (1678) as well as of Christian Thomasius's polemical treatises, especially his *Das Recht evangelischer Fürsten in theologischen Streitigkeiten* ("The Right of Protestant Princes in Theological Controversies") (1669). They all start out from Pufendorf's characterization of the church as a *societas* (see the impressive list of works concerned presented by Schlaich, *loc. cit.,* 49–51) but then divide, at times in a rather blurred way, into the two trends of Territorialism and Collegialism, both agreeing in their rejection of the episcopal theory. The chief representatives of Territorialism are Christian Thomasius, Hermann Conring, Caspar Ziegler, and Johann Brunnemann. They are joined, in the Enlightenment phase of the movement, by Justus Henning Boehmer. Their doctrine assigns the *ius circa sacra* or governance of the church (*Kirchenregiment*) to the prince as a right inherent in his lordly power as such and not as merely accruing to it by virtue of the de facto transfer of episcopal rights, as had been suggested by the episcopal theory. In consequence, the prince ceases to be a *duplex persona.* The Old Testament kings (David, Jehosaphat, Hezekiah) and the Christian Roman emperors (Constantine the Great, Theodosius I, Justinian I) are invoked as prototypes of Christian princes in the exercise of governing the church. The Territorialist position adopted the recognition of the *ius circa sacra* as indigenous to lordship from Hugo Grotius (*De Imperio Summarum Potestatum circa Sacra,* 1647) and, ultimately, from Thomas Erastus (died 1580); see *Johannis Brunnemanni De jure ecclesiastico tractatus posthumus . . . , Francofurti & Lipsiae,* 1709, 8; Johannes Heckel, *Cura religionis,* 290–98; Joseph Lecler, *Toleration,* II, 308–14.

According to Territorialist doctrine the church can lay no claim to the exercise of power (*imperium*). Her function is one of service (*ministerium*). It is not part of the state but only a voluntary association or *collegium*. It consists solely of teachers and auditors, not of rulers and ruled. It is a society of equals (*societas aequalis*). Hence it possesses no right of excommunication. Ownership of a power of this kind would make it a state within the state (*status in statu, imperium in imperio*). In this way a separation of state and church is effected and the road is paved for freedom of conscience. In Thomasius's words, the noblest of the regalia belonging to a prince in matters of religion (*circa sacra*) is the prerogative to tolerate dissidents and to protect them against persecution. Thus it is precisely the absolute state, whose sovereignty extends over the church, that becomes the patron saint of liberty of conscience (cf. Mendelssohn's observations on the toleration enjoyed under the rule of Frederick the Great, below, pp. 78–80). Notwithstanding all this, there is an inner contradiction in the Territorialist doctrine. The assertion of princely power in the realm of the church—the *ius circa sacra*—ill accords with liberty of conscience, as was noticed by the Collegialist Pfaff. This inner contradiction did not escape Mendelssohn either. Hence his radical rejection of all *iura circa sacra*, be they claimed by the state or by the church (see below, pp. 83–84). Concerning the early phase of Territorialism see Martin Heckel, *Staat und Kirche*, 109–27; 241–44; for later (rational) Territorialism, see Schlaich's article in *Zeitschrift der Savigny-Stiftung für Rechtsgeschichte*, vol. 84, Canonistic Section, LIII (1967), 269–340, especially 328 (inner contradiction); Idem, *Kollegialtheorie*, 118–29.

The other doctrine, Collegialism, defended the right of the church as a corporation (*collegium; societas*) to administer its internal affairs in complete independence from the state, this right being one of *directio*, not of *imperium*, and applying to the order of service (*ius liturgicum*), the appointment of the clergy (*ius vocationis*), and the collection of funds (*ius collectandi*). It also claimed the right to expel members that contravened the statutes of the church (*ius excommunicationis*). It called these rights *iura circa sacra collegialia* as distinct from the prerogatives of the state (*iura majestatis*) which extended to churchly matters only insofar as the security of the commonwealth was concerned (*ius inspectionis*).

Notwithstanding this outspoken claim to internal autonomy, the Collegialists were prepared to recognize the princely *ius circa sacra*—a de facto reality—on the assumption that it had been voluntarily ceded by the church and was being exercised in the name of the church; see Mosheim, *Kirchenrecht*, 210f.; the inner contradiction of this theory is pointed out by Schlaich, *Kollegialtheorie*, 37ff.; concerning the Collegialist *potestas ecclesiastica*, see ibid., 226–31.

In light of the above account, Mendelssohn's brief remark about the "vagueness" still to be found in the textbooks of ecclesiastical law would seem to be fully justified. His statement that the clergy "will not or cannot give up all claims to a constitution" refers, no doubt, to Collegialism, particularly to its insistence on the *ius excommunicationis* ("a claim to power and rights, yet no one can state who should exercise them"); see Canz, *Disciplinae*, §2655ff., where the question is discussed whether the *potestas excommunicandi* belongs to the prince or to the church. The fact that Mendelssohn speaks summarily of ecclesiastical law without specifying the trend or trends to which he refers should cause no surprise. The division—current today—into the three major trends (Episcopalianism, Territorialism, Collegialism) appears for the first time in Daniel Nettelbladt's *De tribus systematibus doctrinae de jure sacrorum dirigendorum,* which was published in 1783, the year in which Mendelssohn's *Jerusalem* came out; see Schlaich, *Kollegialtheorie,* 17; 33f.

35, 4   Mendelssohn now turns his attention away from ecclesiastical law—to which he will briefly return later (pp. 79–84)—in order to discuss two thinkers—Hobbes and Locke—who deal with the problem of church and state on a philosophical level, one more congenial to his taste. Yet he was obviously conscious of the importance of the debate in the ecclesiastical law schools which had recourse not only to reason, natural law, and Scripture but also to canonical law, the "Confessions," and the secular juridical sources. The attention he paid to that debate reflects his keen awareness of the fact that in it the acuteness of the problem was most concretely envisaged. The philosophical discussion moved on a more remote and abstract plane but it too grew out of the ecclesiastical law background. Hobbes's theory was, in a sense, the philosophical formulation of radical Territorialism (Erastianism), while Locke's position represented the essence of Collegialism. Hence it was a happy choice on Mendelssohn's part when he selected these two philosophers for the purpose of clarifying his own ideas on the subject. (He had done so already in the Draft.) He thereby remained, as it were, within the horizon of the problems staked out by the ecclesiastical lawyers.

35, 4–7 Thomas Hobbes (1588–1679) developed his doctrine of the indivisibility of the sovereign power under the impact of the religious strife that rent political life in England, created disorders and led eventually to civil war (1642–53) and to the temporary abolition of the monarchy (1653–60). He himself spent the years 1640–51 as a refugee in Paris. The "fanaticism" referred to by Mendelssohn applies to the Presbyterian opposition in Parliament which sought to obstruct any strengthening of royal power. As recent research has shown, Hobbes conceived of his theory already prior to the outbreak of hostilities (1642), in anticipation of the dangers in store; see Windfried Förster, *Thomas Hobbes und der Puritanismus*, Berlin, 1969, 14. He described the events in his *Behemoth, the History of the Causes of the Civil Wars of England, from 1640 to 1660* (written around 1668; published without his consent in 1679; re-edited in *Tracts of Mr. Thomas Hobbs (sic) of Malmesbury*, London, 1682). Mendelssohn does not seem to have known this work. His library contained, however, a German translation of the *History of the Reformation in England* by Gilbert Burnet (1643–1715), the Latitudinarian Bishop of Salisbury (*Verzeichnis*, 45, no. 521, only vol. II listed).

35, 7–10 Similarly, Leo Strauss, *The Political Philosophy of Hobbes* (Oxford, 1936; 6th ed., Chicago, 1973), ch. 7, describes the political goals of Hobbes in terms of bourgeois liberalism in search of protection and security. Likewise Michael Oakeshott in the Introduction to his edition of Hobbes's *Leviathan* (Oxford, 1960, lv–lviii) and C. B. MacPherson, *The Political Theory of Possessive Individualism: Hobbes to Locke* (Oxford, 1962). Other interpreters see in Hobbes a spokesman of the totalitarian state; cf. Förster, *loc. cit.*, 16f.

In Hobbes's language "safety" stands for the Latin term *salus* (which denotes also welfare, prosperity). The office of the sovereign, he says, is meant to procure the safety of the people, and safety is defined in terms that transcend mere security; see *De cive*, XIII.4: Per *salutem* autem intelligi debet non sola vitae qualitercunque conservatio, sed quatenus fieri potest vita beata; *Leviathan*, XXX (*OL*, III, 240): In *salute* autem *populi* comprehendo non solum civium vitam, sed etiam commoda vitae; Oakeshott, 219: But by safety here, is not meant a bare preservation, but also all other contentments of life, which every man by lawful industry, without danger, or hurt to the commonwealth, shall acquire to himself. Hobbes echoes here the Aristotelian definition of the purpose of the state; see Aristotle, *Politics*, I.i.8; III.iv.2–3. Leo Strauss, *loc. cit.*, 33 seems to have ignored Hobbes's definition of *salus* (safety) in *De cive* and *Leviathan*.

35, 10–12   In *De cive*, VI.13 (*OL*, II, 224) Hobbes speaks of *Imperium Absolutum* and in *Leviathan*, XVIII (*OL*, III, 138–39; Oakeshott, 113–19) he says of the twelve rights of the sovereign that they represent the indivisible unity of the supreme power; that they are "essential and inseparable" (*essentialia et inseparabilia*). The *summa potestas* which is said to be indivisible denotes in the first place the inseparability of the secular power but implies also the indivisibility of secular and spiritual authority. In this world there is but one government. He who talks of temporal rule (*regimen temporale*) as distinct from spiritual rule (*regimen spirituale*) uses meaningless words (*verba inania*) with the intention of obscuring men's awareness as to whom obedience is due (*Leviathan*, XXXIX; *OL*, III, 337; Oakeshott, 306). Dividing the power of the commonwealth is tantamount to dissolving it (ibid., XXIX; *OL*, III, 234; Oakeshott, 213); cf. F. C. Hood, *The Divine Politics of Thomas Hobbes* (Oxford, 1964), 165.

35, 12–15   *De cive*, VI.9 (*OL*, II, 221): ejusdem summi imperii est . . . declarare . . . quid suum, quid alienum, quid justum, quid injustum, quid honestum, quid inhonestum, quid bonum, quid malum appellandum sit; *Leviathan*, XVIII (*OL*, III, 136): Regulae ergo, quibus definiuntur meum et tuum, et in actionibus bonum, malum, licitum, illicitum, a quibus de-

pendet pax civium, ab habente potestatem summam prae-
scribendae sunt; Oakeshott, 117: These rules of propriety, or
meum and *tuum,* and of good, evil, lawful, and unlawful in
the actions of subjects, are the civil laws. . . .

35, 15–17 Cf. *De cive,* I.10 (*OL,* II, 164f.): Natura dedit uni-
cuique jus in omnia: hoc est, in statu mere naturali . . . uni-
cuique licebat facere quaecunque et in quoscunque licebat, et
possidere, uti, frui omnibus, quae volebat et poterat. (In the
state of nature every one has the right to everything as a
means to self-preservation.) *Leviathan,* XIV (*OL,* III, 103;
Oakeshott, 85) mentions this right in connection with the second law of nature, which counsels the abandonment of it; see
Hood, *loc. cit.,* 49. It was this doctrine of everyone's right to
everything (*jus omnium in omnia*) and its corollary, the fiction
of a war of all against all (*bellum omnium in omnes*) that provoked most of the criticism. Samuel Pufendorf objected that a
right of all to everything was incapable of taking effect (a
point that had not been ignored by Hobbes; see *De cive,* I.11;
OL, II, 165) and therefore could not be called a right (*De jure
naturae et gentium,* 2nd ed., 1684, I, 7, 13). What Hobbes
called natural right he described as a mere natural faculty
(ability); ibid., III, 5, 3. Cf. Denzer, *Pufendorf,* 87; 113. He
also attempted to interpret Hobbes in a modified sense: The
latter's true meaning was that the *jus omnium in omnia* denoted
every man's ability to use his natural faculties in accordance
with the dictates of reason; ibid., I, 6, 10; II, 2, 3. It was Spinoza, Pufendorf points out, who undoubtedly equated right
and might; ibid., II, 2, 3; see Strauss, *Hobbes,* 28.

Richard Cumberland's critique of Hobbes, with which Mendelssohn was familiar (see *JubA* II, 320; 426), stressed the
"absurd consequences" following from the doctrine of everybody's right to everything; see his *De legibus naturae,* I, xxx–
xxxii. Mendelssohn himself took issue with Hobbes's theory
(*jus omnium in omnia* and *bellum omnium in omnes*) as early
as in his Open Letter (*Sendschreiben*) to Lessing (see *JubA*
II, 99, 101; 392; 394). For the importance of Hobbes's theory
for the evolution of the modern doctrine of natural law, see
Strauss, *Natural Right and History,* 165–202; Karl-Heinz Ilting,
art. "Naturrecht," in Brunner, *Grundbegriffe,* IV, 178–292.

35, 17–19 *De cive,* V.2 (*OL,* II, 210); *Leviathan,* XIII (*OL,* III, 99): Manifestum igitur est, quamdiu nulla est potentia coerciva, tamdiu conditionem hominum eam esse quam dixi bellum esse uniuscujusque contra unumquemque; Oakeshott, 82: "Hereby it is manifest, that during the time men live without a common power to keep them all in awe, they are in that condition which is called war; and such a war, as is of every man, against every man." The war of all against all is the natural state (*status naturalis*), since in the precivil (and extracivil) condition human passions like vanity, obstinacy and desire have free play; *De cive,* I.4–6 (*OL,* II, 162f.). Pufendorf (*De jure naturae et gentium,* II, 2, 8 and passim) denied the right of labeling the condition of man in the natural state as one of universal war. One had to consider the fact that man is characterized not only by the instinct for self-preservation but also by socialibility (*socialitas*), a quality that derives from a sense of infirmity and dependence on others (*imbecillitas*) and that functions as a moral norm; see Krieger, *Politics of Discretion,* 92f.; Denzer, *Pufendorf,* 92–96; 102f.; 111; 113; 120. Pufendorf refers more than once to Cumberland's critique of Hobbes, which proceeded from the assumption of man's natural "benevolence"; see Denzer, *loc. cit.,* 120; 263. He admits, however, that the absence of security in the *status naturalis* involves the danger of anarchy and, hence, renders the remedy provided by the social contract (*pactum sociale*) a necessity, a view adopted also by the Territorialist trend of ecclesiastical law (Christian Thomasius; J. H. Boehmer). This consideration became part and parcel of political theory and is found also in Locke's *Two Treatises of Government,* II, 19.

Mendelssohn knew Cumberland's and Pufendorf's critique of Hobbes's doctrine of the natural state already through his translation into German of Rousseau's second *Discours* (see *JubA* VI.2, 96). In his random notes on this work by Rousseau (*JubA* II, 8) he shares the latter's view that the war of all against all, far from belonging to the state of nature, is but the result of societal development: "It is the Hobbesians who take these ideas from the present civil condition and transfer them to the primitive age." Cf. *JubA* II, 98. For an analysis of Rousseau's view, see Brandt, *Rousseaus Philosophie,* 56f.

35, 24-25 The term "civil liberty" and the sense in which it is used by Mendelssohn reflect the influence of the more advanced phase of the German natural law school (Achenwall; Nettlebladt) which, in contrast to the older school (including Wolff), designated by *libertas civilis* the freedom of the citizen, not that of the sovereign. According to previous usage *libertas civilis* denotes the independence of the sovereign or of the state as a whole. The subject has no claim to specifically civil liberties. All he owns is natural liberty (*libertas naturalis*) to the extent it survives the curtailing of it by the social contract. This residual natural liberty must not be confused with civil liberty. The latter as a prerogative of the citizen is possible only by a revolution in terminology which divorced its meaning from the concept of the sovereign and applied it to the citizen; see Klippel, *Politische Freiheit*, 59ff.

In *Leviathan*, XXI (*De libertate civium*"; "Of the Liberty of Subjects") Hobbes, too, differentiates between (1) *libertas civilis* that belongs to the sovereign; (2) *libertas civitatis* that belongs to the state and represents the ideal for which the ancient Greeks and Romans fought; and (3) *libertas civium* that denotes the freedom of the individual citizen, it being understood that such freedom is but a remnant of the original natural liberty left intact by the laws of the state. The silence of the laws on certain matters leaves room for certain areas of the precivil state of nature to remain unimpaired. There is no *libertas civilis* as such that the subject may claim. Thus Mendelssohn is right in saying that Hobbes had no taste for civil liberty. The matters held by Hobbes to remain within the compass of *libertas civium* are spelled out in the English version of *Leviathan*, XXI (Oakeshott, 139): "the liberty to buy, and sell, and otherwise contract with one another; to choose their own abode, their own diet, their own trade of life, and institute their children as they themselves think fit; and the like."

Hobbes does, however, attempt to safeguard the liberty of the citizen to a degree not to be suspected in the light of Mendelssohn's rather summary remark. In the same chapter he refers to a number of rights which the social contract did not mean to take away and which constitute the "true liberty" of the subject. Included in these is the right to disobey the sovereign's command to kill, wound, or maim oneself; to deprive oneself of things necessary to life; to incriminate oneself; etc. Mendelssohn may have considered such right of disobedience a human rather than a civil right, while applying the latter category to such matters as freedom of expression, of religion, and of the press (which were denied by Hobbes).

35, 27–28   *Leviathan,* XVII (*OL,* III, 127): Leges enim naturae, ut justitia, aequitas, etc., et uno verbo, *facere aliis quod fieri vellemus nobis,* absque metu potentiae coactivae, passionibus naturalibus, quales sunt ira, superbia, cupiditasque omnis, contrariae sunt; Oakeshott, 109: For the laws of nature, as justice, equity, modesty, mercy, and, in sum, *doing to others, as we would be done to,* of themselves, without the terror of some power, to cause them to be observed, are contrary to our natural passions, that carry us to partiality, pride, revenge, and the like.

35, 29–30   God's right itself derives from his power; see *De cive,* XV.5 (*OL,* II, 334): In regno naturali, regnandi et puniendi eos, qui leges suas violant, jus Deo est a sola potentia irresistibili; *Leviathan,* XXXI (*OL,* III, 256): Regni divini naturalis jus, quo Deus illos, qui leges naturales violant, affligit, non ab eo derivatur, quod illos creaverit, cum non essent; sed ab eo, quod divinae potentiae resistere impossibile est; Oakeshott, 234; The right of nature, whereby God reigneth over men, and punisheth those that break his laws, is to be derived, not from his creating them, . . . but from his *irresistible power.*

35, 31–32   *De cive,* XVIII.1 (*OL,* II, 414f.): quia obedire opportet Deo magis quam hominibus orta est difficultas, quo pacto obedientia tuto iis praestare possit, si quando imperatum fuerit aliquid, quod Christus fieri prohibet; *Leviathan,* XLIII (*OL,* III, 434): . . . Deo obediendum potius esse quam homini cuicunque; Oakeshott, 384: It is manifest enough, that when a man receiveth two contrary commands, and knows that one of them is God's, he ought to obey that, and not the other, though it be the command even of his lawful sovereign. . . .

35, 32–36, 4   The forms of public worship (*cultus publicus*) ordained by the state are to be observed by all citizens as the approved symbols of honoring God (*signa honorandi Dei*); see *De cive,* XV. 16 (*OL,* II, 345f.). A different cult is licit only if practiced privately and in secret (*cultus privatus*); ibid.,

XV.12 (*OL,* II, 339). The act of faith (*fides*) cannot be commanded by the sovereign: Leges obligant; ad credendum vero nemo obligari potest, sed ad actiones tantum et verba, si opus sit (*Leviathan,* XLII; *OL,* III, 417; Oakeshott, 371); the reason being that faith is a gift of God (*donum Dei*) and, hence, it cannot be compelled; see *Leviathan,* XXVI; XLII; *OL,* III, 208; 36of.; Oakeshott, 187; 326f. (For the history of this view, cf. Altmann, *Die trostvolle Aufklärung,* 244–68.) To invoke the dictate of conscience whenever it opposes the command of the sovereign is impermissible. It is mistaken and contrary to the interests of the state to hold every action disapproved by the conscience to be sinful, for the conscience is merely a human judgment (*judicium*) subject to error, and as a private opinion it has to yield to the law as the "public conscience"; see *Leviathan,* XXIX (*OL,* III, 232f.; Oakeshott, 211f.) In *De cive,* XII.2 (*OL,* II, 286) Hobbes had argued somewhat differently that it was indeed a sin to act against one's conscience—a view that goes back to Thomas Aquinas; cf. Altmann, ibid.—yet acting at the command of the sovereign and contrary to one's conscience was committing not one's own sin but the sovereign's. This viewpoint is still maintained in *Leviathan,* XLII (*OL,* III, 361f.; Oakeshott, 327) where the case of Naaman the Syrian (2 Kings, 5: 17–18) is cited in corroboration of it.

36, 8–9 Similarly Leibniz in a letter to Kettwig dated November 6/7 (*Textes inédits,* ed. by G. Grua [Paris, 1948], 653) where Hobbes is praised for having "said many excellent, though not exhaustive verities concerning civil matters and the principles of justice" (De rebus civilibus principisque justi vera multa et praeclara, sed non sufficientia dixit). In an undated letter Leibniz (*Schriften,* I, 86f.) tells Hobbes that so far he had found nothing in his theory of the natural state and the social contract that he felt he had to oppose (Hactenus nihil habeo, quod resistam). (Both letters are quoted *in extenso* by Schiedermair, *Leibniz,* 162.)

36, 11 The charge of paradoxicalness had been raised against Hobbes before; see Pufendorf, *De jure naturae et gentium,* II, 2, 3; VIII, 1, 2 and Leibniz, "Méditation sur la notion commune de la justice," in Georg Mollat, ed., *Rechtsphilosophisches aus Leibnizens ungedruckten Schriften* (Leipzig, 1885), 58: Un

philosophe Anglois célèbre, nommé Hobbes qui s'est signalé
par ses paradoxes, a voulu soutenir presque la même chose,
que Trasymache: car il veut que Dieu est en droit de tout faire,
parce qu'il est tout puissant. C'est ne pas distinguer le droit et
la fait. Car autre chose est, ce qui se peut, autre chose ce qui
se doit. Cf. also Rousseau, *Du contrat social*, I, 3.

36, 13–14   On Spinoza's "merit" see *Jub*A I, 14; 18f.

36, 15–18   Mendelssohn refers here to Pufendorf's and Leibniz's
critiques of Hobbes; see Pufendorf, *loc. cit.*, I, 6, 10 (against
Hobbes, *De cive*, XV. 5) where the fundamental distinction
between coercing (*cogere*) and obliging (*obligare*) is pointed
out; see Denzer, Pufendorf, 84; 129ff.; Leibniz, *Essais de
Théodicée*, Appendix 2, §12.

36, 29–37, 9   Mendelssohn understands Hobbes to base the obligation (*obligatio*) of honoring covenants solely upon fear, in the
case of a covenant entered into in the civil state the fear being
one of punishment by the civil authority. His objection is that
an obligation founded upon fear cannot be termed an obligation since it will last only as long as it is supported by fear.
Once fear subsides, it ceases to be valid. This objection on the
part of Mendelssohn ignores, however, Hobbes's explicit thesis
that natural laws (*leges naturales*), of which fidelity to covenants (*fidem observandam esse*) is a part, imply a moral obligation; that they are binding upon the conscience (*in foro
interno*), although they are not laws in a legal sense. Hobbes
recognizes therefore the distinction between might and right,
even though the way he expresses himself is often ambiguous
and inconsistent (see Ilting, *loc. cit.*, 284f.). He expressly calls
a breach of covenant (*fidei violatio*) unjust (*injusta*); see
De cive, III. 1; 3. He says, moreover, that even covenants entered into upon fear, as in the case of extortion, are to be
observed both in the natural and the civil state; see *De cive*,
II. 16; *Leviathan*, XIV; *OL*, III, 108; Oakeshott, 91. Only covenants expecting performance in the future and depending on
trust will be invalid upon reasonable suspicion that one of the
parties will not perform. Yet this applies only to covenants entered into in the state of nature, not to those enacted in the
civil state, where there are no grounds for suspicion since the

power of the sovereign constrains people from violating their faith; see *De cive*, II.11; *Leviathan*, XIV; *OL*, III, 107; Oakeshott, 89f. As Hobbes points out, covenants concluded upon fear must be valid, for otherwise the social contract (*pactus civilis*), upon which the commonwealth is founded, would likewise lack validity since it is solely motivated by fear; see Hood, *loc. cit.*, 120.

37, 10–12 *De cive*, XIII.2; 4 (*OL*, II, 298f.); *Leviathan*, XXX (*OL*, III, 240); Oakeshott, 219; cf. the note on 35, 7–10.

37, 12–17 The sovereign is not subject to civil law (*Leviathan*, XXVI; *OL*, III, 197; Oakeshott, 173). He cannot be accused of injustice, for what he does is authorized by the institution of the commonwealth (by the social contract) and is, in a sense, the deed of every one of his subjects by whose authority he acts and none of whom can commit an injustice to himself. The principle here invoked is the old juridical rule *volenti non fit injuria;* see *Leviathan*, XVIII (*OL*, III, 135); Oakeshott, 115f.; *De homine, OL*, II, 115. Yet to God, the author of the law of nature, the sovereign has to render account of his actions; see *Leviathan*, XXX (*OL*, III, 240); Oakeshott, 219. David committed no injustice to Uriah but he sinned before God. Hence his confession: "Against Thee, Thee only, have I sinned" (Ps. 51: 6); see *Leviathan*, XXI (*OL*, III, 162); cf. Hood, *loc. cit.*, 141; 145–59. Similarly Mendelssohn in his (Hebrew) *Commentary on Ecclesiastes, JubA* XIV, 187: The people has no right to judge the king; he has to give account to God alone.

37, 17–19 Cf. *De cive*, XII.1 (*OL*, II, 285f.): *Eritis sicut dii* (= reges); *Leviathan*, XX (*OL*, III, 157f.); Oakeshott, 135: Genesis 3:5: Ye shall be as gods, knowing good and evil; *Leviathan*, XXX (*OL*, III, 243): *Non habebis coram me deos alienos; Oakeshott,* 222: Thou shalt not have the Gods of other nations; and in another place concerning *kings,* that they are *Gods.* See also Locke's early tract on the *Civil Magistrate* (MS quoted by Peter Laslett, ed., *Locke's Two Treatises of Government,* 2nd ed. [Cambridge, 1970], 20): "to those whom the Scripture calls Gods.' Hobbes designates the state as "Leviathan" or *mortalis Deus* (*Leviathan*, XVIII; *OL*, III, 131; Oakeshott, 112: that *mortal god*).

Mendelssohn's critique of Hobbes relates chiefly to the latter's ideas on natural law. It only briefly touches on his theory of state and church. This may seem rather strange since the avowed purpose of the *Jerusalem* is a discussion, in the first place, of precisely that subject. Yet his subsequent exposition clearly shows that there is a large area of agreement between his own and Hobbes's notions on church and state. He was closer to the Erastian doctrine professed by Hobbes that one might suspect. This applies above all to his rejection of every form of ecclesiastical power. In his views concerning the right of excommunication he went far beyond the restrictions suggested by Hobbes. Specific points of agreement will be indicated as we go along. What Mendelssohn repudiates are the encroachments upon the sphere of religion which Hobbes advocates.

37, 27-28   John Locke (1632-1704) witnessed the fateful and disastrous interaction of religion and politics in the years prior to the "glorious revolution" (1688). At first he inclined toward Hobbesian Erastianism but later changed his views under the influence of the first earl of Shaftesbury and became the spokesman of the liberal Whig party. His *Two Treatises of Government* (London, 1690) opposed Sir Robert Filmer's highly influential *Patriarca: or the Natural Power of Kings* (1680) which denied the natural liberty of men and set in its place the patriarchal royal power inherited from Adam. Locke refuted the "biblical" arguments adduced by Filmer. He rejected absolutism and recommended a maximal amount of civil liberty. *Two Treatises* was not directed against Hobbes but it implied a stand against his doctrine as well; see Laslett, *loc. cit.*, 67-91. This work—Locke's most important political statement—remained almost unknown in Germany until the latter part of the 18th century; see Klippel, *Politische Freiheit*, 47; 88f.; 129f. This fact helps to explain the absence of any reference to it by Mendelssohn.

37, 28-30   Locke wrote the first of his Letters concerning Toleration in the winter of 1685/86 during his exile in Amsterdam. The original Latin edition (*Epistola de Tolerantia*, Gouda, 1689) is dedicated to Philipp van Limborch, the learned bishop of the Remonstrants (Arminians). Translations into

Dutch, French, and English appeared in the same year. William Popple wrote the English version under the title: *A Letter concerning Toleration* (London, 1689; 2nd revised edition: London, 1690). In refutation of attacks by Jonas Proast, Locke published *A second letter concerning toleration* (London, 1690), *A third letter for toleration* (London, 1692) and a fragmentary fourth letter which appeared posthumously in 1704. Mendelssohn refers to *letters* but may have actually read only the first of them in a French translation. He owned (see *Verzeichnis*, 25, no. 131.32) the two-volume enlarged edition of *Oeuvres diverses de Monsieur Jean Locke* (Amsterdam, 1732; 1st edition in one volume, Rotterdam, 1710) which contains but the first "Lettre sur la Tolérance." Apparently, the other letters were little known in Germany. In his bibliography of works dealing with toleration C. M. Pfaff (*Academische Reden*, 129) lists only the first.

37, 30–31 Locke, *Works*, VI, 9: "The commonwealth seems to me to be a society of men constituted only for the procuring, preserving, and advancing their own civil interests (*bona civilia*). Civil interest I call life, liberty, health, and indolency of body; and the possession of outward things, such as money, lands, houses, furniture, and the like (vitam, libertatem, corporis integritatem, et indolentiam, et rerum externarum possessiones, ut sunt latifundia, pecunia, supellex etc.). It is the duty of the civil magistrate, by the impartial execution of equal laws, to secure unto all the people in general, and to every one of his subjects in particular, the just possession of these things belonging to his life." In *Two Treatises* (II.131) the purpose of the state is defined as the safeguarding of "the Peace, Safety, and publick good of the People"; for "Salus Populi Suprema Lex" (II.158). (See also II.3.) It is earthly goods, above all property, which it is the duty of the state to protect, property in its widest sense denoting the rights of the individual in their totality; see Laslett, *loc. cit.*, 102. Already in his early phase, in which there is no mention of the social contract, Locke recognized the function of the state to consist in the "preservation of property, quiet and life of every individual"; "in a peaceable enjoyment of all the good things of this life" (see Euchner, *Locke*, 198ff.; 290f.).

It is this exclusive stress on mundane matters as the sole
purpose of the state which Mendelssohn opposed (see below,
pp. 38, 15–39, 6). The total separation of church and state
advocated by Locke appeared to him even more objectionable
than Hobbes's unification of civil and spiritual power in the
hands of the sovereign. It signified to him the state's abandonment of the task of education by leaving it entirely to the
church. Already Pufendorf had considered this to be irreconcilable with the responsibilities incumbent upon the state (see
Lezius, *Toleranzbegriff*, 18–30).

37, 31–33 Locke, *Works*, VI, 10f. offers three arguments in support of the thesis that state authority must confine itself to the
advancement of purely civil interests: (1) Nobody can accommodate his faith to the precepts of another; hence the social
contract cannot invest the civil magistrate with the care for
men's eternal felicity, the latter being a matter of faith. (2)
The state wields the power of external coercion; but external
coercion has no effect in matters of faith. To persuade and to
command are two different things. (3) Even assuming that
coercive measures do have an effect in matters of faith, they
would not be conducive to eternal felicity because the latter
is incompatible with coercion of conscience. See also ibid., 4,
118, 212. According to Mendelssohn's account of Locke, the
incompetence of the state in matters of religion is implied in
the very definition of the state's purpose. The view that the
care for man's eternal felicity is not part of the functions of
the magistrate as envisaged in the social contract is also shared
by the German Territorialists (Thomasius; J. H. Boehmer);
see Altmann, *Die trostvolle Aufklärung*, 263–268.

Mendelssohn records Locke's view that the state is not to
concern itself with the citizens' convictions regarding their
eternal felicity—a point conceded, by the way, even by Hobbes
so far as the inviolability of the *forum internum* is concerned—
yet nothing is said here about Locke's plea for liberty of external worship, including the so-called "indifferent things"
(*adiaphora*) which previously (in the tract of 1660) he had
considered to be subject to state control. As he did in his
account of Hobbes, Mendelssohn refers only to those aspects
of Locke's doctrine that provoke his criticism.

37, 33–38, 4 Locke, *Works*, VI, 40: "The magistrate ought not to forbid the preaching or professing of any speculative opinions in any church, because they have no manner of relation to the civil rights of the subjects. If a Roman Catholic believe that to be really the body of Christ, which another man calls bread, he does no injury thereby to his neighbour. If a Jew does not believe the New Testament to be the word of God, he does not thereby alter any thing in men's civil rights." Ibid., 52: ". . . those whose doctrine is peaceable, and whose manners are pure and blameless, ought to be upon equal terms with their fellow-subjects. . . . Nay, if we may openly speak the truth, and as becomes one man to another, neither pagan, nor Mahometan, nor Jew, ought to be excluded from the civil rights of the commonwealth, because of his religion." Cf. Thomas Jefferson, *Notes on Virginia* (1782): "The rights of conscience we never submitted, we could not submit. We are answerable for them to our God. The legitimate powers of government extend to such acts only as are injurious to others. But it does me no injury for my neighbor to say there are twenty gods, or no God" (quoted by Anson Phelps Stokes, *Church and State in the United States* [New York, 1950], I, 335). For Locke's influence on the American Constitution, see Klippel, *Politische Freiheit*, 8of.

38, 8–9 Locke spent over three years (1675–79) in France and more than five years (1683–89) in Holland.

38, 12–15 Alluding to Locke's definition of the church (*Works*, VI, 13): "A Church . . . I take to be a voluntary society of men, joining themselves together of their own accord, in order to the public worshipping of God, in such a manner as they judge acceptable to him, and effectual to the salvation of their souls. . . . No member of a religious society can be tied with any other bonds but what proceed from the certain expectation of eternal life. A church then is a society of members voluntarily uniting to this end."

38, 24 Robert Bellarmine (Roberto Francesco Romolo Bellarmino; 1542–1621), one of the most brilliant figures of the Counter-Reformation, joined the Jesuit Order in 1560, became professor of theology at the newly established Collegium Romanum in 1576 and subsequently rose to the position of its

rector. He became a cardinal in 1599 and was archbishop of
Capua from 1602 to 1605. In 1930 he was canonized. His works
include *Disputationes de controversiis christianae fidei adversus hujus temporis haereticos* (3 vols., Ingolstadt, 1586–
93); *De aeterna felicitate sanctorum libri quinque* (Antwerp,
1616) and *De ascensione mentis in Deum per scalas rerum
creatarum opusculum* (Cologne, 1617). The work referred to
by Mendelssohn and inaccurately named by him *De Romano
Pontifice* is Part iii of the *Disputationes: Tertia Controversia
Generalis De Summo Pontifice quinque libris explicata*. In
Justus Ferre's edition of Bellarmine's collected works (*Bellar-
mini Opera Omnia*, Paris, 1870–74; reprint: Frankfurt a.M.,
1865) it is found in vol. I, 449–615 (books i–ii); vol. II, 5–185
(books iii–iv). It propounds the thesis (shared by the politi-
cally active Jesuit Robert Persons and by Cardinal William
Allen) that the Pope has a rightful claim to "indirect power"
over the secular realm; and that he may therefore depose
kings, as in fact Pius V's bull *Regnans in Excelsis* (1570) had
sought to do in the case of Elizabeth I (see Lecler, *Toleration,*
II, 358f; 410; for a discussion of this doctrine see Idem, *L'Église
et la souveraineté de l'État,* 96ff.). At the request of the *Curia
Romana* Bellarmine (using the pseudonym Matthaeus Tortus)
published a refutation of King James I's tract *Triplici Nodo
Triplex Cuneus* in 1608. Therein he disputed the king's thesis
that royal power derived directly from God and that the imposition of the oath of loyalty on the Roman Catholics in
England was therefore legitimate. Bellarmine contended that
sovereign power came from the people's transfer of sovereignty and was willed by God only generally inasmuch as He
willed political order to prevail (*Opera,* XII, 27; 115–203). Cf.
Franz Xaver Arnold, *Die Staatslehre des Kardinals Bellarmin*
(Munich, 1939); James Brodrick, *The Life and Work of
Blessed Robert Francis Cardinal Bellarmine by His Eminence
Cardinal Ehrle, S.J.* (London, 1928; 2 vols.); abbreviated edition: J. Brodrick, *Robert Bellarmine, Saint and Scholar* (West-
minster, Md., 1961); E. A. Ryan, S.J., *The Historical Scholarship of Saint Bellarmine* (New York, 1936).

38, 25 By the "frightful concatenation of his arguments" Mendelssohn means the reasons (*rationes*) and arguments (*argu-*

menta) presented in *De Summo Pontifice,* bk. v, ch. vii (*Opera,* II, 156–59) as well as the historical examples (*exempla*) adduced in the following chapter (viii) in corroboration of the thesis (laid down in ch. vi): *Papam habere summam temporalem potestatem indirecte.* The claim to "indirect" sovereignty made on behalf of the pope is defined as the right accruing to him secondarily and as necessary consequence from his spiritual power (*potestas spiritualis*) to interfere with the secular realm whenever this seems to be required for the sake of the spiritual (*in ordine ad bonum spirituale; per ordinem ad spiritualia; Opera,* II, 155f.; XII, 26). The church as such, so the argument has it, is not entitled to secular power, a view that dares to contradict the more radical theory asserting papal authority in both realms. The kingdom of the church is not of this world (John 18:36) and the "power of the keys" (*potestas clavium*) handed to Peter (Matth. 16:19) relates solely to the kingdom of heaven (*Opera,* II, 151f.). Yet Peter was exhorted "Feed my lambs" (John 21:15) and this implies the duty incumbent upon the pope as Peter's successor to prevent the promotion of heretical doctrines by princes disloyal to the church (*Opera,* II, 148–55; 159). Hence the *potestas ecclesiastica* can and should coerce the temporal power in every way necessary for the attainment of its purposes; it has the right to dethrone kings and transfer dominion to others; to rescind laws and introduce new ones (*Opera,* II, 156).

In support of this doctrine Bellarmine offers five reasons which, in turn, are strengthened by arguments and, finally, by examples from history. (It is Bellarmine's *rationes* that are quoted and refuted in Hobbes's polemic against the Cardinal; see *Leviathan,* XLII.) The overriding viewpoint in Bellarmine's reasoning is the consideration that the temporal welfare of man, which is the sole concern of the state, is subordinate to the eternal salvation of the soul of which the church takes care. The relation of church and state is analogous to that of spirit and flesh (*spiritus et caro*). The body is subjected to the mind and has to obey its commands (*Opera,* II, 155f.). Hence both the spiritual and the temporal sword are rightfully at the disposal of the pope, as Bellarmine claims by invoking the authority of Saint Bernard of Clairvaux and Pope Boniface

VIII (*Opera*, II, 157f.). The doctrine which limits the *potestas spiritualis* to an "indirect" right is likewise presented in the names of some older authorities (*Opera*, II, 148; XII, 26).

Viewed in historical perspective, Bellarmine's theory represents the high point of a development that can be traced back to Cardinal Thomas de Vio Cajetan's endeavors to secure the undiminished recognition of papal primacy against pre-Reformation Gallicanism and Lutheranism (see Cajetanus, *De divina institutione pontificatus romani pontificis*, ed. Friedrich Lauchert [Münster i.W., 1925], ix–xvii). In Bellarmine's case the issue is no longer the primacy of the pope within the church but the effectual assertion of ecclesiastical authority over against the temporal. His doctrine was considered dubious and antiquated even in some Catholic circles (see Lecler, *Toleration*, II, 376; 411). As Mendelssohn indicates in his footnote, Pope Sixtus V placed Bellarmine's name on the index because his theory vindicated to the papacy merely "indirect" power over princes. The incidence of the pope's death in 1590 prevented the publication of the index, and his successor, Urbanus VII, restored Bellarmine's integrity (see X. M. Le Bachelet, *Bellarmin avant son cardinalat* [Paris, 1911]; idem, "Bellarmin à l'index. Documents nouveaux," in *Études*, vol. 111, April 1911, 227–46; quoted by Dominique Bourel, trans., *Jérusalem* [Paris, 1982], 194, note 10).

39, 4–6 An attempt at refuting Bellarmine's doctrine was made already during his lifetime by the Catholic lawyer William Barclay of Aberdeen (1541–1606), a resident of France, in his *De Potestate Papae, an quatenus in principes saeculares jus et imperium habeat* (Paris, 1600 and subsequent editions; French translation: Pont-à-Mousson, 1611; English translation: London, 1611). Barclay made skillful use of Bellarmine's arguments against direct papal power in order to reject indirect power as well. He pointed out that the political dependence of the church on the state as it existed at the time of the apostles was grounded in natural law and, hence, was immutable. An extensive reply to this argument and to numerous others is given in Bellarmine's treatise *De Potestate Summi Pontificis in Temporalibus adversus Gulielmum Barclaium* (*Opera*, XII, 1–113) where the doctrine developed in *De*

Fines civitatis sunt vitae sufficientia, tranquillitas & securitas (*Jus Naturae*, vol. 24, VIII.13). He had pointed out the closeness of his definition to Aristotle's (*Politics*, I.i.8; III.iv.3); see *Jus Naturae*, VIII.10. The "good life," which Aristotle required in addition to "mere life" if the purpose of the state was to be fulfilled, meant comfort (*sufficientia*) over and above security. In Mendelssohn's view, the end of the state included the promotion of eternal felicity as well. His concept of man's perfection has a temporal as well as eternal dimension.

40, 22–35 Mendelssohn defines government as a coercive power motivating the will, thereby causing right action, that is, action conducive to public welfare; and he describes education as the means by which an inner conviction (*Gesinnung*, lit., mental attitude) is formed that produces right action without any prompting by governmental power. Mere actions as such derive from reasons that motivate the will alone (*Bewegungsgründe*), whereas convictions flow from reasons that persuade by their truth (*Wahrheitsgründe*). The distinction between these two kinds of reason is taken over from Wolff who defines *Bewegungsgründe* as "sufficient reasons for willing and not willing" (*German Ethics*, §496). Education, Mendelssohn says, promotes insight into *Wahrheitsgründe*, government provides the other kind of motivating reasons when moral persuasion fails. For want of something better, coercion by state power will have to suffice, yet, on principle, the state must not allow moral education to pass out of its hands. As it is concerned with the happiness of its citizens, it has to establish public institutions designed for both ends. Hence both law and morality are under the aegis of the state. Mendelssohn does not share Thomasius's endeavor to separate the two by assigning the law to the state and morality to religion (see Rüping, *Thomasius*, 67). In his view the law is inseparable from morality. Kant followed the Thomasius school (see Altmann, *Die trostvolle Aufklärung*, 169–81; 192f.; 195ff.)

41, 1–9 Religion as such is concerned with man's relation to God alone but indirectly serves as a motivating power of the persuasive kind for interhuman behavior. Cf. Garve, *Ferguson*, 205: "Religion we call the soul's conviction in relation to God. The sanction which religion gives to the laws rests on the influence it has upon the principles and conduct of man."

41, 9–21   The "inquiries" referred to Mendelssohn may have found
in some treatise based on the old canon law as distinct from
Protestant ecclesiastical law. At Mendelssohn's time there existed already an extensive body of writings on the *jus ecclesiasticum* (including rational Territorialism and late-Collegi-
alism) which reflected a view of the church as a generic
concept. They define the church as a society (see the note
to 34, 30–35, 3) devoted to religious purposes, leaving the
specific content of those purposes out of account since it is
held to be irrelevant to the juridical sense of the term church.
Among the writings making this point are the following:
Gottlieb Hufeland (*Ueber das Recht protestantischer Fürsten* . . . [Jena, 1788], 45) deliberately omitted the term
Christian when defining the church because of his declared
intention to deal with the church "only generally." Johann
Lorenz von Mosheim stated in his *Allegemeines Kirchenrecht
der Protestanten* (Helmstädt, 1760), 427f.: "Whether the ecclesiastical (*geistliche*) society be divine, true or false, pagan,
Christian, Jewish or Mohammedan, does not concern us here
seeing that we want to demonstrate the rights of ecclesistical
society by way of reason." It was in line with this approach
when a 19th-century manual of ecclesiastical law flatly
pointed out: "There are as many churches as concepts of religion and religious persuasions. Juridically speaking, there
may be even a *Jewish* church" (C. F. Glück, *Darstellung des
Kirchenrechts der Katholiken und Protestanten* [Augsburg,
1839], 26). Cf. Schlaich, *Kollegialtheorie,* 67; 97; also 63; 89f.;
107. Hence Mendelssohn's generic use of the term church
was anything but a daring innovation. He did not use the
term society (*societas*) when defining the church but designated it as one of the two "public institutions for the formation [*Bildung*] of man." The notion of the church as a *societas*
as used in both Territorialism and Collegialism carried under-
tones of an earlier Christian tradition; see Schlaich, *loc. cit.,*
53–58; for the notion *societas perfecta,* see ibid., 28, note 59;
Anton Bodem, *Das Wesen der Kirche nach Kardinal Cajetan*
(Trier, 1971), 74–77; Bellarmine, *Opera,* II, 157. As for the
dual aspect of *Bildung* see *JubA* VI.1, 115f., where this concept is subdivided into culture and enlightenment.

41, 22–26 Mendelssohn first draws a picture of the state as governing by education. In such a state the civil laws are complied with freely, that is on the prompting of a sense of benevolence. The element of coercion, that is, the fear of punishment, recedes into the background. The submission to sovereign power and to the laws that derive from the social contract assume here the features of a constantly renewed voluntary resolution of man to act in the interests of the common good; see Altmann, *The Quest for Liberty*, 48f. The state governing by coercion is portrayed below, pp. 43, 29–44, 18.

41, 26–28 Cf. below, pp. 42, 29–33; 56, 32–57, 29; *JubA* VI.1, 53; 129. Mendelssohn sees in the social contract a sacrifice of natural liberties that is compensated for in abundant measure by multiple gains. The "moral bond" of society is therefore secured by the awareness that in the state every one gains more than he loses. Among those increments he singles out the sense of happiness that is afforded by the exercise of benevolence in civil life. The political theories inspired by Hobbes saw the quid pro quo which justified the social contract in a less idealistic light. Pufendorf (*De officio hominis et civis* [1673], II, 103) considered the "utility" of the *pactum sociale* to consist solely in the safety it provided; it was the latter and nothing else that made up for the loss of natural liberty incurred by submission to the sovereign power. Similarly, Locke (*Two Treatises*, II.130–31) describes the giving-up of equality, libery, and executive power which man owns in the state of nature as motivated by every one's expectation "the better to preserve himself his remaining Liberty and Property."

Kant (*Werke*, VII, 122) repudiated the notion that through the social contract man "sacrificed" *part* of his natural liberty in return for some purpose gained. In his view the social contract meant the *total* abandonment of natural ("wild, lawless") liberty by man in order to find his true liberty undiminished in his autonomous submission to his legislative will. In stressing the total surrender of natural liberty in favor of moral (civil) liberty Kant followed Rousseau's concept of the social contract as the denaturing and moralizing of man, without, however sharing Rousseau's view of the complete submergence of the private will in the general will; see Altmann, *The Quest for Liberty*, 48; 62f.; Idem, *Die trostvolle Aufklärung*, 204–7.

41, 31–32   It is a favorite idea of Mendelssohn's that man cannot be happy without the exercise of benevolence; see below, p. 47, 20–21; *JubA* VI.1, 47, 10ff. and the note *ad locum* (p. 224); 159f.

41, 33–42, 2   For Mendelssohn's rejection of the so-called "selfish system" and his adoption of Rousseau's distinction between *amour de soi* (love of oneself) and *amour-propre* (egotism) see *JubA* VI.2, 188f.; XIII, 179f. The "sophists" are the representatives of the "selfish system" (Hobbes, Mandeville, Helvétius) who derive all altruistic acts from the instinct of self-preservation and egotistical concerns. The "benevolent system" subscribed to by Cumberland, Hutcheson, Butler, Spalding, and Mendelssohn recognizes an authentic sociability in man; see *JubA* VI.1, 38f.; 222f.

42, 3–4   By "form of government" (*Regierungsform*) Mendelssohn understands the constitution of the state, which Kant (*Werke*, VI, 437f.) calls "form of the state" (*Staatsform*) or "form of rulership" (*forma imperii*) and which he distinguishes from the "form of government" (*forma regiminis*), the latter denoting the manner of spirit (republican as against despotic) in which the business of government is conducted. This conceptual differentiation, which goes back to Bodin, is echoed in Pufendorf, and underlies Montesquieu's distinction between nature and principle of government (*De l'esprit des lois*, III.1), is not found in Mendelssohn; see *JubA* VI.1, 133.

For the question as to which constitution of government is the best, cf. Aristotle, *Politics*, IV.i.2 and passim; Hobbes, *Leviathan*, XLII (*OL*, III, 404f.; Oakeshott, 361f.), where Bellarmine's discussion of this question is referred to; Locke, *Two Treatises*, II.90 (where the absolute monarchy is said to be "inconsistent with Civil Society"); Pufendorf, *De jure naturae et gentium*, VII.5.22 (where the question is said to be inappropriate). The young Mendelssohn favored the republic but the mature man came to appreciate the merits of enlightened absolutism; see *JubA* VI.1, 108; 133; Altmann, *Die trost-volle Aufklärung*, 107f. On Kant's concept of republicanism, see ibid., 108f.

42, 5–22 This relativist view of the forms of constitution shows the unmistakable influence of Montesquieu; see *De l'esprit des lois*, I, iii: Il vaut mieux dire que le gouvernement le plus conforme à la nature est celui dont la disposition particulière se rapporte mieux à la disposition du peuple por lequel il est établi. The recognition of the climatic factor comes from the same source (I, iii; XIV; XVII). Rousseau (*Du contrat social*, III, viii and passim) also acknowledges the connection between form of government and climate. On Mendelssohn's admiration for Montesquieu see Altmann, *The Quest for Liberty*, 38f. The view that forms of government follow one another cyclically goes back to Polybius's *anacyclosis* theory and to Aristotle (*Politics*, V.x). It tallies with Mendelssohn's view of history; see below, pp. 95–97.

43, 1–4 Pufendorf (*De jure naturae et gentium*, III.6.5) sees no reason why the duty of almsgiving should not be enforced by the state, notwithstanding its (essentially noncoercible) character as one of the "duties of humanity" (*officia humanitatis*). He recalls John Selden's (*De jure naturae et gentium*, VI.vi) reference to rabbinic law which provides for a compulsory levying of charitable contributions imposed by the courts in case of refusal to comply voluntarily with one's duty. Cf. Joseph Karo, *Bet Yosef, Ṭur Yoreh De'ah*, §248 where the Talmudic sources and the divergent views of the later authorities are discussed. Maimonides, Jacob ben Asher, and Joseph Karo codify Raba's view which legitimizes coercion by the courts in cases of unjustified refusal. Mendelssohn considers it inadvisable for the state to administer charity, preferring as he does private initiative. Kant, on the other hand, opposed private charity for juridical and pedagogical reasons; see Altmann, *Die trostvolle Aufklärung*, 215.

43, 14–16 Cf. *JubA* II, 328: "Finally, the fourth main instrument to bring imagination into accord with reason is the vivid understanding, that is transforming, by examples, the general motives of reason into sensual ideas as it were. . . . By now it has become evident what is required in order to make the principles of practical morality properly effective and productive of a permanent and unchangeable readiness for virtue. They have to be vivified by examples . . ." (cf. Altmann, *Frühschriften*, 383f.). "Examples" are said to be one of the means by which abstract principles of morality are transformed into "sensual ideas" as it were, that is, into concretely perceived objects of the understanding which kindle the imagination and activate the will as if by second nature. Likewise, in our present passage Mendelssohn wants to point out that it is the vivid understanding (*anschauende Erkenntnis*)—cf. above, 42, 28 and 43, 5—brought about by the impact of examples that causes principles to "pass into morals." He amplifies the notion of "example" by adding "authority," which is but an exalted form of example to follow.

43, 16–28 In his polemic against Bayle (*JubA* II, 24) Mendelssohn had described religion as one of the most eminent motives for virtue. Here he stresses its political function. In the state which governs by education religion plays a helpful role by imparting a higher sanction to the civil obligations. The ideal church stands therefore at the side of the ideal state, thereby proving itself a "pillar of civil happiness." In this perfect condition there is no conflict between church and state. Both share in the task of moral education. The dogmatic aspects of religion are left out of account. They are not negated but considered unimportant from the point of view of the state. The inner autonomy of the church remains intact. No trace of Erastianism mars this picture. Nor is the church conceived as a merely useful bond (*vinculum*) of society and state, a mode of evaluation of religion that goes back to antiquity and was widespread in the 18th century (see Martin Heckel, *Staat und Kirche*, 112f.; Schlaich, *Kollegialtheories*, 79; 108). What Mendelssohn has in mind is religion as a partner enjoying equal rights with the state, not as of mere instrumental value. It is the inclusion of eternal felicity among the purposes of the state that ensures the status of the church as an equal.

43, 29–35 Cf. the descriptions of the morally reduced and corrupted state in *JubA* VI.1, 118; 134f.; 145. It is this kind of state which confines its attainable purpose to mere "peace and security" (see below, 44, 7).

44, 21–22 In Kant's famous phrase (*Werke,* IV, 175): "Do reason as much as you want and on whatever subject you want as long as you obey!"

45, 9–21 Mendelssohn sees the "essential difference" between state and church (religion) in the contrast between coercive power (which belongs exclusively to the state by virtue of the social contract) and the persuasive power of teaching (which is the only one that belongs to the church). In elaborating this crucial difference he resumes a topic already dealt with prominently in the Preface to *Menasseh ben Israel.* In what follows he gives it a more extensive airing. The thesis that the church has no claim whatever to the right of coercion (*Zwangsrecht*) is going to be argued on the basis of natural law. To be sure, the view that the church is by its nature a *ministerium,* not an *imperium;* that all compulsory power is essentially alien to it; and that within it there is room only for "teachers and auditors" had already become a common assumption of both Territorialists and Collegialists (see Schlaich, *loc. cit.,* 122; 134; 270). Mendelssohn's achievement consists in the juridical conception with which he supports this viewpoint. The excursus on natural law that follows at this point lays the groundwork for the principle of separation of church and state as well as for the far-reaching demands for toleration that flow from that principle. The excursus established Mendelssohn's reputation as an authority on natural law.

45, 30–31 Mendelssohn's definition of the term "right" (*jus*) (see also *JubA* II, 292; III.1, 280; GS, III, 195; IV.1, 596) follows closely Wolff's which derives man's rights from the duty of self-preservation (and includes the duty to promote one's happiness): *Lex naturae dat nobis jus ad ea, quae ad felicitatem consequendam, conservandam & augendam requiruntur* (*Jus naturae,* II.ii.284; *Philosophia moralis sive Ethica,* I.ii.159). The term *authority* (*Befugnis*) is used by Mendelssohn as the equivalent of "right" in the sense of "moral capacity." The latter term translates *facultas moralis,* known in the natural law schools also as *qualitas moralis,* or *facultas moralis activa;* see Grotius, *De jure belli ac pacis,* I.i.4; Pufendorf, *Ele-*

menta, I, 8; Thomasius, *Institutiones*, 25; 37; Leibniz, *Textes inédits*, II, 611; 811. Pufendorf opposes *jus* as *facultas moralis activa* to Hobbes's notion of right as flowing from physical capacity. Natural power does not constitute a right. Power can coerce but it cannot obligate, that is, acquire a right which imposes an obligation on another person; cf. Denzer, *Pufendorf*, 129ff.

45, 32–46, 2 The notion of "moral capacity" is amplified by the criterion of its consistency with "the laws of wisdom and goodness," that is, with justice, for Mendelssohn defines justice as goodness commensurate with wisdom; see below, 46, 16; *JubA* II, 291f.; 321. He adopted this definition from Leibniz (see *Principes de la nature et de la grace*, §9; *Essais de Théodicée*, Appendix II, 12; for more references, see Altmann, *Die trostvolle Aufklärung*, 176). Already Wolff, *Theologia naturalis*, I, §1067 had given it preference over Ulpian's classical definition of justice as "giving every one his own" (*suum cuique tribuere*). Mendelssohn understood Leibniz's definition to mean that one who practices justice desires happiness not only for himself but for others as well (hence is good) and that, at the same time, he seeks to obtain the benefit of all by the choice of the best means (hence is wise). Mendelssohn calls wise goodness "natural justice."

46, 5–7 Pufendorf (*De officio*, I.i.1) defines duty as "an act of man in discharge of an obligation (*pro ratione obligationis*) in conformity with a legal prescription." Similarly Wolff, *German Ethics*, II.1.221; *Philosophia practica universalis*, I, I.ii.224. Mendelssohn defines duty as *obligatio* (*Schuldigkeit*) without reference to the law.

46, 12–15 Cf. *JubA* II, 280: "To every duty there corresponds a right." This assumption of a regular correspondence of right and duty derives from Pufendorf (see Denzer, *loc. cit.*, 88; 150). The jurists of the Thomasius school disagreed. In their view there was no necessary reciprocity of this sort; see Rüping, *Thomasius*, 107; 109; 115; 131.

46, 16–47, 6 The distinction between perfect and imperfect rights and duties is found already in Mendelssohn's earlier writings (*JubA* III.1, 368f.; 271; 28of.); cf. Altmann, *Die trostvolle Auf-*

klärung, 177–79. This division goes back to Grotius (*De jure belli ac pacis*, I, 4) who differentiated between the moral claim (*aptitudo*) to charity (which implies no legal right) and the claim to one's property (*facultas*) (which is legally enforceable). Pufendorf amplified this schema by distinguishing between rights and duties that are either "perfect" (compulsory) or "imperfect" (nonactionable, hence noncompulsory); see *De jure*, I, i, 19; I, vii, 7–9; *Elementa*, I, vii, 1; VIII, ii, 5. He sought to explain this difference by pointing out the varying degrees of importance attaching to the provisions of natural law, some of these being concerned with the mere existence (*esse*), others with the well-being (*bene esse*) of society (cf. Aristotle, *Politics*, I, vii, 8). The duties of humanity (*officia humanitatis*), which aim at the well-being of men, are imperfect, that is, noncoercible duties and the rights corresponding to them confer no title to coercion. Imperfect duties are of two kinds, innocuous permissions (*res innoxiae utilitatis*) which demand no sacrifice, only a show of favor, and gratuitous donations out of benevolence or pity which represent a "more sublime degree of *humanitas*" (see Denzer, *loc. cit.*, 150f.; Schneiders, *Naturrecht*, 86–91). Wolff adopted and further developed this division. According to him, perfect rights and duties are laid down to prevent any injury (*laesio*) of the external condition of any member of society; they flow from the law "not to hurt anyone" (*neminem laedere;* cf. *JubA* III.1, 368) and are compulsory. Imperfect rights and duties serve the perfection (*perfectio*) and happiness (*felicitas*) of our fellow men. Duties of this kind are termed "duties of humaneness" (*officia humanitatis*) and they must not be enforced. They are to be left to the conscience which alone can pass judgment (*judicium*) whether to exercise them in a given case. The obligation concerning them is an internal one (*obligatio interna*), although their social aspect makes them also an external obligation; see Wolff, *Jus naturae*, I, iii.655–74 (*Werke*, Thomann, II, Vol. 17, 430–43; *Philosophia practica universalis*, I, I.ii.234–37).

Mendelssohn appears to have disregarded the objections raised against this theory by Thomasius and his school. Their contention was that an "imperfect right" such as "the right to petition for alms" (*jus petendi eleemosynam*) was no right whatever but merely a permission, and, more importantly, that, strictly speaking, the *officia humanitatis* did not qualify for inclusion among the duties of strict law (*jus strictum*) but rather belonged to morality; see Rüping, ibid. This rejection of the very concept of imperfect rights and duties and the concomitant exclusion of moral precepts from the law (*jus*) was shared by Thomasius, Gundling, Gerhardt, Köhler, Achenwall, and others. The clearcut separation of law and morality, *justum* and *decorum*, advocated by them found its most striking expression later in Kant who assigned the *officia humanitatis* to ethics and sharply distinguished between legality and morality; see Schneiders, *Naturrecht*, 326–37. Mendelssohn's theory of natural law is still imbued with the Pufendorf-Wolff tradition which considers the duties of *humanitas* to be an integral part of natural law, serving as they do the felicity of man. This basic view has far-reaching implications for his theory of the state; see Altmann, *Die trostvolle Aufklärung*, 192–216.

47, 7–19   Mendelssohn's view of natural property, that is, of property in the state of nature prior to all contracts, can be traced back to two sources. First, to Wolff's *Jus naturae*, Part II (1742), chs. I–II, and, second, to Locke's *Two Treatises*. Wolff assumes, like Grotius (*De jure*, I, ii), an original condition in which property was shared by all (*communio rerum primaeva*) insofar as the products of nature were concerned. He holds this right to common things (*jus in res communes*) to be an innate right (*jus connatum*) which extends to the satisfaction of actual wants and implies a perfect right (*jus perfectum*) to resistance (*jus resistendi; jus belli*) in case it is challenged (I.10, 11, 33, 40, 45, 57). Mendelssohn, who was highly conversant with Wolff's doctrine on the origin of property (see *JubA* XII.1, 44; XII.2, 48), refers here distinctly to this "original joint ownership of goods." Wolff goes on saying that private property (*res propriae; res singulorum*) exists also in the state of nature and that the right to dispose of and use property (*jus proprietatis*) called *dominium* constitutes a perfect right. In the *status naturalis* private property is acquired by virtue of a declaration that a certain hitherto ownerless object is claimed for exclusive use, that is, subjected to one's own *dominium.* Such a declaration is legally valid if the seizure (*occupatio*) of the object effectively permits the exercise of the right of possession. Wolff calls this kind of acquisition of ownerless property *modus acquirendi originarius* (II.108, 116, 118, 122, 132, 136, 173–76, 185–86). He considers it independent of the consensus by others, whereas Grotius (II, ii–x) and Pufendorf (*De jure*, IV, 5, 3; IV, 5, 9; IX, 6, 2; IV, 13, 3–5; *De officio*, I, 12, 2) require at least the tacit consent of others to make it legally valid, the reason being that they regard private property not a natural right but an artificial creation (see Denzer, *Pufendorf*, 152–55). Mendelssohn follows Wolff in affirming "natural property."

In the way Mendelssohn determines the *modus acquirendi* by which natural property is made one's own in the state of nature he departs, however, from Wolff. In this respect he takes his cue from Locke, who as one of the first to do so, if not as the very first, derived property (in contradistinction from possession which is a matter of self-preservation) from labor: In the same way in which man has a property in his own body and in the "Work of his Hands" ("the Labour of his Body"), he makes what nature has provided his property if he transforms it into a product of his own effort since he thereby has "mixed" it with his labor (*Two Treatises*, II.26–27). This extremely important and historically influential theory (see Laslett's edition of *Two Treatises*, 2nd ed., notes to pp. 304–6; Euchner, *Locke*, 80–95; Medick, *Naturzustand*, 75–97) was adopted by Mendelssohn in the form in which it appears in Adam Ferguson's *Institutes of Moral Philosophy* (Edinburgh, 1769), Part V, ch. VII ("The Law of Acquisition by Labour"), 202–4. Ferguson's work was known to him in Garve's annotated German edition and a comparison of our passage with that text (pp. 173–75) leaves no doubt that Mendelssohn's list of "the goods to which a man has an exclusive right" reformulates what is found there.

47, 20–31   Having established the perfect right to one's property, Mendelssohn discusses the imperfect duty to exercise beneficence. He is following Wolff who in his *Jus naturae*, Part IV, ch. I lays down this particular duty: "Men are naturally obliged to each other to render mutual benefits (*sibi invicem*

obligantur ad beneficia mutua) as much as is in their power"
(§23). Wolff had pointed out that acts of beneficence gave
joy to the recipient and happiness to the benefactor, sentiments which the latter ought to make the deliberate purpose
of his deeds so as to become conscious of their being "good for
himself as it were" (*tanquam sibi bonum*); see §§33–35. Mendelssohn gave this thought a new turn: "Man cannot be happy
without beneficence." Whereas perfect rights and duties relate
to man's self-preservation (mere "existence"), the *officia humanitatis* are designed to promote perfection and felicity ("the
improvement of his existence"), a differentiation that goes
back to Pufendorf and, ultimately, to Aristotle; see note to 46,
16–47, 6.

47, 32–48, 6   To the duty to exercise benevolence there corresponds the right to expect beneficence; cf. note to 46, 12–15;
46, 16–47, 6. Mendelssohn defines goods as the "means of attaining happiness" (45, 33–34).

48, 7–30   Cf. Wolff, *Jus naturae*, Part I, ch. III.658: "No man has
the right to compel another to exercise duties of *humanitas*"
(*Nemo hominum habet jus ad officia humanitatis alterum
cogendi*); see also §§657, 659, 660, 666. In cases of collision
the rule obtains: "If several people need your help . . . those
are to be preferred to whose perfection you are obliged [to
contribute] for a special reason" (§668). Mendelssohn elaborates this point by emphasizing that the obligated person alone
has the "right to decide" on the exercise and modalities of the
duty. He obviously follows Garve, *loc. cit.*, 415 (Editor's
Notes): "A duty the obligatory nature of which depends on circumstances known solely to the obligated person must not be
enforced by compulsion. How can the mendicant judge the
issue? He would have to know all my circumstances, my property, the poor already supported by me and those I still must
support, my total condition."

48, 30–49, 2   The view that in the state of nature all positive duties
and rights are imperfect (noncoercible) while duties of omission (*neminem laedere*) alone are perfect (coercible) is one
that Mendelssohn took over from Garve, *loc. cit.*, 414f.: "Omis-
sions can be enforced by compulsion; positive actions (except

for contracts) must be petitioned for. All compulsory duties
have for their sole aim the prevention of injury. They want to
ensure our peaceableness, our refraining from injurious actions. All duties of conscience are concerned with the purpose
of seeing to it that we prove ourselves useful, active and productive. Not to injure depends only on my will, to prove useful
depends also on my abilities and circumstances." Thus Garve
suggests two criteria by which duties of conscience may be
distinguished from compulsory duties: (1) omission or commission of action; (2) obligation to act (or not to act) in all
circumstances or only in certain circumstances. Mendelssohn
elaborates these two viewpoints into a coherent theory: Whenever the obligated person faces an unambiguous, clear-cut
duty (as in the case of *neminem laedere*), he is subject to
coercion. Whenever he can be presumed to face a collision of
duties (as in all cases that involve *officia humanitatis*), the
decision lies with his conscience (cf. *JubA* III.1, 289f.; VI.1,
132). Mendelssohn calls "the rule that in the state of nature
man is independent, that is, under no positive obligation to
anyone" (49, 16–18) a "universal law of nature" (49, 24). In
concert with other lawyers (Pufendorf, Wolff) he identifies
natural liberty (*libertas naturalis*), that is, the liberty obtaining in the state of nature, with independence but he endows
this independence with a moral character. He interprets it as
the liberty to decide in matters of *officia humanitatis* without coercion, according to the dictates of one's conscience.
"This right," he says further below (52, 8–9), "constitutes
man's natural liberty which makes up a great portion of his
happiness." (Cf. Altmann, *Die trostvolle Aufklärung*, 180f.;
185f.; 187f.)

49, 36–50, 23 In other words, the duty to educate children derives
from two sources: the law of nature and a tacit contract between the spouses. The obligation based on the law of nature
is no more than an *officium humanitatis* and, as such, cannot
be enforced while the *pactum* concluded between husband
and wife gives each one a perfect, coercive right to demand
participation of the other in the children's education. Wolff,
Jus naturae, Part VII, ch. II assumes this duty to rest on
natural law and two contracts, one between the parents and

180   COMMENTARY

another, which is but a quasi one (*ex quasi contractu*), between parents and children (§§270, 634, 636). Mendelssohn
dispenses with the latter.

50, 24–30   By the "double principle" adopted by teachers of jurisprudence Mendelssohn apparently understands the differentiation between matrimony (*matrimonium*) and paternal society
(*societas paterna*), that is, family; see Wolff, *German Politics*,
ch. 2: On Matrimony; ch. 3: On Paternal Society; *Jus naturae*,
Part VII, ch. II: *De societate conjugali seu matrimonio*; ch. IV:
De societate paterna. Similarly Pufendorf, *De jure naturae*, VI,
i: *De matrimonio*; VI, ii: *De potestate patria*; Idem, *De officiis*,
II, 2: *De officiis conjugalibus*; II, 3: *De officiis parentum et
liberorum*. Mendelssohn wants to derive all rights and duties
of marriage as well as of family from a single principle. In
fact, the definitions of matrimony and paternal society given
by Pufendorf and Wolff largely overlap; see Pufendorf, *De
jure naturae*, VI, i, 2–5; *De officiis*, II, 2, 3; II, 3, 1; Wolff,
German Politics, §§16, 18, 80.

50, 30–34   This definition of marriage (matrimony) agrees with
Wolff's (*Jus naturae*, Part VII, ch. II.270): "A society entered
into by male and female for the sake of the procreation and
education of offspring is called a conjugal society or *matrimonium*." In Kant's view, the procreation and education of
children, though it might be regarded as nature's purpose, is
not necessarily required as a purpose legitimizing marriage;
see *Metaphysics of Morals*, Jurisprudence: Part I, §24 (*Werke*,
VII, 81f.). Similarly Francisco de Vitoria in his *Relectia de
matrimonio*; see *Relecciones theológicas del Maestro Fray
Francisco de Vitoria*, ed. Luis G. Alonso Getino, II (Madrid,
1934), 439–504.

50–52, Note   The Vienna court case mentioned by the anonymous
author refers, as Jacob Katz (*Zion* XXIX.1–2, 1964, 126f.) has
shown, to Josel Arnstein, a son of the highly respected Adam
Isaac Arnstein, purveyor to the Vienna royal household. Josel
was a brother of the banker Nathan Arnstein (1748–1838)
who was raised to the Austrian baronetcy. He was the only
one among the five brothers to convert to Christianity. He had
married the daughter of a Jewish family by the name of Stre-

litz in Berlin (1777) and Mendelssohn may have been a friend
of her father's. Our surmise rests on the assumption that she
was the daughter of the Berlin merchant Abraham Strelitz,
one of the elders of the community (see *JubA* XIX, lxix). How
deeply Mendelssohn was affected by the case is attested not
only by his remarks in the present note but also by a letter to
Herz Homberg dated October 4, 1782 (*JubA* XIII, 83). It may
be noted that immediately after publication he sent a copy of
Jerusalem to Homberg via Nathan Arnstein (*JubA* XIII, 112,
116). As for the legal position, one should bear in mind that
according to the then authoritative manual of law concerning
Jews, the *Tractatus de juribus Judaeorum* by the Altdorf
jurist Johannes Jodocus Beck, Nürnberg, 1731 (p. 14), conversion to Christianity by one of the Jewish partners in marriage was not considered a valid reason for divorce. It seems
that the purpose of this ruling was to facilitate the conversion
of Jews. What provoked Mendelssohn's energetic protest was
the anonymous author's expression of hope that the case would
be decided in favor of "tolerance," against the religious scru-
ples of the wife.

50, 34–52, 2 See below, pp. 56, 21f.

52, 8–12 See above, note to 48, 30–49, 2; Klippel, *Politische Freiheit*, 31–38. The right to decide according to one's conscience
is a "spiritual good" (53, 35–54, 1) the denial of which
amounts to an act of injury (*laesio*), that is, to an "external
act of injustice" which calls for coercive redress.

53, 14–55, 13 Mendelssohn expounds here his theory concerning
the validity of contracts. The legally effective transfer of property does not consist in its delivery (*traditio*) but in the promise
made by the owner and in the acceptance thereof expressed by
the recipient. This is evident in the case of immovable or intangible (spiritual) goods where delivery is impossible. The decisive factor is the declaration of will on both sides. Hence the
object transferred is not the property as such but the (perfect)
right to it and, ultimately, the right freely and independently
to dispose of it. Mendelssohn, therefore, defines the contract
as "the cession, by the one party, and the acceptance, by the
other party, of the right to decide cases of collision involving

certain goods which the promising party can spare" (54, 35–55, 3). The validity of the contract, which implies the duty to abide by it, is said to be a corollary of the fact that the right to dispose of the property concerned was ceded as such (55, 5–8) and has passed into the rightful possession of the party that accepted it. If the original owner's right to decide is to have any meaning, his declaration of will must take effect. In the last resort, therefore, it is natural liberty as defined by Mendelssohn which furnishes the ground for the validity of contracts.

55, Note   Ernst Ferdinand Klein (1743–1810), a Breslau lawyer, had been invited by Count von Carmer, Grand Chancellor of Prussia, to come to Berlin in order to assist in the drafting of the new legislation (*Allgemeines Landrecht*) which was to become the crowning achievement of the reign of Frederick the Great. He arrived in Berlin toward the end of 1781. What brought him into contact with Mendelssohn was a special assignment to work out a reform of the antiquated and obnoxious procedure of Jewish oath-taking in the public courts. Carmer requested Klein to consult, to this end, with a number of Jewish notables, particularly Mendelssohn. There ensued a warm personal relationship; see *JubA* VII, 278–93; XIII, 49–52; 78ff.; 162; 245f.; 255ff.; 258ff.; Altmann, *Mendelssohn*, 496–500 and passim.

For Ferguson's theory of contracts see his *Institutes of Moral Philosophy* (quoted in note to 48, 30–49, 2), 204–7 (The Law of Acquisition by Contract; Laws of Contract in General); Garve's German edition, 176–80. In his notes (p. 417) Garve expressed agreement with Ferguson's view. It is the expectation aroused by a promise that establishes a right to the thing promised. (Similarly Ludwig J. F. Höpfner, *Naturrecht*, §19.) This theory remained a bone of contention between Mendelssohn and Garve (see Garve's letter, *JubA* XIII, 195f.). In his reply to Herz Homberg's objections Mendelssohn pointed out that in all manuals of natural law that had come to his notice he had found much that was "still obscure and vague" in dealing with the nature of contracts and that he had endeavored to improve matters by establishing "solid principles" (*JubA* XIII, 133f.).

56, 21-24 Cf. above, p. 40, 11–18; *JubA* VI.1, 52f. Like Wolff (*Jus naturae*, Part VIII, ch. I, §26: *homines civitates constituere debere*), Mendelssohn sees in the relinquishing of the state of nature and in the entering into civil society the fulfillment of a duty that derives from man's own nature and represents an "inner call."

56, 30–31 Cf. Locke, *Two Treatises*, II.79, 81.

56, 35–57, 2 By "nature" Mendelssohn understands here the natural conditions of life that operate in human society. Nature, he says (57, 4–7) has endowed men with the forces which, by their interplay, impel the formation of society.

57, 7–24 As a rule, Mendelssohn does not differentiate between state and society (see note to 40, 8–22). Here he does draw a line between the formation of society and the *pactum sociale* by which the state comes into being. In the terminology of the ecclesiastical lawyers of the period: Society originates by a *consociatio inter homines* (a *pactum sociale* in the narrow sense of the word) which establishes a *societas imperfecta* of equals whereas the state is established by a pact of submission that creates a *societas perfecta inaequalis* (see Schlaich, *Kollegialtheorie*, 86). Mendelssohn's designation of the state as a "moral person" (cf. *JubA* VI.1, 241) goes back to Pufendorf (see J. W. Gough, *The Social Contract*, 2nd ed. [Oxford, 1957], 47, 122f.).

57, 24–29 Cf. above, pp. 43, 29–45, 8.

57, 30–58, 20 Wolff, *Vernünftige Gedanken* (1752) discusses in Part II man's duties to himself, in Part III his duties to God, and in Part IV those to one another. Alexander Gottlieb Baumgarten, *Ethica philosophica* (1751) has a similar tripartite division of duties but avoids the term "duties to God" (*officia erga Deum*) in the title of the chapter dealing with the subject—using instead *religio*—while the headings of the following chapters are *officia erga te ipsum* and *officia erga alia* respectively. Yet he does use the formula *officia erga Deum* in the text (§22). Wolff makes the point that God does not need us for this perfection. Our duties to him call for actions motivated by the divine perfections and are meant to honor him (§§651–52). Baumgarten derives the obligatory character of

religion from the latter's ability to make us more perfect
(§11). By duties to God he understands both the exercise of
pious acts (*actiones piae*) and the appropriate state of mind
(*habitus*) (§22; see Mendelssohn's translation of the text,
JubA VI.2, 237; 240f.).

Mendelssohn could hardly have objected to the way Wolff
and Baumgarten interpreted the term "duties toward God,"
yet he obviously considered it necessary to counsel against the
continued use of this term. He felt that it had engendered
mistaken notions of glorifying God by persecuting infidels.
In reality God demanded nothing but the fulfillment of our
duties to ourselves and others. The obligation to act benefi-
cently derived from our fellow men's need of help. God who
was in no need of our assistance could therefore ask for no
benevolence or sacrifice on our part. Hence no collisions between His and our own claims were possible. This absence of
colliding duties removed the ground for any contractual ar-
rangement such as existed in the sphere of interhuman relations and took the form of the *pactum sociale* (see 59, 17–28).
What Mendelssohn aims at is the clarification of the essential
difference between state and church.

The view (58, 35–59, 3) that God "desires no service from
us" echoes Job 35: 6–7: "If you sin, what do you do to Him?
. . . If you are righteous, what do you give Him; what does
He receive from your hand?" Yet in the Jewish tradition the
notion of "service" ('*avodah*) does play a notable role. It signifies the sacrificial cult and, after the destruction of the Second Temple, the act of prayer and the study of the Torah (cf.
Sifrey, 'Eqev, 41; b. Ta'anit 2a; Midrash Tehillim 66, 1). Moreover, the Kabbalists speak of the fulfillment of the divine commandments as acts that have an impact on the realm of the
Sefirot, answering a divine "need" (*ṣorekh gavoah*). Anti-
Kabbalists like Elijah del Medigo (*Beḥinat Ha-Dat*, ed. I. S.
Reggio [Vienna, 1833], 67f.) and Leone Modena (*Ari Nohem*
[Leipzig, 1840], 95) opposed this view and Mendelssohn most
certainly shared their opinion. He saw in prayer the expression
of a human rather than a divine need; see *JubA* XIII, 334.
Kant may reflect Mendelssohn's discussion of the subject when
he says: "There are no special duties to God in a universal

religion, for God can receive nothing from us; we cannot act upon Him nor on his behalf" (*Religion within the Limits of Reason alone*, Book IV, Part I, note at the beginning). The notion is characteristic of Deism; see Matthew Tindal, *Christianity as old as the Creation* (1731), 36.

58, 27–29   See note to 56, 35–57, 2.

58, 32–33   Mendelssohn considers reason "sacred" (*heilig*); cf. *JubA* XII.1, 32.

58, 34–35   Cf. Kant, ibid. (opening statement): "Religion is (subjectively regarded) the recognition of all duties as divine commandments." This definition seems to derive from Tindal; see *loc. cit.*, 272; Lechler, *Geschichte*, 328.

59, 10–11   The enigma posed by this remark is solved when one considers the fact that the year 2240 of the Christian era coincides with the year 6000 of the Jewish chronology. According to a tradition recorded in the Talmud (b. Sanhedrin 97a–b; 'Avodah zarah 2a), the world is to last 6,000 years. The year 2240 (6000) signifies therefore the end of the world. With a tinge of good humor Mendelssohn expresses the hope that by that time mankind will have learned to follow principles of reason. He was justified in assuming that some Christian readers would understand the eschatological meaning of the date, for the rabbinic doctrine of the 6,000-year duration of the world had been taken over by the Christian chroniclers (Julius Africanus, Hippolytus and others) after Eusebius of Caesarea had adopted the Jewish scheme of world chronology. The doctrine is mentioned in Cardinal Bellarmine's *Chronologia brevis*, Luther's *Supputatio annorum mundi* (Werke, Weimar Edition, LIII, 22) and Melanchthon's *Chronicon* (*Corpus Reformatorum*, XII, 711ff.); see E. A. Ryan, S.J., *The Historical Scholarship of Saint Bellarmine*, New York, 1936, 66f.

59, 12–28   Compulsory rights are claims to goods. They are perfect rights either by acquisition or by contract, that is, by the transformation of imperfect (petitionary) into perfect rights. The church, a society devoted to purely religious purposes, has neither a perfect nor an imperfect right to goods (which are means of obtaining temporal happiness), and since it has no right to claim property, the citizens will not be faced with cases of collision involving claims for the material benefit of the church. Hence no contract is feasible that would give the church a perfect, coercive right to levy contributions. That is to say, there are simply no grounds for the conclusion of a social contract between the church and the citizens analogous to the *pactum sociale* by which the compulsory power of the state is established. Similarly Locke, *Works*, VI, 15f.: "The end of a religious society . . . is the public worship of God, and by means thereof the acquisition of eternal life. All discipline ought therefore to tend to that end, and all ecclesiastical laws to be thereunto confined. Nothing ought, nor can be transacted in this society, relating to the possession of civil and worldly goods. No force is here to be made use of, upon any occasion whatsoever: for force belongs wholly to the civil magistrate, and the possession of all outward goods is subject to his jurisdication."

59, 28–60, 2   Cf. Locke, *Works*, VI, 16: "The arms by which the members of this society are to be kept within their duty, are exhortations, admonitions, and advice."

60, Note   Spinoza, *Tractatus Theologico-politicus*, V.5 quotes the same verse (and verse 9 of the same chapter) in corroboration of the view that the divine law attaches no importance to the sacrificial cult and other ceremonies as means of attaining eternal felicity (*ad beautitudinem*).

60, 2–7   Hitherto Mendelssohn's rejection of claims to compulsory power on the part of the church related to property alone since it was argued on grounds of natural law. It is now extended to rewards and punishments (church discipline) which, as he points out, are a form of bribery and coercion, and the argument shifts to the "nature" of religion itself. The way he pleads his case is reminiscent of the manner in which both Territorialists and Collegialists in 18th-century Germany described the exercise of power and compulsion as incompatible with the character of the church; cf. Schlaich, *Kollegialtheorie*, 86, 134. Yet in denying the church the right to property he took up a highly controversial position. The *jus ecclesiasticum Protestantium* had expressly vindicated this right by arguing that it belonged to all societies; see Mosheim, *Allgemeines Kirchenrecht*, 479–83; Schlaich, *loc. cit.*, 165, 227, 286.

60, 8–61, 3 In the Tannaitic period the rabbis earned their livelihood as artisans, farmers, or merchants. The rabbinic statement (b. Nedarim 37a; Bekhorot 29a) quoted by Mendelssohn reflects that state of affairs. The development which led to the practice of remunerating rabbinic functions and to fixed salaries as an accepted feature started in the Talmudic period (200–500 c.e.); see Simcha Assaf, *Be-'Oholey Ya'aqov* (Jerusalem, 1943), 40ff. The form of payment denoted by the term *sekhar baṭṭalah* (compensation for loss of time), to which Mendelssohn refers, was an attempt to legalize the acceptance of emoluments; see Jacob Katz, *Masoret U-Mashber*, Jerusalem, 1958, 120.

61, 4–20 The social contract gives the state the right of coercing citizens with respect to certain actions but does not authorize it to coerce opinions, principles, convictions. The reason given is twofold: (1) The social contract does not include the yielding of a coercive right with respect to convictions; (2) convictions are by their very nature noncoercible. Reason (1) is discussed in a number of textbooks of ecclesiastical law; see Pufendorf, *De habitu*, §6; Thomasius, *Das Recht*, propositions iii, iv, v; Fleischer, *Einleitung*, New Preface; Pfaff, *Academische Reden*, I, 12; III.2 and 13. Reason (2) figures in J. H. Boehmer, *Ius ecclesiasticum Protestantium*, II, Halle, 1762, *Dissertatio praeliminaris de iure circa libertatem conscientiae*, 18f. Cf. Denzer, *Pufendorf*, 210ff.; Schlaich, *Kollegialtheorie*, 78, 81ff.; Idem, *Der rationale Territorialismus*, 282f.; Rüping, *Thomasius*, 66–69; Altmann, *Die trostvolle Aufklärung*, 263–68.

Reason (1) is not elaborated by Mendelssohn. He puts the emphasis on reason (2) and he does so, it seems, because his particular view of the purposes of the state requires it. The first reason is based on the assumption that the state is established solely for the sake of security. From this it follows that the social contract has no concern with religion or opinions. Hence these matters cannot be subjected to state authority. Mendelssohn, who assigns to the state also the care for the citizens' happiness in this world and the next and who, thereby, includes right convictions among the concerns of the magistrate needs the second reason to ensure liberty of conscience and of expression. He therefore makes use of Boehmer's argument but gives it a new slant. Boehmer had pointed out that, according to the dictates of right reason (*recta ratio*), only such liberties could have been transferred to the sovereign as *had to be* for the sake of obtaining the purpose of the state. What could not have been transferred was the right to form one's own ideas and religious convictions, for the ability to seek the truth was an individual gift and no one could think, judge, and believe in another person's stead. Mendelssohn, however, starts out from the assumption that a transfer of rights through contracts in general involves a renunciation of an original right to dispose of one's goods. He points out that such an act of renunciation is possible only in the case of goods capable of transfer. Convictions are not goods one could renounce because of benevolence or for any other reason nor are they a piece of property amenable to compulsory rights acquired by contract. They simply do not belong in the class of "goods," that is, of "means of obtaining temporal happiness" but are ends in themselves. Hence the right to our convictions is "inalienable."

61, 26–28 Cf. J. H. Boehmer's distinction between *tolerantia* and *approbatio; tolerantia publica* and *tolerantia privata; tolerantia necessaria* and *tolerantia voluntaria seu gratiosa*. The latter is said to be a kind of toleration to which the sovereign may set certain limits (*certos limites*). Thus the public exercise (*publicum exercitium*) of a disapproved religion (*reprobatae religionis*) may be legally restricted, and citizens who adhered to such a faith could be ordered to leave the country in the way of an "honorable emigration" (*honesta emigratio*), even if they were citizens of good standing. The distinction between *toleratio* and *approbatio* has a particularly harsh bearing upon the legal position of "infidels" (*infideles*), that is, Jews and Muslims; see Boehmer, *Jus ecclesiasticum protestantium*, Lib. V, Tit. VII, §§lxxii–lxxvi; clxxx–i; Tit. VI (*tolerantia infidelium*). Pfaff likewise distinguishes between toleration and approbation. The state is said to be authorized to confer special privileges on a certain religion and to make it the "dominant religion." The toleration of the Jews is to be limited by "many restrictions"; see *Academische Reden*, V.3; VI.6, 11, 15, 16. Mosheim declared: "There may be many reasons why a government may deny civil legitimacy to a morally altogether legitimate church"; see *Allgemeines Kirchenrecht*, 439f.; cf. Altmann, *Die trostvolle Aufklärung*, 268–72.

62, 20 The question which form of government—monarchic, aristocratic, or democratic—suits the church was extensively discussed by Cardinal Robert Bellarmine in *Disputationes de controversiis*, Book I (*Opera*, I, 451f.), the result of the discussion being that a mixture of all three with a leaning toward the monarchy, was the best. Hobbes, *Leviathan*, XLII (*OL*, III, 404f.; Oakeshott, 361f.) commented that it was inappropriate for pastors, who wielded no rulership (*imperium*), to pose the question as to the best form of the state (*quae forma civitatis optima sit*), [let alone of the church]. They were called pastors (*pastores*) because they were to govern (*regerent*) men not by rulership (*imperio*) but by doctrine and arguments (*doctrina et argumentis*). This criticism was repeated by subsequent authors; see Pufendorf, *De habitu*, §32; Pfaff, *De originibus juris ecclesiastici* (Tübingen, 1720), 88; Mosheim, *loc. cit.*, 28f.; J. L. Fleischer, *loc. cit.*, §28. The very question was rejected as "absurd" (Pufendorf), "most insipid" (Pfaff), "useless" (Mosheim), and "tasteless" (Fleischer). It was the general view of the ecclesiastical lawyers that the church as a society of equals (*societas aequalis*) knew of no regimen whatever. Mendelssohn consented to this view.

62, 21–28 The question raised by Mendelssohn forms the subject of Christian Thomasius's and Enno Rudolph Brenneysen's jointly written treatise "The Right of Protestant Princes in Theological Controversies" (*Das Recht evangelischer Fürsten in theologischen Streitigkeiten*, Halle, 1713). The two authors oppose the doctrine held by Grotius according to which all theological disputes, including such as have recourse to "the revealed word of God," are subject to the "commanding judgment" (*judicio imperativo*) of the prince (prop. VII, pp. 75ff.). A historical survey of the views propounded in this matter is found in Gottlieb Hufeland's work *Ueber das Recht protestantischer Fürsten unabänderliche Lehrvorschriften fest-zusetzen* (Jena, 1788). Mendelssohn expresses the view that it is only the individual's ability of persuasion by rational argument that has a right to decide in cases of religious dissent. No authority is entitled to lay down any doctrine by way of command. He denies the right both of state and church to act as the judiciary in questions concerning religious truths. Neither had acquired such a right by contract. The individual retains the liberty of conscience vis-à-vis authoritarian claims by both church and state. Cf. Spinoza. *Tract. Theol.-pol.*, VII, §93.

62, 28–30   The state was established for the sake of peace and security. From this purpose flows the sovereign's right of supervision with respect to all spheres of public activity (*jus inspectionis generalis majestaticum*), including the church; see Pufendorf, *De habitu*, §44: "On the rights of princes concerning the church; in the first place on the general supervision of the church's activities; . . . seeing to it that nothing be done therein that is prejudicial to the state" (*ne quid in sui prae-judicium ibi agatur*). Canz, *Disciplinae*, §2459 (§2246 in the edition used by Mendelssohn) defines the sovereign's right (*ius majestaticum*) as "the right (*facultas*), belonging to the prince, of being on guard lest the state suffer any harm through the teachings of the church" (*nequid respublica detrimenti capiat per ecclesiae instituta*). (This is one of the passages which Mendelssohn excerpted in preparation for his writing *Jerusalem;* see *JubA* VIII, 97.) Cf. also *Disciplinae*, §2466f. and Mosheim, *loc. cit.*, 425; for further references see Schlaich, *loc. cit.*, 249, note 69.

62, 30–63, 2   Locke, *A Third Letter for Toleration* (*Works*, VI, 414) also brackets atheism and Epicureanism together. In the 17th and 18th centuries atheism was widely considered asocial in character and, hence, a danger to the very existence of the state. It was assumed that oaths taken by atheists could not be trusted and that the moral law, promises, and contracts were not held by them to be binding; see Lecler, *Toleration*, II, 486. Hence toleration by the state was not to be extended to them. Cf. Locke, *A Letter concerning Toleration* (*Works*, VI, 47): "Those are not at all to be tolerated who deny the being of God. Promises, covenants, and oaths, which are the bonds of human society, can have no hold upon an atheist." Boehmer, *loc. cit.*, Lib. V, Tit. VI, §xxxvi declares that atheism subverts the foundation of the state and dissolves the bond of civil society (*vinculum civile*); it recognizes "no veneration of God, no fear of a divine being, and no judgment of the conscience" (*nullum Dei cultum, nullum Numinis timorem, nullum conscientiae iudicium*). Hence the sovereign had the right to expel atheists from his country in order to prevent the spreading of their doctrine. Boehmer refers to Wolff's statement in his *German Politics*, §368: Atheists are not to be tolerated in the state notwithstanding the fact that atheism does not necessarily lead to amorality (cf. Wolff, *German Ethics*, §§21–22). Pfaff, *Academische Reden*, VI.1 describes a variety of types of atheism and suggests that toleration be denied only to those atheists who conduct themselves immorally and actively propagate their unbelief. These were to be "chased out of the state." Mosheim, *loc. cit.*, 437–39 shows a more tolerant attitude. Though he reiterates the charge that atheists are no respecters of oaths, he wants to see them tolerated as long as they fulfill their civil obligations. Cf. Altmann, *Die trostvolle Aufklärung*, 272–74; Schlaich, *Kollegialtheorie*, 79f.

63, 2–12 In his Notes to Bayle's *Pensées diverses sur les comètes* (*JubA* II, 21) Mendelssohn had opposed Plutarch and Bayle by trying to show that idolatry was preferable to atheism. Here he leaves the question open. To the literature on the subject quoted by Bamberger (pp. 372–76) one should add: C. M. Pfaff, *Academische Reden*, VI.2, where reference is made to the opinions of Bayle, Thomasius, Toland, and Wolff on the one side and of Welch, Lange, Bilfinger, and himself on the other. For Plutarch's notion of superstition (*deisidaimonia*) see Morton Smith, *De Superstitione*, in: *Plutarch's Ethical Writings and Early Christian Literature*, ed. Hans Dieter Betz (Leiden, 1975), 1–35.

63, 13–28 The "purpose" of the state being the promotion of the perfection and happiness of its citizens (cf. above, pp. 40–42), the sovereign is not permitted to stifle the free use of reason. The state must not favor any positive religion but should support natural religion as the common ground of all religions and the moral foundation of the state. Ecclesiastical lawyers of the rational persuasion had come to subscribe to this view; see Schlaich, *loc. cit.*, 78f. They held that the foundation of the state rested on natural religion, that is, on the belief that God existed and took care of things human (*religionis naturalis primum principium est, Deum et esse, et ab eo curari res humanas*). In Mendelssohn's view natural religion not only secured the foundation of the state but also contributed to the realization of its final purpose, the perfection and happiness of men. Without belief in God, providence, and a future life—the three dogmas of natural religion—all striving for perfection would lose its meaning (cf. *JubA* III.2, 68).

63, 29–31   The question whether requiring the attestation of one's religious orthodoxy by oath (*juramentum religionis*) as a precondition for ecclesiastical appointment could be regarded as a commendable practice was widely discussed in Germany and England. In most Lutheran principalities clergymen (and teachers) were admitted to office only upon taking an oath affirming that they subscribed to the teachings of the faith laid down in the "symbolic books," that is, in the confessional writings summarized in the *Konkordienbuch* (Dresden, 1580); see RGG³, III, 1776–79. In his satirical novel *Leben und Meinungen des Herrn Magisters Sebaldus Nothanker* (1773; 4th ed., 1799; reprint Berlin, 1960) Friedrich Nicolai, Mendelssohn's publisher and friend, had described the lamentable fate of a Lutheran minister of religion "who at taking office had sworn to the symbolic books yet in his heart of hearts was anything but orthodox" and who was soon dismissed "because of heresy and deviation from the symbolic books to which he had solemnly pledged allegiance" (pp. 21 and 46 of the reprint edition). That the legitimacy of such oath-taking had become a matter of public concern is shown by Mendelssohn's letter to Nicolai (*JubA* XII.2, 51) in which he wrote: "Perhaps I am already tired of the disputes about the symbolic books that may still have some undiminished attraction for other readers." In England it was the "Thirty-Nine Articles" of the Anglican Church (1563; final version 1571; see *The Oxford Dictionary of the Christian Church* [London, 1957], 1349) which the clergy was required to sign at ordination and which had run into some trouble; see below, note to 68, 7–33.

64, 4–23 Mendelssohn's first argument against the legitimacy of religious oaths follows directly from his definition of the social contract as a cession of certain perfect rights to temporal goods for the sake of promoting the public welfare. No contract had given the state the authority to demand declarations of conscience that were not needed for the benefit of society and that, moreover, concerned inalienable goods (convictions). This argument, however, does not take into account the possible admissibility of contracts by which a church obligates a minister of religion as an appointed official to teach certain beliefs and by which disciplinary measures (such as dismissal from office) become a matter of contractual stipulation. (For arrangements of this kind within the collegialist system, see Schlaich, *loc. cit.*, 99ff.).

64, 24–68, 6 The second argument relates to the nature of religious oaths. Normally, oaths have for their purpose the prodding of the conscience to make a true, factual statement about matters clearly present to the mind, matters that had been perceived by the external senses and that carried with them unmistakable evidence. In the case of religious oaths a statement has to be made about matters of faith which by their very nature are more or less elusive because they are objects of the internal senses, matters of thought and reflection. Mendelssohn points out the cruelty of such an imposition. He employs here the distinction between external and internal senses known from medieval psychology; see Harry A. Wolfson, *Studies in the History of Philosophy and Religion*, I, 250–370.

66, 30 The terms *confusion* and *indistinctiveness* reflect the Leibniz-Wolffian notion of "confused" and "indistinct" ideas as opposed to "clear" and "distinct" ones; see Altmann, *Frühschriften*, 94f.

68, 7–33 The fictional counterargument reflects the Collegialist view of the church as a society administering its own affairs and possessing the right to stipulate conditions when making appointments of officials (see note 64, 4–23). Mendelssohn rejects such legal justification of religious oaths. He makes a further point. Some of those who sincerely believed in the propositions to which they swore may, after the passage of time, no longer do so, in which case they will be exposed to grave inner conflict. It is in this context that he refers to the Anglican bishops. It was clearly not his intention to accuse them of perjury but to point out that in submitting to the oath-taking procedure in the first place they showed "little regard" for the sanctity of oaths. With what rights, he added, did one therefore single out the Jews for, allegedly, being prone to the same offense?

This polemical question was introduced with good reason. In the late spring of 1782 Mendelssohn had acted as consultant of the Prussian Government on matters related to the proposed reform of Jewish oath-taking in public courts. In reply to an inquiry by Ernst Ferdinand Klein (see note to p. 55) he had shown that neither the Talmud nor the rabbinic codes condoned false oaths taken with a *reservatio mentalis*. In Jewish law the sanctity of oaths was considered inviolable (see Altmann, *Mendelssohn*, 497–99). He felt outraged when, in a review of Dohm's treatise, Johann David Michaelis, the eminent Orientalist, had expressed serious doubts about the reliability of Jewish oaths (*Orientalische und Exegetische Bibliothek*, XIX, 1782, 8, 21). In our passage Mendelssohn gave vent to his feelings, and his remark, directed as it was against Michaelis, struck home when Michaelis reviewed *Jerusalem* (*Bibliothek*, XXII, [1783], 69–72; 165–70). He accused Mendelssohn of having slandered the English bishops, a charge which Mendelssohn refuted with great aplomb in the *Berlinische Monatsschrift*, III (January 1784), 24–41 (see *JubA* VIII, 205–24 where the relevant texts are reproduced and commented upon; Altmann, *Mendelssohn*, 530f.).

How correctly Mendelssohn assessed the situation in England may be gauged from a passage in Richard Price's *Observations on the Importance of the American Revolution* (London, 1785), 36f.: "The Church Establishment in England is one of the mildest and best sort. But even here what a snare has it been to integrity? . . . What struggles has it produced in its members to accommodate their opinions to the subscriptions and tests which it imposes? What a perversion of learning has it occasioned to defend obsolete creeds and absurdities? What a burthen is it on the consciences of some of its best clergy, who, in consequence of being bound to a system they do not approve, and having no support except that which they derive from conforming to it, find themselves under the hard necessity of either prevaricating or starving?—No one doubts but that the English clergy in general could with more truth declare that they *do not,* than that they *do* give their unfeigned assent to all and every thing contained in the thirty-nine Articles and the Book of Common-Prayer; and yet, with a solemn declaration to this purpose, are they obliged to enter upon an office which above all offices requires those who exercise it to be examples of simplicity and sincerity.—Who can help execrating the cause of such an evil?" As early as 1667 David Jenkins had written in *A Proposition for the Safety and Happiness of the King and Kingdom* (pp. 18–24) that religious oaths were useless since nobody would change his principles even though he had taken an oath; yet one grew embittered if in order to be able to swear one "loosened the reins of conscience." Oaths caused such havoc in honest souls that he wished for their abolition. This is strikingly reminiscent of Mendelssohn's complaint about the "lightheartedness" of such oaths and the "little regard" which those who took them showed for their sanctity, a point elaborated in the reply to Michaelis; see *JubA* VIII, 213–24.

68, 34–70, 3 Mendelssohn exonerates those who cease to assent to sworn propositions and nevertheless fail to resign their ecclesiastical office. The arguments he attributes to them in self-defense reflect those he had adduced above. He offers the additional consideration that any contractual stipulation of loyalty to the sworn propositions is null and void because it is impermissible to connect adherence to certain beliefs with external benefits such as tenure of office. To do so, he points out, is tantamount to following an "erroneous conscience." This remark (made in the footnote) is not without irony. In the textbooks of ecclesiastical law the *conscientia erronea* denotes the conscience of dissidents or infidels which is said not to be entitled to the rights that may be claimed by the correct conscience (*conscientia recta*). For Mendelssohn's use of the term "erroneous conscience" see also below, pp. 71, 32; 72, 11;

JubA VII, 305; for the notion of *conscientia recta* as used by Wolff and Baumgarten, see Altmann, *Frühschriften*, 342ff. The history of the concept of *conscientia erronea* is discussed in Altmann, *Die trostvolle Aufklärung*, 255–63; 275.

70, 14–15   Gen. 1:26–27; 9:6.

71, 29–72, 20   The question posed by Mendelssohn is taken up by Kant in his essay "Answer to the Question: What is Enlightenment?" which appeared in *Berlinische Monatsschrift*, IV (December, 1784), 481–94 (*Werke*, IV, 169–76); see E. G. Schulz, "Kant und die Berliner Aufklärung," *Akten*, 60–80. Kant extended the scope of the discussion so as to include all types of officeholders bound by an oath of loyalty. He suggested that a distinction be drawn between the duty to abide by the accepted norms when acting in an official capacity and the right to publicly raise questions as to their legitimacy when engaged in the exercise of scholarship. Somewhat paradoxically, he called the circumscribed use of reason in the exercise of one's public office (church or state) a "private use of reason" and he termed the reasoning of the scholar who freely expresses his criticism of conventional beliefs a "public use of reason." Mendelssohn took the opportunity of commenting on Kant's view when the latter was made the subject of debate in the Berlin Wednesday Society. The remarks he offered (*JubA* VIII, 225–29) made the point that under certain conditions one was entitled to propose innovations in doctrinal matters even in one's official capacity. For a full discussion of the issue as discussed by Mendelssohn, Kant, and Johann Friedrich Zöllner, who led the debate in the Wednesday Society, see Schulz, ibid.

72, 26–27   More precisely: only insofar as they *express* convictions.

73, 5–17   Cf. the description of "true, divine religion" in Mendelssohn's Preface to Menasseh ben Israel's *Vindiciae Judaeorum* (*JubA* VIII, 18); "bands of love": see Hosea 11:4.

73, 13–15   Cf. below pp. 123–25.

73, 18–74, 4   Mendelssohn had made the same point in his Preface to *Vindiciae Judaeorum*, including the suggestion that "very much inner religion" may be found among dissidents; see *JubA*, VIII, 23.

74, 5–16 Cf. "Preface" (*JubA*, VIII, 24): "To introduce church discipline without hurting civil happiness seems to be a problem still awaiting its solution in politics. It is like the answer of the supreme Judge to the prosecutor: Let him be in your hands; but spare his life! Break the barrel, as the commentators add, but don't let the wine run out!" The reference is to Job 2:6 and b. Baba Batra 16b (quoted by Rashi, *ad locum*). For the concern of the ecclesiastical lawyers in this respect see Altmann, *Essays*, 170–89, where Mendelssohn's attitude, especially vis-à-vis Dohm, is discussed.

75, 9–20 The Athenian philosopher referred to is Xenocrates, who from 339 to 315 C.E. was head of the Academy (not of the Stoa) and who converted his fellow Athenian Polemo from a life of debauchery to one of virtue and devotion to philosophy, which led to his eventually becoming himself the head of the Academy (311–270). The story of the conversion is frequently reported or alluded to; see Eduard Zeller, *Die Philosophie der Griechen*, II, i, 933f., where all the references can be found. Mendelssohn's description of the scene is an embellished account of the event as told by Diogenes Laertius who pictures Polemo as a young man "drunk and wreathed" (*ebrius et coronatus*) who with his friends burst (*irrupit*) into the school of Xenocrates. Unperturbed, the latter continued his lecture which happened to deal with the subject of temperance, thereby conquering the mind of the intruder and converting him; see *Diogenis Laertii De clarorum philosophorum vitis, dogmatibus et apophthegmatibus libri decem*, ed. C. Gabr. Cobet (Paris, 1850), lib. IV.3, pp. 97–98.

77, 2–3 The "universally held principle" opposed by Mendelssohn concerns the ecclesiastical right of excommunication (*jus excommunicationis*) which had been upheld by the Collegialists (Pfaff; Canz) as well as by Locke (see Altmann, *Die trostvolle Aufklärung*, 243). However, not all Collegialists considered it to be applicable in all circumstances. Mosheim pointed out that in case this right was exercised by the sovereign it was "almost impossible" to free it from civil consequences (*Allgemeines Kirchenrecht*, 416f.), a view that comes somewhat close to Mendelssohn's. The reference is to the so-called "minor ban" (*excommunicatio minor*) which is confined to

198 COMMENTARY

the denial of participation in the sacraments, not to the major ban or anathema (*excommunicatio major*) which was universally rejected because it involved a violation of civil rights (*diminutio capitis*) and was tantamount to an infringement of state prerogative, the church acting like a state within the state (*status in statu*); see Altmann, *loc. cit.*, 235–42. Mendelssohn opposes both forms of the ban, and he does so not merely on account of its civil consequences, which he considers inevitable also in the case of the minor ban, but also because he considers this right to be irreconcilable with the essence of religion.

77, 3–4   Viz., in the "Preface" to *Menasseh ben Israel;* see *JubA* VIII, 18–24.

77, 4–8   Cf. Wilhelm Dohm, *Ueber die bürgerliche Verbesserung der Juden* (1781), 124; for Mendelssohn's "inquiry" see Preface (*JubA* VIII, 17) and the Mendelssohn-inspired critique of Dohm's proposal in Moses Wessely's *Anmerkungen zu der Schrift des Herrn Dohm, über die bürgerliche Verfassung [!] der Juden* (Altona, 1782; published under the initials of Johann Christoph Unzer); see Altmann, *loc. cit.*, 229f.; for Dohm's suggested compromise solution see *JubA* XIII, 29f. and note, p. 356; Altmann, "Letters from Dohm to Mendelssohn," in *S. W. Baron Jubilee Volume* (Jerusalem, 1974), I, 51ff.

77, 8–13   Mendelssohn interprets Dohm's proposal by hypothetically assuming an enfeoffment of the autonomous Jewish "colony" with the right of excommunication; cf. "Preface" (*JubA* VIII, 21f.).

78, 18–19   Cf. Spinoza, *Tract. Theol.-pol.*, Praefatio, §12.

78, 19–80, 2   Cf. *JubA*, XI, 338, lines 31–34; Hermann Conrad, *Staatsgedanke und Staatspraxis des aufgeklärten Absolutismus* (Opladen, 1971); Klippel, *Politische Freiheit*, 102ff.; 106f.

78–79, Note   Mendelssohn expresses his regret at not having mentioned the name of Isaak Iselin (1728–82), the Swiss philosopher and political writer (see *JubA* XI, 500f.), when, at the beginning of his Preface, he bestowed praise on Reimarus (the "Fragmentist"), Lessing, and Dohm on account of their pleas for unrestricted toleration. He takes this opportunity to clarify a misunderstanding on Iselin's part. In the latter's review article on Mendelssohn's edition of *Vindiciae Judaeorum* and, especially, on the Preface (*Ephemeriden der Menschheit,* X [October 1782], 429–31) the following passage is found: "Mr. Mendelssohn somewhat laboriously refutes there [i.e., in the Preface, *JubA* VIII, 12–16] a statement [in an earlier issue of *Ephemeriden;* see *JubA* VIII, 12] which he attributes to the editor [*Verfasser,* i.e., Iselin] and which he assumes to imply that middlemen (*Zwischenhände*) are a useless burden upon human society [the notion rejected by Mendelssohn]. Such a view never occurred to the editor [*Verfasser*] of *Ephemeriden.* . . . He thinks about middlemen exactly as Mr. Mendelssohn does." In the present note Mendelssohn explains that his criticism had not been directed against the editor [*Verfasser*] but against the author of that essay (J. A. Schlettwein). The term *Verfasser,* which commonly denotes an author, is used here by Iselin and, following him, by Mendelssohn in the sense of *editor,* according, seemingly, to Swiss usage.

Iselin's review article, while praising Mendelssohn to the skies, showed its author to be imbued with anti-Jewish sentiment of the type common to radical Deism. In his concluding paragraph Mendelssohn gives a dignified reply. The reference he makes is to the notorious *Observations d'un Alsacien sur l'affaire présente des Juifs d'Alsace* (1779) by François Hell.

80, 3–15   Cf. *JubA* XIII, 63. The Berlin theologians named in that letter are Teller, Spalding, and Büsching. In addition, the Leipzig neologist preacher Zollikofer is mentioned. In the early 18th century many theologians had expressed regret at the ecclesiastical lawyers' suggestion that the ban be abolished, and had blamed the current disarray in the church upon the loss of "church discipline" (Mosheim, *loc. cit.,* 399).

80, 33–81, 3   *Göttingische Anzeigen von gelehrten Sachen,* III (Sept. 1782), 889–94, where the full passage reads (893f.): "There follows a noteworthy section about ecclesiastical rights. The author recognizes no right over persons and things connected with doctrinal opinions and founded upon them. Neither can positive laws and contracts make such a right possible in his opinion; for by contracts only imperfect rights could be transformed into perfect ones. In cases, however, in

which in the absence of a contract, there was neither duty
nor right all [subsequent] contracts and all agreements in the
world remained empty sounds, words spoken to the winds,
bereft of power and effect. All this is new and harsh. First
principles are negated, and all dispute comes to an end."
Thereupon follows the passage about a fictitious case to
which Mendelssohn responds further below (81, 34–82, 8).

81, 6–9 The legend that Pythagoras had a golden hip is reported
by Aelianus, Plutarch, Diogenes Laertius, Porphyry, and Iam-
blichus; see Zeller, *Philosophie der Griechen*, Part I, Section I,
1st Half, 7th ed., 396, note 1; Idem, *Vorträge und Abhandlun-
gen*, I (Leipzig, 1865), 44.

81, 34–82, 8 See note to 80, 83–81, 3, end.

82, Note For Jewish law and custom concerning circumcision
(*hilkhot milah*) see *Ṭur* and *Shulḥan 'Arukh, Yoreh De'ah*,
§§260–66.

83, 2–5 See above, 71, 29–72, 20.

84, 1–7 In Territorialism the term *jus circa sacra* designates the
rights of the sovereign in churchly matters (*potestas regia
circa ecclesiastica*). The Dutch Territorialists, following the
pattern of the Zwinglian and Anglican state church, included
in the *jus circa sacra* complete control over the synods, church
legislation, and appointment to ecclesiastical office, leaving
merely the spiritual functions of the clergy to the jurisdiction
of the church. They considered the *jus circa sacra* an integral
part of the state's sovereignty. The German ecclesiastical lawyers of the 17th century, though adopting the same premiss,
increasingly sought to limit that right to the externals (*ex-
terna*) of the church; see Martin Heckel, *Staat und Kirche*,
245f.; Johannes Heckel, *Cura religionis*, 224–98. Collegialism
differentiated between the *jura circa sacra collegialia*, which
belong to the authority of the church, and the *jura circa sacra
majestatica*, which are the province of the state, and affirmed,
in opposition to Territorialism, the legitimacy of the *potestas
ecclesiastica* (also denoted as *jus sacrum* or *jus ecclesiasticum*
and here referred to by Mendelssohn as "ecclesiastical power")
as a right exercised in the governance of the church (*Kirchenregiment*); see Schlaich, *Kollegialtheorie*, 226, 296. The Col-

legialists arrived, however, at the theory that for certain reasons the actual exercise of the *potestas ecclesiastica* had been
transferred to the sovereign, a doctrine that goes back to
Pufendorf, was developed by Pfaff and, finally, taken over by
Canz and Mosheim; see ibid., 235–46.

It is clearly the Collegialist understanding of the term *jus
circa sacra* and, in particular, the right of excommunication as
claimed by the lawyers of that school which Mendelssohn has
in mind. The term *enfeoffment* used by him here most probably refers to the transference of the governance of the church
upon the sovereign (a "visible person"), it being assumed that
this prerogative originally rested with the church itself (an
"invisible person"). He knew about the theory of transference,
no doubt, from Canz's *Disciplinae morales omnes* (for the relevant passages see Schlaich, *loc. cit.*, 243–45, 259). His rejection
of the *jus circa sacra*—irrespective of who may have been enfeoffed therewith—was based on the correct assumption that
the transference theory of Collegialism had taken the social
contract for its model (see Schlaich, *loc. cit.*, 236). In his view
no *pactum sociale* between the church and the state was feasible. Besides, no rights connected with doctrinal opinions,
even assuming that they might be valid within the church,
could be transferred to the sovereign.

84, 7–11 Hobbes distinguishes between the passing of a sentence
by which a man is to be excommunicated and the execution of
the judgment. The former he assigns to the (membership of
the) church, the latter to the clergy; see *De cive*, XVII.25
(*OL*, II, 405): *de peccato quidem judicare, ecclesiae est; pas-
torum vero judicatos ab ecclesia ejicere;* similarly *Leviathan*,
XLII; *OL*, III, 369f.; Oakeshott, 332.

84, 22–85, 23 Mendelssohn quotes passages from the treatise *Das
Forschen nach Licht und Recht* (pp. 12–14; 18; 23–24) which
seek to show how far his view of religion as expressed in the
Preface was removed from the Mosaic Law, the latter being
described here as an "ecclesiastical law armed with power."
The "Searcher" expresses full agreement with Mendelssohn's
reasoning for noncoercive natural religion (*JubA* VIII, 77)
but accuses him of inconsistency. How could he reconcile his
enlightened stance with continued adherence to the faith of

his fathers? In contrast to the radical Deists (Matthew Tindal and Thomas Morgan in England; Voltaire in France; Hermann Samuel Reimarus and Johann Salomo Semler in Germany), all of whom considered the Old Testament as irrelevant for the New, the anonymous author still shared the traditional view: "The essence of Christianity is also the faith of your fathers as it was transmitted to us, yet cleansed of the onerous statutes of the rabbis and augmented by new elements which nevertheless derive from the faith of your fathers and are explained as the fulfillment of Old Testament prophecies" (p. 10). Hence he believes that he is justified in recommending Christianity to Mendelssohn as a faith compatible with that of his fathers.

Concerning radical Deism see John Leland, *A View of the Principal Deistical Writers*, 5th ed., I (London, 1766); Gottfried Victor Lechler, *Geschichte des englischen Deismus* (Stuttgart and Tübingen, 1841); Leslie Stephen, *History of English Thought in the Eighteenth Century* (many editions); H. S. Reimarus, *Apologie oder Schutzschrift für die vernünftigen Verehrer Gottes,* ed. Gerhard Alexander (Frankfurt a.M., 1972). Semler wrote in 1777: "The books of the Old Testament . . . have no connection with the Christian religion. They are neither the foundation nor the content of Christianity" (quoted by Wolfhart Pannenberg, *Wissenschaftstheorie und Theologie* [Frankfurt, 1973], 385). This view represented a relapse, as it were, into the Gnostic attitude to the Old Testament which Tertullian had combated in his *Adversus Marcionem.*

85, 24–86, 6 Mendelssohn faces up to the possibility that his concept of true religion may contradict the Bible (the "word of God") and he demonstrates his faith in the authority of Scripture by considering the steps he would have to take in such an eventuality. The prayer for "illumination" is taken from the Book of Psalms (43:3). The hypothetical form in which his deliberation is expressed is a clear indication, however, that he is by no means laboring under "disquieting doubts" but actually feels that he is on sure ground. The phrase "bring reason into captivity under the yoke of . . ." (see 2 Cor. 10:5) is a necessarily inadequate rendition of the German text where the missing word at the end of the sentence is "gefangennehmen" (bring into captivity). Since in English the verb cannot be placed at the end, the ellipsis loses some of its pungency.

86, 8 On "Mr. Mörschel" see Introduction, p. 11.

86, 20–87, 2 *Das Forschen*, 24f (*JubA* VIII, 81). The concluding passage quotes John 4:23.

87, 4–14 The simile of the two floors is already found in the Draft. What provoked Mendelssohn to use it was a passage in *Das Forschen*, 23 (*JubA* VIII, 80): "How can you . . . continue to adhere to the faith of your fathers and shake the entire edifice by removing its cornerstones?" Kant comments: "Mendelssohn very ingeniously makes use of this weak spot in the customary presentation of Christianity wholly to reject every demand upon a son of Israel that he change his religion. For, he says, since the Jewish faith itself is, according to the avowal of Christians, the substructure upon which the superstructure of Christianity rests, the demand that it be abandoned is equivalent to expecting someone to demolish the ground floor of a house in order to take up his abode in the second story. His real intention is fairly clear. He means to say: First wholly remove Judaism itself out of your *religion* (it can always remain, as an antiquity, in the historical account of the faith); we can then take your proposal under advisement. (Actually nothing would then be left but pure moral religion unencumbered by statutes.) Our burden will not be lightened in the least by throwing off the yoke of outer observances if, in its place, another yoke, namely confession of faith in sacred history—a yoke which rests far more heavily upon the conscientious—is substituted in its place" (*Religion within the Limits of Reason Alone*, trans. Theodore M. Greene and Hoyt H. Hudson [New York, 1960], 154; *Werke*, VI, 315).

Kant realized that in Mendelssohn's eyes the Christian dogma was a far heavier yoke than the ceremonial law (cf. the latter's phrase—unbeknownst to Kant—in the Draft: "Christianity is a yoke in spirit and truth"). Yet what he misjudged was Mendelssohn's attitude to the historical element in Judaism. Far from wishing to discard it, he considered it an integral and indispensable part of the Jewish religion. Nor was he ready to take conversion "under advisement" in case Christianity eliminated its "historical" dogma. It was the advent of the messianic period when pure monotheism reigned supreme which Mendelssohn expected to bring about the abolition of the ceremonial law; cf. *JubA* VII, 102–6 where he discusses the faith of the Unitarians, and VII, 97f. where he describes the universal religion of the messianic period. See also *JubA* XIII, 134, where he upholds the necessity of the ceremonial law until such a time arrives.

87, 14–23   Christian efforts of this kind were made in a number of 18th-century writings which sought to refute the vilification of the Old Testament by radical Deists. Thus, Thomas Morgan's *The Moral Philosopher* (3 vols., 1737, 1739, 1740) evoked numerous replies, such as: John Chapman, *Eusebius* (2 vols., 1739, 1741); John Leland, *The divine Authority of the Old and New Testaments asserted* (2 vols., 1739, 1740); Moses Lowman, *Dissertation on the Civil Government of the Hebrews in which the Justice, Wisdom and Goodness of the Mosaical Constitution are vindicated* (1740); William Warburton, *The Divine Legation of Moses . . .* (2 vols., 1738, 1741).

87, 26–88, 11   See Mörschel's Postscript to *Das Forschen* (*JubA* VIII, 91–92). The references given by the author are to the Preface to *Menasseh ben Israel*. Whereas the "Searcher" sees in Mendelssohn a believer in the Mosaic revelation, Mörschel thinks he is a Deist in disguise, that is, a person who considers the truths of natural religion sufficient to secure man's salvation. He himself professes a rational belief in revelation without clearly defining it. For his references to statements made by Mendelssohn in the course of the Lavater affair see *JubA* VII, 9, lines 32–34; ibid., lines 18–20.

Mendelssohn treats Mörschel with a tinge of irony but does do "justice" to his "searching eye" and actually devotes the major part of *Jerusalem* II to the theme of reason and revelation raised by Mörschel. The question brought up by the "Searcher" (Cranz) is addressed only briefly toward the end of the book.

88, 27–89, 7   Cf. *JubA* VII, 362 where the same assurance is given.

The surmise that the Jews were in possession of secret documents concerning the origins of Christianity had been voiced
by Rousseau; see Altmann, *Mendelssohn*, 226; 238f.; 844,
note 11.

89, 25–90, 9   The view presented here—Mendelssohn's fundamental thesis on the question of reason and revelation—is basically
stated already in his letter to Elkan Herz (*JubA* XIX, 151)
dated July 22, 1771; see also *JubA* VII, 95: "The religion of
my fathers, insofar as its fundamental principles are concerned, knows nothing of mysteries to be believed and not to
be comprehended. Our reason may comfortably start out from
the first axioms of human knowledge and be sure to meet, in
the end, religion on this very road. Here no conflict exists between religion and reason. Similarly *JubA* XIII, 70; III.2, 196–
99. Mendelssohn adopts the Deistic stance which rejects the
credibility of "mysteries" of the faith not open to verification
by rational argument. In his view assent can be given only to
propositions that represent clear and distinct ideas and are
amenable to demonstration or are, at least, broadly conceivable by sound common sense. On the Deistical position see
Sullivan, *Toland*, 222f. and passim.

Mendelssohn does not share Locke's and Leibniz's distinction between propositions to be rejected because they are
contrary to reason and propositions to be admitted because
they are not in violation of reason but superrational, that is,
above comprehension; see Locke, *Essay Concerning Human
Understanding*, IV, 18, 7–8; Leibniz, *Essais de Théodicée*,
§23. For a discussion of Locke's and Leibniz's respective positions see Sullivan, *Toland*, passim; E. Crous, *Die religionsphi-
losophischen Lehren Lockes* (Halle, 1910); Leopold Zschar-
nack, *John Locke's Reasonableness of Christianity* (Giessen,
1914); August Wilhelm Dieckhoff, *Leibnitz Stellung zur Of-
fenbarung* (Rostock, 1888); Margrit Muff, *Leibnizens Kritik
der Religionsphilosophie von John Toland* (Dissertation, Zu-
rich, 1940). Like the Deists and Socinians, Mendelssohn considered the "mysteries" of the Christian faith (trinity, incarna-
tion, transsubstantiation) to be contrary to reason (see *JubA*
VII, 91ff.). In the doctrinal content of Judaism he found no
mysteries of any sort. It should be noted, however, that the

image of Judaism he had in mind was the "true," "original" Judaism (see below) and that, on his distinct admission (*JubA* VII, 9), some later accretions had "darkened" the pristine "splendor" of its truths, the reference being most probably to certain kabbalistic notions. He was also undoubtedly conscious of the designation of the deeper meaning of scriptural truth as "mysteries" (*razim; sodoth*) in Jewish mystical literature (see Gershom Scholem, *Ursprung und Anfänge der Kabbala* (Berlin, 1962, 33, 182, 337); Idem, *Kabbala* ([New York, 1974], 13, 41, 398). He himself mentioned in his Hebrew *Commentary on Kohelet* (*JubA* XIV, 148) the *sensus mysticus* (*sod*) as part of the fourfold meaning of Scripture. Yet he obviously perceived the difference between the "mystery" of the faith according to the Christian understanding—which was beyond comprehension—and the notion of *sod* in the Kabbala which implied only esotericism, not incomprehensibility.

Mendelssohn's distinction between natural revelation "through nature and things" and supernatural revelation "through word and script" derives, it seems, from Spinoza (*Tract. Theol.-pol.*, XIV, §38): "Philosophy has universal concepts (*notiones communes*) for its foundation, and it can be derived from nature (*ex natura*) alone; faith, however, has stories and language for its foundation and it can be derived from Scripture and revelation alone (*fidei autem historiae et lingua, et ex sola Scriptura et revelatione petenda*)." Here philosophy and faith are distinguished in terms of the difference between *nature* on the one hand and history, *language*, and revelation on the other. Mendelssohn adopts the key words of this division, but whereas Spinoza finds truth in philosophy alone, Mendelssohn acknowledges the "eternal truths" of natural religion in their philosophical as well as prephilosophical (commonsense) expression. What Spinoza calls "stories" he regards as history.

90, 10–11 "new and harsh"; see above, p. 81.

90, 17 Mendelssohn underpins his Spinozistic division with the aid of first principles borrowed from Leibniz's typology of truths.

90,20–93, 15 Leibniz distinguishes between *vérités de raison* (*nécessaires; universelles; éternelles*) and *vérités de fait* (*posi-*

tives; des choses contingentes et singulières). The truths of the
first kind are said to be grounded in God's intellect and to constitute geometrical necessity (which is unalterable even by
God), whereas those of the second kind are said to follow
from God's will and to represent moral necessity (which can
be suspended by God on occasion). This distinction is clearly
designed to serve, among other things, the admissibility of
miracles; see Leibniz, *Essais de Théodicée*, §§2–5. On the
subject as a whole see Leibniz, *Monadology*, §§33–44; *Textes
inédits*, ed. Grua, II, 287; 303; 325; *Nouveaux Essais*, I, i. 77;
III, v, 301; IV, iv, 446; Schiedermair, *Leibniz*, 142–150; 214–
220; 230ff.; H. G. Knapp, "Notwendige und zufällige Wahr-
heiten," in: *Studia leibniziana*, X.1 (1978), 60–86; Christian
August Crusius, *Entwurf der nothwendigen Vernunft-Wahr-
heiten, wiefern sie den zufälligen entgegen gesetzet werden*
(Leipzig, 1745, 3rd ed., 1766).

  Leibniz grants "moral" evidence or certitude not only to the
vérités de fait represented by statements concerning the permanent order of the universe but also to singular events (historical truths) attested by creditable witnesses. He thereby
facilitates the acceptance of "revealed" truths in addition to
that of miracles: "Besides, I include among the truths that
have *a posteriori*, not a *priori* certitude all historical truths
(*veritates historicas*) which come to our notice through sense
experience or authority in case they are revealed (*quales sunt
revelatae*)" (Leibniz, ed. Gerhardt, II, 259). To Leibniz the
mysteries of the Christian faith are on a par with miracles,
and they receive their verification through miracles. Miracles
are, as it were, transient mysteries, and mysteries are, in a
way, permanent miracles (see Muff, *op. cit.*, 98f.). It is on this
point that Mendelssohn parts company with Leibniz whose
division of truths he otherwise adopts and accentuates. While
he follows Leibniz in admitting the possibility of miraculous
events—they do not contradict truths of reason; they are
merely exceptions to the ordinary truths of fact which God
may suspend—he denies that miracles prove anything in the
realm of eternal verities of reason, that is, in the sphere of
metaphysical truth. The cleavage between the historical and
the metaphysical—the "ugly ditch" which Lessing had found

an obstacle necessitating a leap of faith from the one to the other—was unbridgeable to Mendelssohn too (see below).

For Leibniz the historical truths are but a special case of the *vérités de fait*. Mendelssohn elaborates these *choses singulières* into a more distinct category, giving the historical a status of its own. His purpose in so doing is to demarcate the domain of revealed legislation from the realm of natural religion which forms the doctrinal content of Judaism. The revealed law is embedded in, and part of, a sequel of events. The Sinaitic (Mosaic) constitution is "a matter of history" (*eine Geschichtssache*) which can be trustfully affirmed as such (*JubA* VII, 88). This is what also medieval Jewish philosophers like Judah Hallevi had affirmed. For Mendelssohn, however, historical truth has an epistemological character distinct from the metaphysical. Its *modus persuadendi* differs from that of metaphysical truth which is a truth of reason. It is "only" historical truth, i.e. something accepted on trust. It is valid only for those who received from their forebears the written record of certain events. It is revealed by "word and script," not by "nature and thing." By stressing its historical facticity Mendelssohn differs from Spinoza who saw in the biblical "stories" (*historiae*) a mere means of strengthening obedience (*Tract. Theol.-pol.*, IV, §19; V, §§39–40; 44–45). In a way similar to the stress on the encounter with God in history which characterizes some modern theologians' understanding of revelation (Richard Niebuhr; John Baillie; Martin Buber), Mendelssohn anchors revelation—as he sees it, the revelation of the law—in the historical sphere. Its nature is an act of covenant. In contrast to the Deists—and, later, Kant, who sought to eliminate the historical element from religion—he regarded the historical as an integral part of Judaism, and he could do so because he identified revelation with the historical givenness of the law. It therefore makes perfect sense that to him revelation is a matter of "word and script." By contrast, the metaphysical doctrines of Judaism are not revealed but taught by "nature and thing" (God's revelation in nature: "The heavens declare the glory of God"; see below, p. 126).

93, 16–94, 21 Mendelssohn explains the reason that motivated him to keep natural religion and revelation apart; see the Introduction, pp. 21–22.

93, 23–33 The consideration of what does and what does not "befit" God's wisdom can be traced historically to early Greek philosophy and patristic literature. It arose from the criticism of the myths in which the gods were portrayed in a manner offensive to moral standards and the dignity of the divine. The criterion applied led to the formation of the term *theoprepés* ("that which is befitting the deity"); see Werner Jaeger, *Early Christianity and Greek Paideia* (Cambridge, Mass., 1961), 128. A similar concept is tacitly assumed in Maimonides' discussion of the attributes of God (*Guide of the Perplexed*, I, 26; 46; 47; 59). What concerns Mendelssohn is not the problem of anthropomorphism but the moral principle involved in an exclusive revelation.

94, 13–21 Mendelssohn reverts here to the argument which he had put forward already at the time of the Lavater affair (*JubA* VII, 12; 73) and is expressed in a letter to Rabbi Jacob Emden dated October 26, 1773 (*JubA* XIX, 178). In that letter he had taken issue with Maimonides' verdict that a "righteous heathen" will have a portion in the world to come only if he observes the laws given to Noah and his descendents as divinely revealed laws (*Mishneh Torah*, Melakhim, viii, 10–11). "These words," he wrote to Emden, "are to me harder than flint. Are, then, all dwellers on earth . . . , except for us, doomed to perdition if they fail to believe in the Torah that was given as an inheritance only to the congregation of Jacob? . . . What, then, is expected of the nations unto whom the light of the Torah did not shine and who received no tradition either, except from ancestors not to be relied upon? Does God act tyrannically with his creatures by destroying them . . . without their having committed any wrong?" (cf. *JubA* VII, 11, note c). Spinoza, *Tract, Theol.-pol.*, V, §§47–48 had already attacked the Maimonides passage (known to him in a corrupt reading which aggravated the problem); see the treatment of this topic by Stephan Schwarzschild, "Do Noachites have to believe in revelation?" *JQR* LII (1962), 297ff.; LIII (1963), 30f.; Marvin Fox, "Maimonides on Natural Law," in *Diné Israel*,

III (Tel-Aviv, 1972), xii–xv; Isadore Twersky, *Introduction to the Code of Maimonides* (*Mishneh Torah*) (New Haven and London, 1980), 455, note 239. For Deistic models of Mendelssohn's argument see the Introduction, 21f.

94, 22   The "true" Judaism is identical with the "ancient" Judaism (100, 29) in its pristine purity, free from "human additions and abuses" (*JubA* VII, 9).

94, 22–95, 31   Mendelssohn upholds the concept of reason as a more or less static entity in the light of which natural religion is understood to be independent of time and space. As Julius Guttman has shown ("Mendelssohn's *Jerusalem*," 370), we find in Mendelssohn's "Counterreflections" (1769) two contradictory views concerning the religious development of mankind. In one place (*JubA* VII, 74–75) he speaks of a primitive condition at the dawn of history in which the truths of natural religion are but dimly apprehended by their "first discoverers" and conveyed by them to the people in indistinct and confused fashion with an admixture of superstitious ideas. Only gradually are these "prejudices" superseded by rational views. This evolutionist theory, Guttmann suggests, may reflect some influence of Voltairean and Humean concepts and point to the notion of a natural history of religion rather than of natural religion. In another place (ibid., 98), however, Mendelssohn returns to the older theory of paganism as a corruption of the original religion of pure reason and it is this view which he adopts throughout the *Jerusalem*.

That the truths necessary for the attainment of felicity in both worlds are evident to sound common sense—on this term see *JubA* VI.1, 232f.—and that their philosophical demonstration by subtle arguments is required only to safeguard them against the skepticism of the "sophists" is a view expressed by Mendelssohn on several occasions; see *JubA* III.1, 149; III.2, 197–99; lxvi–lxix. The "babbling of children" (Ps. 8:3) serves here as a metaphor for the simplicity of sound common sense. By "direct and indirect causality" the *causae proximae* and *causae remotae* of the Aristotelians are meant. They designate the causal chain leading up to God, the *causa prima* (see *JubA* XIV, 8of.). To those who choose to ignore the intermediate causes God appears to be the efficient cause operating directly in all happenings of nature (see Maimonides, *Guide*, II, 48). For Mendelssohn's view of Epicurus, Lucretius, Helvétius, and Hume see *JubA* II, 50; VI.1, 141; XI, 181; 265f.; XIII, 1. His remark about the "game" carried on with the word "nature" obviously refers to Lucretius's *De rerum natura* and Helvétius's *Système de la Nature*. The "cycle of ideas" is a notion which has its parallel in the "cycle of forms of government" (above, p. 42). Mendelssohn holds that the refinement of the arts and sciences has no substantial influence upon the average degree of morality (cf. *JubA* XII.1, 215), yet he by no means wishes to deny the progress achieved in the realms of culture and in philosophy in particular (see *JubA* III.1, 150f.; VII, 75; Altmann, *Die trostvolle Aufklärung*, 277f. and below, note to 96, 8–97, 15; Guttmann, *loc. cit.*, 369).

95, 32–96, 2   Mendelssohn dissociates himself from Lessing's anonymously published work "The Education of the Human Race" (Berlin, 1780; L-M, XIII, 413–36), the first 53 paragraphs of which had already appeared in 1777 (L-M, XII, 447ff.). Lessing conceived of the "education" of mankind as a process leading from childhood to youth and, finally, to mature manhood and as being represented by Judaism, Christianity, and the "new eternal gospel" respectively. The last of these three stages he considered to be identical with an autonomous, rational type of religion which he envisaged on the pattern of Joachim of Fiore's (ca. 1132–1202) "Ecclesia Spiritualis." With the notion of a Divine "education" of humanity in two stages of revelation (Moses; Jesus) Lessing had been familiar through his sustained research in patristic literature in his earlier years. While his "Education of the Human Race" had a decidedly theological tinge, another anonymous publication of his which appeared almost simultaneously (1778) applied the concept of growth and development to politics. In this book, "Ernst und Falk," a dialogue on Freemasonry, the "new gospel" is replaced by an ideal society in which all differences dividing men (state; religion; social status) are obliterated. (See Reinhart Kosellek, *Kritik und Krise* [Freiburg and Munich, 1959] and Ion Contiades' postscript to his edition of the text, 1968, 134f.) In the light of "Ernst und Falk" one may be

justified in attributing to Lessing's "The Education of the
Human Race" a more general tendency than its theological
language would suggest. It probably meant to express a definite theory of progress in history and this is no doubt how
Mendelssohn understood it. Philosophically viewed, Lessing's
theory rests on Leibniz's perspectivalism, which puts dynamic
development in place of the uniform constancy of reason and
attaches a value of its own to every stage of the monadic
process; see Henry E. Allison, *Lessing and the Enlightenment*
(Ann Arbor, 1966); Ernst Cassirer, "Die Idee der Religion,"
31ff.

96, 8–97, 15   Cf. Mendelssohn's letter to Hennings, *JubA* XIII,
65f.; VI.1, 19–24; 40–43; 48–50; XII.1, 43:51f.

In his essay "On the Adage: This may be right in theory but
does not do for practical purposes" (1793), §3, Kant criticizes
Mendelssohn's allegedly pessimistic view of history. He starts
from the assumption that what Mendelssohn asserted in the
present passage was the occurrence of inescapable periodic
relapses of mankind into moral depravity, all human effort
therefore amounting to a kind of labors of Sisyphus. Mendelssohn is said to have believed, as did the Indians, that the
earth was "a place of atonement for old sins," as if it were
God's desire to have an opportunity of meting out punishments in plentiful measure. But nothing of this sort is found
in Mendelssohn. True, he does not assume any progress of
mankind as a whole as far as the average degree of moral
culture is concerned, yet he does not profess belief in moral
relapse either. He considers the measure of morality (virtue-
vice; happiness-misery) to remain more or less static in all
periods. What he emphatically denies is the doctrine of an
upward trend in the sphere of religion since he is convinced
that the eternal truths of natural religion are accessible at all
times and in all places (see note to 94, 22–95, 31). On the
other hand, he definitely admits progress in the arts, sciences,
and philosophy, even if development in these realms is held
by him to proceed in oscillatory fashion rather than by rec-
tilinear and steady motion (96, 14–16, 30–35). Notwithstanding his denial of *steady* progress (which, by the way, is shared
by Kant), Mendelssohn regards it as the task of man in every

period to promote, as best he can, the progress of enlightenment and culture (see *JubA* VI.1, 118). In view of the main thesis put forward in the present passage it is somewhat surprising to find that in a letter written in 1770 he declares: "As for man, both the genus as a whole and each individual are capable of infinite progress" (*JubA* XII.1, 215). On Mendelssohn's view of history see Hans Liebeschütz's essay in *Studies in Jewish Religious and Intellectual History*, ed. Siegfried Stein and Raphael Loewe (University, Alabama, 1979), 167–82.

97, 16–98, 35   See above, p. 90, 6; *JubA* III.2, 196. Mendelssohn's interpretation of Exodus 20:2 offered here agrees with the ideas expressed in his Pentateuch Commentary (*Be'ur*) *ad locum*. The passage concerned reads (in translation): "The simple literal meaning of this verse shows that, by uttering the words 'I am the Lord thy God,' the Lord, be He blessed, addressed solely those who already believed in his existence; that, therefore, the Holy One, be He blessed, descended upon Mount Sinai not in order to teach his people [the truth] that He exists and that his existence is a necessary one and unlimited in time or whatever true and eternal propositions of reason there are. For these are the results of reflection and contemplation upon the works of God, . . . and he who has not reached that stage will have to accept those rational propositions from some intelligent man on trust. There is no way of establishing, or confirming, them in the heart of one who (having reached no conclusion) still ponders the issue by [simply] hearing a divine pronouncement declare: I exist! Nor can this be effected by thunderous voices, thick cloud, and the sound of trumpets [Ex. 19:16]. All this offers no attestation and no proof for those speculative propositions of reason unless one already believes that God exists. . . . This pronouncement [Ex. 20:2] had no other purpose than to declare the chosenness of the people . . . whereas with regard to the said speculative propositions of reason the children of Israel can claim no distinctiveness and no superiority over the rest of the nations, all of whom acknowledge God, be He blessed, it being admitted even by the worshipers of strange gods that the supreme and most perfect power belongs to God; as our teachers, of blessed memory, said: 'They called Him *God of gods* [b. Menaḥot 110a], and so also says Scripture [Mal. 1:11], *For from the rising of the sun even unto the going down of the same My name is great among the nations.*' It may be rightly assumed that the poet also had this in mind when saying [Ps. 19:4]: 'Without language, without words, with an inaudible voice,' which is to say that truth is made known to the world without pronouncement and speech [i.e., without a supernatural revelation; cf. below, p. 126]. Pronouncement and speech of whatever kind are intelligible only to those who know the language concerned, whereas that which 'the heavens declare'—they being 'his handiwork'—is intelligible to all inhabitants of the earth. . . . This will explain to you the reason why God did not say: I am the Lord thy God who created heaven and earth and who also created you. The question [why He did not say this?] was put to Rabbi Abraham ibn Ezra by Rabbi Judah Hallevi, of blessed memory [cf. Abraham ibn Ezra, *Commentary on Exodus, ad locum*] and mention of it is made in his *Sefer Ha-Kuzari* [I, 25]."

Mendelssohn's remark that neither the opening sentence of the Decalogue nor "the voice of thunder" and "the sound of trumpets" could mediate a revelation of eternal truths of reason reflects statements found in Spinoza's *Tractatus Theologico-politicus,* as Guttman (*loc. cit.,* 365–67) has shown. Spinoza had pointed out that the voice sounding forth from Mount Sinai was incapable of convincing anybody of God's existence (I, §§14–17); that objects of a spiritual nature can be seen only with the eyes of demonstrative proofs and that mere hearing and repeating of words equal the speech of a parrot or automaton (XIII, §17); that the voice heard at Sinai, which was a "created thing" (*res creata;* I, §§14–15), could not produce any philosophical or mathematical certainty about the existence of God; that its sole purpose was to excite admiration for God and obedience to his laws, God having impressed the people not by arguments (*rationibus*) but by the blaring of trumpets and by thunder and lightning (XIV, §36). Mendelssohn obviously agreed with the tenor of Spinoza's observations. He pointed out that the act of revelation could not—and was not intended to—convey metaphysical truths about God. Yet he refrained from characterizing the events accompanying the legislation as a mere "spectacle" as Spinoza did. He offered no explanation of the "miraculous voice" (97, 31) which Spinoza, following a tradition going back to Philo Judaeus (*Decal.*, 9, 32–35), reaffirmed by Maimonides (*Guide*, II, 33) and rejected by the Kabbalists (see Meir ibn Gabbai, 'Avodat ha-Qodesh [Jerusalem, 5733/1973], 276ff.), interpreted as a "created voice."

98, 1–8   Cf. *JubA* VII, 94; Lessing, L-M, XIII, 6: "If, as a historian I see no objection to Christ's reviving a dead person, must I therefore believe that God has a son who is consubstantial with Him?"

98, 18–20   For the "days of preparation" (*yemey ha-hagbala*), see Ex. 19:10–15.

98, 22–99, 11   Cf. the more explicit account in *JubA* VII, 43–45; 86–88, where Mendelssohn draws a clear line between miracles and the Sinaitic revelation as a legislative act; see Fritz Bamberger, "Mendelssohn's Concept of Judaism," 350–52. A public act of legislation, not miracles performed, established the authority of the Law, and the precept in Deut. 18:15 to obey miracle-working prophets is nothing but a positive commandment. It does not amount to the recognition of miracles as proofs of metaphysical verities. Miracles as such cannot validate religious truths of a doctrinal character which have reference to what is true at all times and everywhere. Nor can verities of the latter kind be disproved by miracles performed by a false prophet, as Mendelssohn points out (quoting Deut. 13:2–6; cf. *Be'ur, ad loc.*). In other words, miracles have a legitimate function only in the realm of historical truths concerning which we depend on reports ("word and script"). They enhance the authority of the reporters who interpret history in terms of divine acts. Traditionally, a miracle authenticates the divine mission of a prophet, the legitimacy of his authority as a messenger of God, not the trustworthiness of historical reports. For an analysis of Mendelssohn's philosophical treatment of miracles see Altmann, *Essays*, 142–53.

99, 12–35   In contrast to Spinoza, Mendelssohn sees in the Torah far more than a code of laws. In his view, the commandments are intimately related to the eternal truths of reason which constitute natural religion. They are said to relate to those truths in the way body relates to soul. The source of the dictum quoted in the name of the "rabbis" is obscure. Mendelssohn may have had in mind a *Zohar* passage (III, 152a) which speaks of the commandments as *gufey torah* (lit. "bodies of the Tora") wrapped up in the narratives as their garments as it were and pointing to an esoteric, mystical meaning which is their soul; see Scholem, *On the Kabbala and Its Symbolism* (New York 1965; 4th impression, 1973), 64. It is also possible that Mendelssohn simply varied the popular adage "Prayer without devotion is like body without soul" by applying the analogy to the commandments and the rational truths to which he saw them related.

In connecting the Mosaic law with the rational truths of natural religion, Mendelssohn, in obvious opposition to Spinoza, raises the meaning of the commandments from a merely political to an eminently religious level; see Guttmann, "Mendelssohn's Jerusalem," 374f. He emphasizes the "depths of insight" that are "concealed" in the Torah. The image used in this context recalls the allegory of the beautiful maiden employed by the *Zohar* (II, 99a–b; see Scholem, loc cit., 55f.).

99, 35–100, 28 Cf. *JubA* III.2, 196–99; 205; 218; especially pp. 69–73 (rejection of J. B. Basedow's principle of "duty to believe" [*Glaubenspflicht*]). The verse (Gen. 15:6) quoted by Mendelssohn is rendered differently in his German translation of the Pentateuch and in a sermon he composed on a patriotic occasion in 1757 (Frederick the Great's victory at Leuthen): "Abram believed in the Eternal, and He accounted this to him as virtue (*Tugend*)."

For the interpretation of *he'emin* (Gen. 15:6) as trust see Rashi *ad loc.*; on the understanding of "belief" in medieval Jewish philosophy see Harry A. Wolfson, *Studies*, I, 583–618; Simon Rawidowicz, *Studies in Jewish Thought*, ed. Nahum N. Glatzer (Philadelphia, 1974), 317–23. Moses Cordovero (*Sefer Or Ne'erav*, Tel-Aviv, 1965, 17a) stresses the obligation to know God by way of Kabbalah, mere belief being insufficient. For the distinction between *belief-in* and *belief-that* in modern analysis see W. Donald Hudson, *Wittgenstein and Religious Belief* (London and Basingstoke, 1975), 176ff.; Dallas M.

High, *Language, Persons, and Belief* (New York, 1967), 146–63; cf. Martin Buber, *Two Types of Faith* (London, 1951).

100, 29 By "ancient" (102, 12: "original") Judaism Mendelssohn understands the Mosaic and early-rabbinic religion prior to the writing down of the oral tradition, i.e., prior to ca. 200 C.E. In his view that primary phase was characterized by the oneness of "life and theory" (*Leben und Lehre*); see below, p. 128f. On the other hand, he speaks also of the Judaism of the "original constitution (ibid.), that is, of the unity of state and religion which gradually disintegrated and reached its end with the destruction of the second Temple in the year 70 C.E. (p. 130f.). His periodization is therefore somewhat ambiguous. It reflects, however, the underlying purpose of placing the ideal image of Judaism in the past and seeing it, in typical Enlightenment fashion, tarnished by later accretions.

100, 29–31 As Fritz Bamberger, *loc. cit.*, 343 rightly remarked, the view here expressed ("Judaism has no symbolic books, no articles of faith") has often been misunderstood. Mendelssohn by no means denied the fact that both the "old" and the latter-day Judaism subscribes to a set of definite beliefs. What he holds to be alien to Judaism is the liturgically expressed status which Christianity accords to the creeds (Apostolic; Nicene) as authoritative *symbola* (formulations) of the faith, and what he considers wholly inadmissible is the institution of religious oaths. Cf. Leo Baeck's essay "Does Traditional Judaism Possess Dogmas?" where Mendelssohn's view is explained and defended against the attacks by Jewish reformers like David Einhorn, Samuel Holdheim, and Leopold Löw, and where it is shown that Judaism has no dogmas in the Christian sense of this term; see Jospe, ed., *Studies*, 41–53. For further discussion of this subject see the essays by Julius Guttmann and Max Wiener, *loc. cit.*, 54–69; 70–111.

100, 33–101, 23 Cf. *JubA* XIII, 70. For a survey of the entire subject see Altmann's article in *Encyclopaedia Judaica*, III, 654–60. Maimonides was by no means "the first" to reduce the content of Jewish belief to "principles" (*'iqqarim*), and it was Isaac Abrabanel, not Luria, who declared that in the Torah everything was fundamental; see Abrabanel, *Rosh Amanah,* ch. 23; annotated English translation by M. M. Kellner (London and Toronto), 194–200.

Lord Herbert of Cherbury's (1583–1648) five religious truths of reason (*notiones communes*) are discussed in his *De veritate* (Paris, 1624) *and De religione gentilium* (London, 1645). They cover the following points: (1) There is a supreme God; (2) This God is to be worshipped; (3) Good conduct and piety form the principal parts of Divine worship; (4) Vice and crime should be expiated and effaced by repentance; (5) Rewards and punishments are to be expected after this life; cf. Basil Willey, *The Seventeenth Century Background* (1962), 111–22; Heinrich Scholz, *Die Religionsphilosophie des Herbert von Cherbury* (Giessen, 1914); G. V. Lechler, *Geschichte des englischen Deismus*, 42.

101, 21–23 and Note   The quotation in the text obviously conflates two distinct rabbinic passages, viz., Mishnah Yebamot I, 4 and b. 'Erubin 13b. The Yebamot passage (see also 'Eduyot IV, 8) mentions a number of halakhic controversies between the schools of Shammai and Hillel, adding the remark: "Notwithstanding that these bind (forbid) what the others loosen (permit), . . . yet the [men of the] School of Shammai did not refrain from marrying women from [the families of] the School of Hillel, nor the [men of the] School of Hillel from marrying women from [the families of] the School of Shammai." The parallel passage in the Tosefta adds: "This [practice was prompted by their desire] to live up to the Scriptural verse (Zech. 8:19), 'Therefore love ye truth and peace.' " See b. Yebamot 14b, where a more extensive version is found. Mendelssohn's quotation in the Note refers to this passage. The 'Erubin passage, on the other hand, reports that the Schools of Shammai and Hillel were in dispute over a period of three years, each claiming the right to determine the final *halakhah* until a voice (*bat qol*) from Heaven proclaimed: "Both these and the others are the words of the living God, yet let the final decision be according to the School of Hillel." Mendelssohn quotes this verdict but omits the last clause, which has no significance in the present context where the issue is not halakhic practice but matters of belief.

The fast days mentioned in the Note are the seventeenth of

Tammuz, the ninth of Ab, the third of Tishri, and the tenth of Tebet. These days of national mourning are supposed to be changed into days of joy when the Jewish people will merit the advent of the messianic future by exercising the love of truth and peace. Cf. the final sentence in *Jerusalem* and *JubA* VI.1, 197.

101, 24–102, 2   Mendelssohn designates "religious doctrines" (viz., the eternal truths of natural religion) as objects of "knowing," and "religious commandments" (viz., the revealed Law, which embraces relevant historical truths) as objects of "believing." Knowledge, he says, can be reduced to principles, whereas Law cannot; here everything is fundamental. He thus applies Abrabanel's statement to the halakhic aspect of Judaism.

102, 2–11   In the story as told in b. Shabbat 31a the negative form of the so-called Golden Rule is used: "Do not to your fellow what you hate to have done to you." This form goes back to Tobit 4:15 and is ascribed also to Rabbi 'Aqiba (*ARN*, ed. Schechter, Version II, ch. 26, p. 27); it appears likewise in the early-Christian *Didachē* (1:2) and other Christian sources. In the Gospels (Matth. 7:12; Luke 6:31) the rule is stated in a positive form: "All that ye wish that men should do to you, do ye even so to them." The positive form is used also by Maimonides, *Mishneh Torah*, Hilkhot Evel, 14:1; see G. F. Moore, *Judaism* (New York, 1958), II, 87f. Mendelssohn quotes neither the negative form found in the story nor the positive one but refers to the biblical text (Lev. 19:18). He thereby combines the Hillel story with a dictum of Rabbi 'Aqiba's (Sifra Lev., *ad loc.;* p. Nedarim IX, 1; see *Genesis Rabba*, ed. Theodor-Albeck, 236f.) which calls the precept "Love thy neighbor as thyself" a "great principle in the Torah" (*kelal gadol ba-torah*). He may have refrained from quoting the negative form of the rule because of the fact that in some writings of the Natural Law School it stood for the precept "do not hurt any one" (*neminem laedere*) and expressed the principle of strict law (*just strictum*), not the "duty of love" (*officium humanitatis*), the latter being identified with the positive form of the Golden Rule.

It should be noted that Spinoza too points out that the "whole Law" is expressed in the precept to love one's neighbor, the main purpose of the Scriptures in both the Old and the New Testament being obedience to God as manifested in loving one's neighbor (*Tract. Theol.-pol.*, XIV, §§6–10). In another context (XIX, §29), however, he follows the statement in Matth. 5:43 by declaring that the Hebrews were told, "Thou shalt love thy neighbor, and hate thine enemy," a rule found neither in the Old Testament nor in rabbinic writings (see M. Kister, "Sayings of Jesus and the Midrash," *Jerusalem Studies in Jewish Thought*, II, 1982, 13). Mendelssohn was clearly concerned to show that the commandment to love one's neighbor was considered central in Judaism.

102, 12–25   Mendelssohn distinguishes between the static character of the written Law and the fluid nature of the oral Law. He also draws a line between actions (laws) and convictions (beliefs), a distinction which is basic to his entire system of thought in *Jerusalem* (see Index s.v. "Convictions and actions"). It should be borne in mind that in Section I (pp. 44–45) he defines religion as an indivisible unity of action and conviction in contradistinction to the state which may be content with mere action. He also distinguishes there between laws (the province of the state) and commandments (the province of religion). This particular differentiation is not upheld in Section II.

102, 25–28   b. Gittin 60b.

102, 30–33   Ps. 119:126; b. Temurah 14b.

102, 34–103, 7   Mendelssohn adopts the term "ceremonies" ("ceremonial law"), which is of Latin origin (*caerimonia*, meaning the sacred; holy dread; sacred rite), from Spinoza who distinguished the "natural divine law" (*lex divina naturalis*) from the "ceremonies" (*ceremoniae*). According to Spinoza, the *lex divina* refers to the true knowledge and love of God (IV, §§9; 14); it is universal by virtue of its being derived from the nature of man and on account of being innate in him as it were (IV, §18; V, §1). The ceremonies, on the other hand, are in themselves "indifferent" acts which were commanded to the Hebrews alone (V, §§1–2), are based on revelation (V, §3), and aim at the temporal and physical well-being of that nation (V, §§6–12). Mendelssohn found the term *ceremonies* convenient for differentiating the revealed Law from the moral laws of natural religion, but whereas Spinoza attributes to the ceremonies (and even to the moral precepts of the Old Testament) a merely political purpose (V, §7), Mendelssohn affirms a close bond between the ceremonial law and the eternal truths of natural religion. Far from being "indifferent," they help to promote eternal, not merely temporal, happiness.

103, 7–27   Cf. T. L. Haering, *Hegel*, 154: "Mendelssohn treats here—as, by the way, Schiller also did—the present paper age with an irony reminiscent of Hegel." As early as 1768 (see GS IV.2, 541) Mendelssohn had characterized the "enthusiasm of our sophistical (*vernünftelnden*) period" as a "prearranged game between poet and reader."

104, 3–4   Isa. 3:5; cf. Mishnah Soṭah IX, 15: "The young shall shame the elders, and the elders shall rise up before the young" (one of the symptoms of the period of terror said to precede the advent of the Messiah).

104, 34–105, 33   As Mendelssohn remarks in a letter to Herz Homberg (*JubA* XIII, 133), much more could have been said here about the origin of language, had this been the right occasion for it. The little which he managed to say in this context differs in several respects from what he had suggested in his early "Epistle to Lessing" (*JubA* II, 106–9) and in his treatise "On Language" (*JubA* VI.2, 5–23) which, no doubt, originated at the same time (see Eva J. Engel, ibid., xi–xxi; 325–27). He himself pointed out that the treatise would have to be reworked in the light of the "important" publications that had appeared afterwards. (On 18th-century literature on this topic see Arno Borst, *Der Turmbau von Babel*, III, Part 2, 1961.) Mendelssohn knew Herder's prize essay "On the Origin of Language" (Berlin, 1772; *Sämtliche Werke*, ed. B. Suphan, V, Berlin, 1891; revised text edition by Vlaus Träger, Berlin, 1959); see *Verzeichnis*, 53, no. 655. He had already previously held the view expounded by Herder that language originated in response to the need to isolate ("separate") the conceptualized characteristics of things perceived, a purpose to be achieved by the attentiveness of reason. He seems to have been impressed, however, by the way Herder showed this process to represent something specifically human and to exclude the possibility of explaining the origin of language by the theory of mere imitative signs. Whereas Mendelssohn had advocated that particular theory before (*JubA* II, 106f.; VI.2, 111–14), he no longer mentions it here. Traces of Herder's influence may be detected also in the manner in which he stresses the eminently human character in the formation of language ("the urge implanted in his [man's] soul") and, moreover, in the division of the signs into natural and arbitrary ones. Yet while Herder identifies general characteristic, concept, and natural sign, Mendelssohn differentiates between concept (characteristic) and sign.

106, 7–13 Mendelssohn had in his library (*Verzeichnis*, 8, no. 73) a copy of the Latin translation of Newton's *Opticks* (1704) which had first appeared in English: *Optice sive De reflexionibus, refractionibus, inflexionibus et coloribus lucis, libri tres . . . Auctore Isaaco Newton. Latine reddidit Samuel Clarke. Londini 1706.*

106, 16–31 The reference is to Evangelista Torricelli's discovery, in 1643, of the principle of the barometer ("Torricellian tube"; "Torricellian vacuum").

106, 35–107, 13 The reference is to Albrecht von Haller's treatise *Von den empfindlichen und reizbaren Theilen des menschlichen Körpers* (1756), a copy of which he had in his library (*Verzeichnis*, 13, no. 203); translated into English by M. Tissot under the title "A Dissertation on the Sensible and Irritable Parts of Animals" (London, 1755); a new German edition by Karl Sudhoff appeared in Leipzig, 1922 (reprint, 1968). When it was first published in Latin, the treatise caused a great sensation but also provoked opposition (see the bibliographical references in: Susanna Lundsgaard-Hansen-von Fischer, *Verzeichnis der gedruckten Schriften Albrecht von Hallers* [Bern, 1959], Index, s.v. *Reizbarkeit*, p. 85). In his preface to the English edition, Tissot hailed Haller's presentation as "the great discovery of the present age," and he compared it with Newton's discovery of gravitation and Torricelli's of the weight and elasticity of the air. Mendelssohn follows his example. On the prehistory of Haller's discovery see Tissot's edition, vi–xiii; 61–67.

108, 12–110, 15   Mendelssohn seeks to show that the transition
from hieroglyphics (pictorial script) to the alphabet (sound-
notation; letter script) was a natural and gradual one. His assumption that hieroglyphics itself eventually came to indicate
sounds probably derives from William Warburton's *The Divine Legation of Moses* (1737–41) where it is said: "When
the picture lost its form, by being contracted into a mark or
note, this mark or note would raise in the mind the sound ex-
pressing the idea of the thing as the idea itself" (4th ed., III,
London, 1765, 153). This theory seems to be confirmed by
modern research; see *Encyclopaedia Britannica*, 1964, XI, 477.
Hegel, on the other hand, assumed that hieroglyphic script indicated only objects "with no reference to sound as a sign";
see "Philosophische Propädeutik," III, 2nd section, §161
(*Sämtliche Werke Jubiläumsausgabe*, III, 211). In his view,
the transition to "the more intelligent" alphabetic script was
caused by the impact of "commerce between the nations"; see
"Die Philosophie des Geistes," in *Werke*, X, 347ff. Cf. also
David Diringer, *The Alphabet: A Key to the History of Mankind*, 3rd ed. (New York, 1968).

110, 26–112, 5   As Haering (*Hegel*, I, 154) remarks, Mendelssohn
draws here "an ingenious parallel between the symbolism of
written characters and that of images of the gods on the one
hand and between the confusion of signs with things and the
confusion of idolatry with the true notion of God on the other,
indeed seeing in the former the direct cause of the latter."
Mendelssohn's attempt at deriving the origin of animal worship from hieroglyphics may have been indebted to both Tin-
dall and Warburton. Cf. Matthew Tindal, *Christianity as Old
as the Creation*, I (London, 1730), 173: "The chief cause of
the Egyptians following into grosser Idolatries than other less
knowing nations, was, no Doubt, owing to the Use of Hyero-
glyphicks in their religious worship: An Ox . . . was at first
only a symbolic Representation; the Meaning of which, the
People in Time forgetting, fell to down-right adoring the
Beast"; similarly Warburton, *loc. cit.*, 197; 201–5. Mendelssohn's acquaintance with Warburton's "The Divine Legation
of Moses" is attested (see *JubA* IV, 323).

112, 5–14   See Christoph Meiners, *Versuch über die Religionsge-
schichte der ältesten Völker besonders der Egyptier* (Göttin-

gen, 1775), 27: "For all nations in their original state base their religion on physics and natural history: all their deities and objects of worship are either celestial bodies or other parts of the corporeal world; they rather adore the most abominable creatures, even inanimate things, than individuals of their own genus" (cf. also pp. 32–34). Mendelssohn's library contained copies of both Meiners's *Versuch* and his *Geschichte des Ursprungs, Fortgangs und Verfalls der Wissenschaften in Griechenland und Rom,* 2 vols. (Lemgo, 1781–82) (see *Verzeichnis,* 23, nos. 94–95; 36, no. 321).

112, 17–20 See *G. E. Lessings Fabeln* (Berlin, 1759); L-M, VII, 446–55, where the use of animals in the fable is discussed. Lessing shows that "the generally known and immutable characters of the animals are the true reason why the fable elevates them to the status of moral entities."

113, 26–27 Mendelssohn quotes the Hebrew proverb *eyn navi' be-'iro* ("No one is prophet in his town"); cf. Matth. 13:57.

113, 33–114, 10 The reference is to Omai, the "wild Indian," who, as Captain James Cook reports, was taken captive on an island in the South Seas and brought to England where his handsome appearance, amiability, and cheerful imitativeness created a sensation. He was presented to the King, visited the Opera, was painted by Reynolds and mentioned by Boswell in his *Journal.* He became the darling of the public, including high society. Eventually he was sent home. See *The Journals of Captain James Cook on his Voyages of Discovery 1776–1780,* ed. J. C. Beaglehole, III, Part One (Cambridge, 1967), lxxxviif.; IV. *The Life of Captain James Cook* (London, 1974), 447–49; Index, 750, s.v. *Omai.*

114, 3–13 The "Temple of Providence" is the place of worship established in Dessau by Johann Bernard Basedow (1723–90) who, influenced by Rousseau, became one of the pioneers of enlightened pedagogy in Germany. He also founded a modern school, the *Philanthropinum,* in Dessau. His "Temple" was to serve the cause of natural religion. A reproduction of its exterior and interior can be found in *Studien über das Philanthropinum und die Dessauer Aufklärung,* Wissenschaftliche Beiträge der Martin-Luther-Universität Halle-Wittenberg, 1970/3, Halle (Saale), 27–28. Mendelssohn mentioned this edifice to his friend August Hennings as early as 1776; see Altmann, *Mendelssohn*, 340.

114, 18–24 Cf. *Midrash Lamentations Rabba*, Introduction, 9 (ed. S. Buber, Wilna, 1899, p. 8). The story is alluded to in Ele'azar Qalir's dirge (*qinah*) for the Ninth of Ab commencing with the words '*al ḥorban bet ha-miqdash;* see Daniel Gold-schmidt, *Seder Ha-Qinot le-Tish'ah be-'Av* (Jerusalem, 1968), 92. I owe this reference to Professor Aaron L. Katchen.

114, 33–115, 26 See J[ohn] Z[ephaniah] Holwell, *Interesting His-torical Events Relative to the Provinces of Bengal, and the Empire of Indostan* . . . *as also the Mythology and Cosmog-ony, Fasts and Festivals of the Gentoo's, followers of the Shas-tah, and A Dissertation on the Metempsychosis, commonly, though erroneously called the Pythagorean Doctrine.* Part I, London, 1765; Part II, London, 1767; 2nd ed., 1766–71; French translation, Amsterdam, 1768. A German translation of Part I is found in Johann Tobias Köhler's *Sammlung neuer Reisebe-schreibungen aus fremden Sprachen, besonders der englischen, in die Teutsche übersetzt* . . . , Vol. I in two parts, Göttingen and Gotha, 1767–69. Vol. II, which was to contain Part II of Holwell's work, remained unpublished. The passage quoted here by Mendelssohn occurs in Part II, Sect. VIII, pp. 106ff. The translation is his. The text immediately preceding it reads as follows: "And it was—that when the Eternal *One* resolved to form the new creation of the *Dunneahoudah* (the universe), he gave the rule of *Mahab Surgo* to his first created Birmah, and became invisible to the whole angelic host. When the Eternal *One* first began his intended new creation of the *Dun-neahoudah,* he was opposed by two mighty *Ossours* (giants), which proceeded from the wax of Brum's ear, and their names were Modoo (discord) and Kytoo (confusion). And the Eternal *One* contended and fought with Modoo and Kytoo five thousand years, and he smote them." It is at this point that Mendelssohn's translation starts, his first sentence providing a sort of *mise en scène.* His is a somewhat shortened version that is accurate except for two errors (corrected in the text). The spelling of names is Germanized (Modu for Modoo, etc.). In his work, pp. 110–16, Holwell provides a commentary on this text.

115, 33–116, 4   This was the view held by Plutarch and Bayle; see note to 63, 2–12. Mendelssohn sees in superstition a product of "luxury, hypocrisy and effeminacy" (*JubA* VI.1, 118), a theory that goes back to classical antiquity (*divitiae-avaritia-ambitio, luxuria-superstitio*); see Edward N. O'neil, *De cupiditate Divitiarum*, in *Plutarch's Ethical Writings and Early Christian Literature*, ed. Hans Dieter Betz (Leiden, 1978), 296f.

116, 14   The reference may be to Plutarch, *Isis and Osiris*, 379E–381D. For Plutarch's monotheistic stance see John Oaksmith, *The Religion of Plutarch* (London, 1902).

116, 17–20   Hosea 13:2.

117, 6–9   The reference is to the school founded by Pythagoras of Samos (b. ca. 580 B.C.E.). It considered numbers and combinations of numbers to constitute the ultimate causes of things; see Eduard Zeller, *Die Philosophie der Griechen*, I, i, 1, 7th ed. (Hildesheim, 1963), 361–617. It may be assumed that Mendelssohn derived his knowledge of this school chiefly from Jacob Brucker's *Historia critica philosophiae*, I (Leipzig, 1767).

117, 34–118, 10   Mendelssohn reduces the doctrine of the "election of Israel," which plays a central role in Jewish theology, to the idea that the Jewish people is destined to preserve "pure," "sound," and "unadulterated" notions of God, that is, to safeguard natural religion (see Julius Guttmann, *loc. cit.*, 375f.). Cf. *JubA* VII, 98; XIII, 134.

118, 15   Following Isa. 43:21.

118, 18–19   The biblical phrase "to enter into God's sanctuary" (Ps. 73:17) is used here and further below (133, 30) in the sense of comprehending the purpose of the divine commandments. One may venture to surmise God's "plan" ("the system of his designs"), he says, but from any such surmise one may not draw practical consequences bearing on the continuing validity or otherwise of the commandments concerned. In Jewish mysticism the "reasons of the commandments" (*ta'amey ha-miṣvot*) are said to be connected with the mystery of Divinity as expressed in the *Ten Sefirot*. Mendelssohn, though remote from kabbalistic thought, nevertheless reflects some of the religious emotion of awe that characterizes its approach to the commandments.

118, 20–23   The attacks made upon the Mosaic law, Mendelssohn implies, indicate a rather immodest "Searcher," the reference being to Cranz. They were to be answered by the "modest searcher."

119, 27–28   Deut. 6:9.

120, 3–7   By the "road of corruption" Mendelssohn means the growing "fissure" in the unity of state and religion that eventually led to the end of Jewish political independence (cf. below, p. 132). The "brilliant circle" is the period of statehood.

120, 8–27   This account of the episode narrated in Exodus 32:1–28 follows the interpretation offered by Judah Hallevi (*Sefer Ha-Kuzari*, I, 92–98) and subsequently adopted by Isaac Abrabanel (*Pentateuch Commentary, ad loc.*), Jacob Abendana (*Leqet Shikhehah, ad loc.*), and by Mendelssohn himself in his *Be'ur, ad loc.;* see David Cassel, *Sefer Ha-Kuzari,* 2nd ed. (Leipzig, 1869), 66, note 1. The salient point of this interpretation is the distinction between idolatry and the representation of God by an image.

120, 36–121, 2   Mendelssohn means to say that one envies only gifts of good fortune, not goodness of character which depends on one's own moral effort. The last clause ("which he finds enviable") is hardly in place since it contradicts the very proposition which the argument seeks to explain.

121, Note   For the complete title of Meiners's work, see note to 112, 5–14.

122, 3–123, 2   Mendelssohn's second note to this passage refers to his translation of the text (Ex. 33:15–34:10) in his Pentateuch edition. There are, however, some slight variants, apart from the abbreviated form of the story as retold here. What motivated him to present an account of it in the context of *Jerusalem* was his desire to offset the reproach of undue harshness which the "Searcher" had directed against the Mosaic legislation. The Mosaic notion of God that emerges from the story is, by contrast, one of kindness, grace, and forgiving. The text was not chosen at random. The verses 34:6–7 which hold the center of attention are the very core of rabbinic theology ("the thirteen attributes of mercy").

123, 8–9 The statement "this, too, is a quality of divine love that for man nothing is allowed to go unpunished" which is quoted here in the name of the rabbis actually derives from Abraham ibn Ezra's *Pentateuch Commentary* (Ex. 34:7) where it reads "this, too, is a quality of mercy" and refers to the words added to the thirteenth quality ("visiting the iniquity of the fathers upon the children, and upon the children's children"). In his *Be'ur, ad loc.*, Mendelssohn explains this statement of Ibn Ezra's in the sense of the Talmudic interpretation (b. 'Avoda zara 4a) according to which God in his mercy distributes the measure of punishment in small coin as it were over a long period rather than at one fell swoop. In the present context he connects Ibn Ezra's saying with the thirteenth quality as such ("and will by no means clear the guilty"). He gives it the meaning that punishment itself is an expression of divine love since it serves man's moral improvement (see the discussion that follows). Similarly, Naḥmanides (*Pentateuch Commentary, ad loc.*) had described the punishment of sins as a means of purifying the soul of its dross as it were.

123, 10–125, 8 This passage reformulates the thoughts Mendelssohn had already voiced in his "Counterreflections on Bonnet's *Palingenesis*" (*Juba* VII, 72–73). It may be assumed that the "venerable friend" mentioned in both places is Johann August Eberhard, enlightened clergyman and later professor of philosophy at Halle University, who lived in Berlin at the time of the Lavater affair (see *JubA* XII.2, 260) and was a devoted friend of Mendelssohn's whose abhorrence of the doctrine of eternal punishment in hell he shared and publicly expressed (see Altmann, *Mendelssohn*, 220; 553–56).

123, 11–13 The question obviously relates to the Protestant doctrine of man's justification by faith, which bids the sinner trust in the divine forgiveness as promised in the Christian revelation. The friend poses the question whether Mendelssohn, who did not accept that revelation, might not wish to receive a "direct," that is, a personal, revelation to this effect. The distinction between two kinds of revelation, one direct and the other by way of tradition, goes back to John Locke, *An Essay Concerning Human Understanding*, II, 4, 18, §3 and passim.

123, 16–20 The "hypothesis" mentioned here was known to Mendelssohn chiefly from Leibniz (*Essais de Théodicée*, I, §§73–74; 126) and Lessing ("Leibniz von den ewigen Strafen," L-M, XII, 461–87); cf. his polemic against Leibniz in "Sache Gottes," *JubA* III.2, 240; 250. The notion that punishment of sin must be proportionate to the offended majesty of God and, hence, eternal is discussed also in medieval Christian and Jewish theology; see Thomas Aquinas, *Summa theologiae*, 1.2, 87, 3–5; Joseph Albo, *Sefer Ha-'Iqqarim*, IV, 36–38. It was rejected by the Socinians and Hobbes; see Leibniz, *loc. cit.*, I, §73; Hobbes, *Leviathan*, Part IV, ch. 44; *OL*, III, 522. In Jewish theology a repudiation of this doctrine is found already in Isaac da Fonseca Aboab, *Nishmat Ḥayyim* (1636); see A. Altmann, "A Theological Controversy within the Amsterdam Rabbinate . . . ," in *PAAJR*, XI (1972), 1–88, esp. 20ff.; 75.

123, 20–21   Cf. above, p. 58f.

123, 34–35   The term "fire of his laws" reflects Deut. 33:2.

124, 9–23   Plato, too, assigns to punishment the purpose of improving man; see *Gorgias*, 477A; *Laws*, XI, 934A. Philo Judaeus, *De confusione linguarum*, 36, 182 considers punishment a benefit; hence the punitive angels who carry out the divinely decreed punishment are said to be included in the general description of the angels as "God's beneficent and merciful and bountiful powers." See Harry A. Wolfson, *Philo*, 3rd ed. (Cambridge, Mass., 1962), I, 382f.

124, 24–26   Leibniz, *loc. cit.*, I, §73 sees one of the purposes of punishment in making an example of a person who committed a misdeed. This notion of *exemplum* (exemplary punishment) underlies the present discussion; cf. *JubA* VII, 73.

125, 9–11   By way of translation Mendelssohn offers here a novel exegesis of Ps. 62:13; for different interpretations of the verse see Rashi and Ibn Ezra, *ad loc.*; Mendelssohn, *Die Psalmen, ad loc.* (*GS* VI, 218).

125, 12–15   For the apologetic tendency of this passage see note to 122, 3–123, 2.

126, 1–2   For Mendelssohn's use of the term "the Judaism of former times" see note to 100, 29 ("ancient Judaism").

126, 17–25   Mendelssohn interprets Ps. 19:1–5 as a hymn celebrating the natural revelation of God as Creator of the world.

This revelation requires no words or script but is legible and audible at all times and in all places; cf. above, p. 93. The translation of the passage in *Die Psalmen* (*GS* VI, 154) shows a number of variants.

126, 33–35   Ps. 103:2–4.

127, 1–4   Mal. 1:11.

127, 15–18   Cf. above, p. 98, 32–35.

128, 14   The "early period" signifies "ancient Judaism" (see note to 100, 29) during which the idea of God's kingship over the nation held sway in its full extent until the time of the prophet Samuel but was on the wane in the subsequent periods until it lost all political meaning when Jewish statehood came to an end (see below, p. 132). The Mosaic law was the legitimate expression of this idea and, as Mendelssohn points out, the severe penalties for transgressions of the law which it demanded made sense in view of the inseparable unity of state and religion which obtained in this particular constitution (pp. 128–30). Yet when "the constitution degenerated" (132, 21: "was undermined"), the *raison d'être* of those punishments vanished; Judaism became a mere "religion" as it were, and as a result the previously "good" was changed into "evil," the formerly "useful" into something "harmful." In other words, the political use of force, which had been legitimate within the realm of the *civitas Dei*, turned into an evil thing, for religion as such can claim no coercive power.

128, 18–19   Cf. Spinoza, *Tract. Theol.-pol.*, XVII, §31: "Therefore in this state civil right and religion . . . were one and the same" (*Quare in hoc imperio ius civile et religio . . . unum et idem erant*); Hobbes, *Leviathan*, XII (*OL*, III, 93): "and thereby in the Kingdome of God, the Policy, and Laws Civill, are a part of Religion; and therefore the 1581 distinction of Temporall, and Spirituall Domination, hath there no place" (*Manifestum ergo est in regno Dei politiam et leges civiles omnes religionis partem esse; ideoque distinctionem dominii temporalis et spiritualis in regno Dei nullam fuisse*); ibid., XXXV (295): "In short, the Kingdome of God is a Civill Kingdome" (*Concludimus ergo regnum Dei esse civile*); Locke, *Works*, VI, 37: "The Laws established in the Commonwealth of the Jews concerning the Worship of One Invisible Deity, were the Civil Laws of that People, and a part of their Political Government; in which God himself was the Legislator."

128, 29–31 Cf. Spinoza, *loc. cit.*, XVII, §31: "He who defected from the religion ceased to be a citizen" (*Qui a religione deficiebat, civis esse desinebat*); Hobbes, *loc. cit.*, XXXV (296): "HOLY . . . is a word, which in God's Kingdome answereth to that, which men in their Kingdoms use to call *Publique*, or the *King's*" (*Sanctum enim, in regno Dei, respondet vocabulo publicum, in civitatibus humanis*).

129, 1–2 Deut. 18:2 ("the Lord is their inheritance"); 10:9.

129, 2–6 Cf. Spinoza, *loc. cit.*, XVII, §78: "Indeed, emigration itself was considered a sacrilege because the service of God which was their constant obligation could be performed only in their own country; . . . For this reason David laments before Saul who had compelled him to go abroad: 'If it be men that have stirred thee up against me, let them be cursed for having driven me out that I should not remain in the inheritance of God, saying: Go, serve other gods' (I Sam., 26:19)." The Talmud (b. Ketubot 110b) infers from the biblical verse quoted that a Jew who dwells outside the Land of Israel is to be considered an idolater as it were; cf. Rashi's *Pentateuch Commentary* on Deut. 11:16, *The Book of Mirrors: Sefer Mar'ot ha-Ṣove'ot* by R. David ben Yehudah he-Ḥasid, ed. Daniel Chanan Matt, Brown Judaica Studies, 1982, 181f.; Moses Cordovero, *Sefer Or Yaqar*, XI, 251 (commenting on *Zohar*, II, 246a), where the Talmudic statement is interpreted to mean that the anguish over one's absence from the Holy Land amounts to a sense of separation from God. Mendelssohn, following Spinoza, gives it a political turn of meaning.

129, 13–15 Ex. 31:17.

129, 21–29 Cf. *Talmudic Encyclopaedia*, ed. S. J. Zevin, XI (Jerusalem, 1965), 291–314 (s.v. *hatra'ah*).

129, 32–34 Deut. 21:23.

130, 1–4 Mishnah Makkot I, 10. Cf. Spinoza, *loc. cit.*, V, §29: "Moreover, [Moses] did not give any particularly severe laws, as everyone will be ready to admit who studied them, espe-

cially when considering the circumstances that were required
for the sentencing of an accused."

130, 5–35 Mendelssohn's reply to the "Searcher" contains the following points: (1) The Mosaic law authorized no ecclesiastical power since according to its constitution the political and
the religious are inseparably one and the same thing. Hence
punishments were not inflicted by the "church" but by the
state as a kingdom of God and what was penalized was rebellion against the state. It is therefore incorrect to say that
the Mosaic law is a case of "statutory ecclesiastical law." (2)
What was considered punishable according to that law was
not unbelief, false doctrines, and error but "misdeeds," actions amounting to lese majesty. (3) After the destruction of
the second Temple (which meant the termination of Jewish
statehood) the rabbis declared the penal code of the Mosaic
legislation suspended (see the following note). Mendelssohn
takes this to imply that Judaism shed its former character as
a state-religion and became a "mere" religion. In consequence, it can no longer lay claim to the exercise of coercive rights or authority to punish. Its sole privilege, like that
of all other religions, is to use the "staff [called] *gentleness*" (see Zech. 11:10: "And I took my staff Graciousness") in
an effort to persuade the hearts and minds of men. What historically happened was an inner transformation in the character of Judaism. Hence it was wrong to maintain, as the
"Searcher" did, that "Ecclesiastical law armed with power has
always been one of the principal cornerstones of the Jewish
religion itself" (see above, p. 85).

130, 24–27 Cf. *Talmudic Encyclopaedia*, VII (Jerusalem, 1956),
354f. (s.v. *diney nefashot*); 377ff. (*diney qenasot*); *JubA* VII,
115; 482. Mendelssohn's assertion that punitive measures by
Jewish courts ceased after the loss of political independence
does not fully correspond to the facts; see ibid., III (1963),
173; Jacob Katz, *Tradition and Crisis* (1961), 98f.; 129; Salo
W. Baron, *A Social and Religious History of the Jews*, 2nd
ed., V (1957), 3–81 ("Communal Controls").

131, 2–3 The term "theocracy," which Flavius Josephus (*Contra
Apionem*, II, 16, 165) had coined as an honorific designation

of the Mosaic constitution, had been debased by the Deistic
critics of the Old Testament through identifying it with fraud-
ulent priestly rule. The chief protagonist of this view had been
Thomas Morgan in his *The Moral Philosopher*, I (London,
1737), 23ff. This denigration of the Old Testament was opposed by a number of theologians who upheld the authenticity
of the Mosaic theocracy. To these belonged Moses Lowman
who wrote a "Dissertation on the Civil Government of the
Hebrews, in which the True Designs, and Nature of their Government are explained, the Justice, Wisdom and Goodness of
the Mosaical Constitutions are vindicated: In Particular, from
some late, unfair and false Representations in the Moral Philosopher" (London, 1740); cf. note to 87, 14–23. In the 17th
century the notion of theocracy does not seem to have met
with vilification. Petrus Cunaeus invoked the Josephus passage according to which all matters obtaining in the Mosaic
state were dealt with by divine authority. See his *De repub-
lica Hebraeorum* (Leiden, 1640; 2nd ed., 1693; English Translation by C.B., London, 1653). Hobbes does not use the
term theocracy. He calls the kingdom established by a covenant (*pactum*) with God a *regnum sacerdotale;* see *Leviathan*,
XL (*OL*, III, 341); *De cive*, III.16 (*OL* II, 365). His view concerning the nature of this kingdom wavers between the notions of theocracy and hierocracy; see Zeev Harvey's discussion of the matter in *'Iyyun*, XXXI.1 (1981), 34f. Spinoza,
Tract. Theol.-pol., XVII, §32 justifies the term theocracy:
"Therefore this government could also be called a theocracy
because its citizens were bound to no other law than the one
revealed by God"; see also §41. Locke, *Works*, VI, 37 designates the Jewish state an "absolute theocracy."

131, 6–132, 5   The "false light" (131, 34: the "false point of view")
which Mendelssohn seeks to "avoid" is the pedestrian cast of
mind which operates with conventional ideas and has no eye
for what is great and unique. He was a sworn opponent of all
classifying (see *JubA* III.2, 189; XIII, 123). In the tendency
to place things into pigeonholes he recognized a source of misunderstanding. As for the requisite manner in which to look
at the Mosaic constitution, he considered it necessary to distinguish, in Platonic fashion, between idea and imperfect re-

ality. Just as there was an earthly and a heavenly Eros ("Amor"), so in politics, too. The Kingdom of God that had been embodied in ancient Judaism had to be regarded as the idea of a celestial politics as it were, as an allegory rather than historical fact—as which, indeed, it could not maintain itself for any length of time. This exalted idea was not to be confounded with the various hierocracies met with as a generic phenomenon in history. Yet Mendelssohn, it seems, did not want to see in biblical theocracy a model to be followed by modern states as had been suggested by Erastians and some Territorialists (see Guttmann, *loc. cit.*, 382). His liberal outlook, which bade him plead for the separation of state and church, was hardly in tune with any such tendency. Hence his insistence on the uniqueness of the Mosaic constitution. Being unique, it was unrepeatable. Only God knows, he says, when and where anything similar will ever occur again. Locke and the Collegialists, too, had counseled against any attempts by Christian states to imitate features of the ancient Jewish state; see L. von Mosheim, *Allgemeines Kirchenrecht*, 216; Locke, *Works*, VI, 38.

132, 6–7   See above, pp. 120, 2–7; 128, 14–17.

132, 7–21   1 Sam., chs. 8–10; cf. Hobbes, *Leviathan*, XXXV, *OL*, III, 293ff.: The *regnum Dei*, which had been "a real, not a metaphorical Kingdom," was "rejected" by the people at the time of Samuel. The prayer "Thy Kingdom come" is said by Hobbes to refer to the restitution of that Kingdom.

132, 29–30   Matth. 22:21. Cf. Hobbes, *loc. cit.*, XX, *OL*, III, 156: "*Postremo Servator noster ipse docet . . . tributa imposita a summa potestate civili solvenda esse, ipse solvens et 'date, inquiens, Caesari eaque Caesari sunt'*"; Mosheim, *loc. cit.*, 423. Jesus' saying agrees with the rabbinic statement formulated by the Babylonian teacher Samuel (2nd to 3rd cent. C.E.): "The Law of the ruling authority is law" (*dina de-malkhuta dina*); see b. Nedarim 28a and parallel passages; *Talmudic Encyclopaedia*, VII, 295–305. Mendelssohn quotes the New Testament saying because it more strikingly expresses the duty of serving two masters and because it sanctions what

COMMENTARY 235

might be considered a dual loyalty by the example of Jesus
which Christian rulers will respect.

133, 3–14 Mendelssohn imparts to the maxim "Serve two masters"
the additional meaning: "Adapt yourselves to the morals of
the land . . . but hold fast to the religion of your fathers too."
Thus he outlines a program for a new form of Jewish existence
among the nations, one which was to become highly relevant in
the period of Emancipation. The Enlightenment stance taken
up by Mendelssohn and his intellectual successors admitted of
no other type of solution. A different road was advocated by
the Romantic philosopher Herder who stressed the national
aspect; cf. Frederick M. Barnard, "Herder and Israel," *Jewish
Social Studies*, XXVIII (1966), 25–33.

What the "lawgiver foretold long ago" are the vicissitudes of
exile and the future return to the land of the fathers (Lev.
26:33–45; Deut. 28:64; 30:3–5). Mendelssohn refers only to the
sufferings foretold ("endure everything . . ."). The hope to
achieve civil equality in exile pushed the messianic expectation of a return to the Holy Land into the background. Besides, he considered the chances for a restoration of Jewish
statehood minimal since he felt that the "natural urge for
freedom" had become defunct among Jews, transmuted as
it was into the "monkish virtue" of mere praying and acceptance of suffering (see *JubA* XII.1, 212). Similarly Spinoza
(*loc. cit.*, III, §55) who made the principles of the Jewish religion responsible for the political condition of the Jews: they
had "rendered them effeminate" (*effeminarent*), a view which
had already been expressed by the 14th-century philosopher
Isaac Pulgar in his *'Ezer Ha-Dath;* see Shlomo Pines, "Spinoza's *Tractatus Theologico-Politicus* and the Jewish Philosophical Tradition," in Seventeenth Century Jewish Thought,
Proceedings of the Harvard Center for Jewish Studies Collo-
quium, 1982 (to be published). Spinoza, nevertheless, believed the restoration of the Jewish state to be possible, and
Mendelssohn, too, weighed the political factors that might
favor the successful accomplishment of such an enterprise in
the future (see *JubA*, XII.1, 211–12). In the present passage
no consideration is given to such remote possibilities.

133, 14–28 Mendelssohn reverts here to reflections which had oc-

cupied his mind when taking issue with Bonnet in the course
of the Lavater affair (*JubA* VII, 91; 87–98). He had denied
the historical correctness of Bonnet's assertion that Jesus abrogated the laws of Moses (cf. below, 134, 13–25). He had
argued that it would be "incomprehensible" were one to assume that God annulled, "tacitly as it were," a legislation that
had been installed "with so many public displays." Hence the
Law remained "obligatory" so long as God did not "revoke it
expressly with the same public solemnity" with which it had
been introduced. A similar argument had been put forward
during the famous Disputation at Tortosa (1413–14) as reported in Solomon ibn Verga's *Shevet Yehudah,* ed. A. Shoḥeṭ
(Jerusalem, 1947), 99f., and Mendelssohn undoubtedly took
it from that source.

Kant in "The Conflict of the Faculties" (Section I, General
Note; *Werke,* VII, 364) comments on this passage: "Moses
Mendelssohn repudiated this suggestion of a 'general conversion of the Jews' in a manner which does honor to his *sagacity*
(by an *argumentatio ad hominem*). So long (he says) as God
does not suspend our law from Mount Sinai as solemnly as He
gave it (amid thunder and lightning), that is to say, until the
day-that-never-will-be, we are bound by it; by which he probably meant to say: Christians, not until you remove Judaism
from *your* own faith, shall we abandon ours as well.—Yet let
his own coreligionists themselves decide whether it does
honor to his good *will* that by this harsh demand he cut off
all hope for the least reduction of the burdens pressing upon
them although, most probably, he regarded the smallest number of them as essential to his faith." Cf. above, note to 87,
4–14.

Mendelssohn's argument is implicitly directed also against
Spinoza who considered the ceremonial laws of the Mosaic
legislation an integral part of the Jewish state and therefore
as abolished by virtue of the destruction of the state (*loc. cit.,*
V, §§13–15). As Shlomo Pines suggested, Spinoza may have
derived this view from Marrano sources. We find it expressed
as the opinion of the Jewish spokesman (Solomon) in Bodin's
Heptaplomeres (written in 1593) where the context makes its
provenience from a Marrano milieu likely; see Pines, "The

Jewish Religion after the Destruction of Temple and State:
The Views of Bodin and Spinoza," in *Studies in Jewish Religious and Intellectual History*, ed. Siegfried Stein and Raphael Loewe (University, Ala., 1979), 228. Yet this view is
already found in early-medieval Jewish sectaries like Judah
Yudgan (8th cent., Persia) and some Karaites in Baṣra; see
Jacob Mann, in *HUCA*, XII–XIII (1937–38), 428f. It obviously
had some vogue in the 13th century since Naḥmanides considered it necessary to reject it; see his *Pentateuch Commentary* on Num. 35:29. Its spread in the 15th century may be
gauged from the sharp polemic it encountered from Ṣemaḥ
ben Solomon Duran in his *Responsa Yakhin U-Boʿaz* (Leg-
horn, 1781), no. 134, fol. 50d.

In his "Counterreflections" (*JubA* VII, 97) Mendelssohn
had discussed also the question as to whether the Mosaic law
was to be abrogated or changed at any time in the future. He
had pointed out that some authorities considered it not im-
probable that the hoped-for "miraculous restoration of the Jewish nation" would occasion "a second public legislation" by the
"Supreme Lawgiver" according to which "many of our present
ceremonial laws might be altered in one way or another." In
the opinion of others the present laws were "altogether immutable." The latter view can be found in p. Megillah, I, 5;
Saadia Gaon, *Sefer Emunot ve-Deʿot*, III, 7; Moses Maimon-
ides, *Mishnah Commentary*, Sanhedrin, X, 9; *Mishneh Torah*,
Yesodey Ha-Torah, IX, 1; Megillah ve-Hanukah, II, 18; *Guide
of the Perplexed*, III, 34. The contrary opinion is expressed in b.
Niddah 61b; *Leviticus Rabba* XIII, 3; *Midrash Tehilim*, 146, 7;
Yalqut Shimeʿoni, §944. An obviously antinomian passage in
Raʿya Mehemna (*Zohar*, III, 124b) served the purposes of the
Sabbatian heresy and was used by Nathan of Gaza; see G.
Scholem, *Sabbatai Ṣevi The Mystical Messiah 1626–1676*
(Princeton, N.J., 1973), 11; 809. Of particular interest is the
following passage in Menaḥem Mendel of Vitebsk, *Sefer Peri
Ha-ʾAreṣ* (Kopys, 1814), Pericope Toledot (quoted by Reuben
Margalioth, *Shaʿarey Zohar* [Jerusalem, 1956], 125a–b): "The
statement of our Teachers, of blessed memory, that in the days
of the Messiah all commandments will be abolished rests on
[the belief] that in the time to come the earth shall be full of

the knowledge of God as waters cover the sea [Isa. 11:9] . . .
and that this knowledge will penetrate to the root of the Torah
and the commandments, that is, to the absolute Unity, the
Eyn-Sof as expressed in the words 'I am the Lord thy God.'
When this goal is reached all commandments will 'let down
their wings' and all statutes will be suspended because the evil
urge will then have been overcome." Mendelssohn reflects
similar notions when, in the passage mentioned (*JubA* VII,
97–98) he declares: At the time when the knowledge of God
will cover the whole earth as waters cover the sea, "divine
wisdom might find it no longer necessary to separate us by
special ceremonial laws from the rest of the nations, and instead it might introduce, by a second public revelation, such
external rites as will unite the hearts of all men in reverence
of their Creator as well as in mutual love and beneficence."

Mendelssohn thus assumed that an abrogation of the Mosaic
law was to be expected in the Messianic future when there
would be "one shepherd and one flock" (using the very phrase
quoted by the "Searcher"). Until then, however, the sons of
Israel were obliged to keep the ceremonial law in order thereby
to safeguard the pure monotheism (see *JubA* XIII, 134). It
may be noted that Jacob Emden, whom Mendelssohn revered
as the leading rabbinic authority in German Jewry (cf. *JubA*
XIX, 114 and passim), likewise held that with the advent of
the Messianic period, that is, with the beginning of the sev-
enth millennium according to Jewish chronology (see note to
59, 10–11), the law would be abolished; see Yehuda Liebes,
"The Messianity of R. Jacob Emden and his Relation to Sab-
batianism," in *Tarbiz*, 49.1–2, 1981. See also Judah Rosenthal,
"The Idea of the Abrogation of the Commandments in Jewish
Eschatology" (Hebrew) in *Meyer Waxman Jubilee*, ed. Judah
Rosenthal (Chicago, 1967), 217–33.

133, 30 Cf. above p. 118, 18–19 and note *ad locum.*

134, 1–12 Mendelssohn adopts the rabbinic distinction between
laws that "depend on the land" and laws that do not and,
hence, are valid also in exilic conditions. The latter kind he
calls "personal commandments," a term borrowed, it seems,
from Naḥmanides' *Pentateuch Commentary* (Deut. 11:18)

where the Hebrew phrase used is *ḥovot ha-guf* ("personal duties").

134, 17–32   The Orientalist Johann David Michaelis remarked apropos of this passage: "One ought to thank Mr. Mendelssohn for his having drawn attention to such an important matter which has been noticed too little: I cannot agree with him that Jesus did not declare the law to be abrogated for the Jews also . . . but that much is certain: Christ never *interdicted* [my emphasis] the retention of the Levitical law. Paul too observed it and, at no time, bade the Jews fall away from the law." See his review of "Jerusalem" in *Michaelis' Orientalische und Exegetische Bibliothek*, 22 (1783), 92f.

135, 25–26   John 10:16, based on Ezek. 37:24. The "Searcher" (p. 44) had recalled that "prophecy" (*Weissagung*).

136, 10–11   Isa. 11:6.

136, 11–35   In the propagation of a union of faiths Mendelssohn saw a recrudescence of religious fanaticism in opposition to the Enlightenment and, therefore, an acute danger to the liberty of conscience. In a letter to his friend Herz Homberg (*JubA* XIII, 134) he characterized the missionary purpose behind all advocacy of religious fraternization as "the unificatory system of wolves" aimed at "transforming mutton and lamb into wolves' flesh." He distrusted the all too eager protestation of tolerance because of his suspicion that it concealed a mere missionary objective (see *JubA* XIII, 179). He perceived the same tendency in Joseph II's Edict of Tolerance which he had first greeted with enthusiasm (*JubA* XIII, 31; 357; cf. Altmann, *Mendelssohn*, 462f.). This kind of suspicion had been reinforced by his past personal experience of evangelical zeal directed at his own person.

    Michaelis wrote in his review (*loc. cit.*, 95): "What Mr. Mendelssohn . . . says against the unification of faiths . . . corresponds so much to my own view that I can heartily commend it to my readers."

136–37, Note   Cf. C. M. Pfaff's differentiation between the theoretical (*professus*) and the propagandistic (*seductor*) atheist; see above, note on 62, 30–63, 2, and Altmann, *Die trostvolle Aufklärung*, p. 273.

137, 4–21   Cf. above, 66, 11–68, 6.

138, 5–18   Cf. *JubA* XII.1, 49–52; VI.1, 54ff.; 225; XII.2, 93–95; Altmann, *Essays in Jewish Intellectual History*, 164f. Mendelssohn offers a metaphysical rationale for his pluralistic view of state and society which was meant to facilitate the civil admission of the Jews.

138, 23–24   Cf. above, 33, 20.

139, 15–16   Zech. 8:29; cf. *JubA* VI.1, 197.

139, Note   This is possibly a reference to the "General Assessment Bill for Support of Christian denominations" which was debated by the American Congress in 1783–84 and contained the clause: "The Christian religion shall in all times coming be deemed and held to be the established Religion of this Commonwealth." Thanks to the efforts made by James Madison, this bill was not passed. Thomas Jefferson wrote his *Notes on Virginia*, which pleaded for the complete separation of state and church in 1782 (see Anson Phelps Stokes, *Church and State in the United States*, I, 334f.), in the year in which Mendelssohn wrote *Jerusalem*. Cf. note on 37, 33–38, 4.

ABBREVIATED REFERENCES

AdB	*Allgemeine deutsche Biographie.* 56 vols. Berlin, 1967–71.
Altmann, *Frühschriften*	Alexander Altmann. *Moses Mendelssohns Frühschriften zur Metaphysik. Tübingen,* 1969.
———, *Mendelssohn*	———. *Moses Mendelssohn: A Biographical Study.* University, Ala. 1973; London, 1973.
———, *Essays*	———. *Essays in Jewish Intellectual History.* Hanover, N.H. and London, 1981.
———, *Die trostvolle Aufklärung*	———. *Die trostvolle Aufklärung. Studien zur Metaphysik und politischen Theorie Moses Mendelssohns.* Stuttgart-Bad Cannstatt, 1982.
ARN	*Aboth de Rabbi Nathan,* ed. Solomon Schechter. Vienna, 1887.
b.	Babylonian Talmud.
Bamberger, "Mendelssohn's Concept of Judaism"	Fritz Bamberger. "Mendelssohn's Concept of Judaism." In Alfred Jospe, ed., *Studies in Jewish Thought,* pp. 343–60. Detroit, 1981.
Borst, *Turmbau*	Arno Borst. *Der Turmbau von Babel.* 4 vols. Stuttgart, 1957–63.
Boehmer, *Jus Ecclesiasticum*	Justus Henning Boehmer. *Jus Ecclesiasticum Protestantium.* 6 vols. 5th ed. Halle, 1756–89.
Cassirer, "Die Idee der Religion"	Ernst Cassirer. "Die Idee der Religion bei Lessing und Mendelssohn." In *Festgabe zum zehnjährigen Bestehen der Akademie für die Wissenschaft des Judentums.* Berlin, 1929.
Denzer, *Pufendorf*	Horst Denzer. *Moralphilosophie und Naturrecht bei Samuel Pufendorf.* Munich, 1972.

Dohm, *Bürgerliche Verbesserung* — Christian Wilhelm Dohm. *Ueber die bürgerliche Verbesserung der Juden.* Berlin and Stettin, 1781.

Euchner, *Locke* — Walter Euchner. *Naturrecht und Politik bei John Locke.* Frankfurt a.M., 1969.

Fleischer, *Einleitung* — J. L. Fleischer. *Einleitung zum geistlichen Rechte.* Halle, 1724; 2nd ed. (quoted here), 1729.

Ferguson, *Institutes* — Adam Ferguson. *Institutes of Moral Philosophy.* Edinburgh, 1769.

Garve, *Ferguson* — Christian Garve, trans. *Adam Fergusons Grundsätze der Moralphilosophie.* Leipzig, 1772.

GS — *Moses Mendelssohn's gesammelte Schriften.* Edited by G. B. Mendelssohn. Leipzig, 1843–45.

Guttmann, "Mendelssohn's Jerusalem" — Julius Guttmann. "Mendelssohn's *Jerusalem* and Spinoza's *Theologico-Political Treatise.*" In Alfred Jospe, ed., *Studies in Jewish Thought,* pp. 361–86. Detroit, 1981.

Hamann, *Briefwechsel* — Walther Ziesemer and Arthur Henkel, eds. *Johann Georg Hamann Briefwechsel.* Wiesbaden, 1955 ff.

Haering, *Hegel* — Theodor Lorenz Haering. *Hegel, sein Wollen und sein Werk.* 2 vols. Leipzig and Berlin, 1929.

Heckel, *Cura religionis* — Johannes Heckel. *Cura religionis, Ius in sacra, Ius circa sacra.* In *Festschrift Ulrich Stutz.* Stuttgart, 1938.

Heckel, *Staat und Kirche* — Martin Heckel. *Staat und Kirche nach den Lehren der evangelischen Juristen Deutschlands in der ersten Hälfte des 17. Jahrhunderts.* Munich, 1968.

Hobbes, *OL* — *Thomae Hobbes Malmesburiensis Opera Philosophica quae latine scripsit Omnia . . . collecta studio et labore Gulielmi Molesworth.* Vol. II, London, 1839; Vol. III, London, 1841 (Reprint: Aalen, 1961).

Hobbes, *EW* — *English Works of Thomas Hobbes.* Edited by William Molesworth. 11 vols. London, 1839.

Höpfner, *Naturrecht* — Ludwig Julius Friedrich Höpfner. *Naturrecht des einzelnen Menschen, der Gesellschaften*

	und der Völker. Darmstadt, 1780; 6th ed. (quoted here), 1806.
HUCA	*Hebrew Union College Annual,* Cincinnati, Ohio, 1924 ff.
Ilting, "Naturrecht"	Karl-Heinz Ilting. "Naturrecht." In Otto Brunner et al., eds. *Geschichtliche Grundbegriffe, Historisches Lexikon zur politisch-sozialen Sprache in Deutschland.* Vol. IV, Stuttgart, 1978.
Jospe, *Studies*	Alfred Jospe, ed. *Studies in Jewish Thought, An Anthology of German-Jewish Scholarship.* Detroit, 1981.
JQR	*The Jewish Quarterly Review.* Philadelphia, 1889 ff.
JubA	*Moses Mendelssohn Gesammelte Schriften Jubiläumsausgabe.* Stuttgart-Bad Cannstatt, 1971 ff.
Kant, *Werke*	*Immanuel Kants Werke.* Edited by Ernst Cassirer. Berlin, 1922 ff.
Klippel, *Politische Freiheit*	Diethelm Klippel. *Politische Freiheit und Freiheitsrechte im deutschen Naturrecht des 18. Jahrhunderts.* Paderborn, 1976.
Krieger, *Politics*	Leonard Krieger. *The Politics of Discretion: Pufendorf and the Acceptance of Natural Law.* Chicago and London, 1965.
Lechler, *Geschichte*	Gottfried Victor Lechler. *Geschichte des englischen Deismus.* Stuttgart and Tübingen, 1841.
Lecler, *Toleration*	Joseph Lecler. *Toleration and the Reformation.* Vol. II. New York, 1960.
Leibniz (Gerhardt)	C. J. Gerhardt, ed. *Die philosophischen Schriften von G. W. Leibniz.* 7 vols. Berlin, 1875–90.
Leibniz, *Philosophische Schriften*	*G. W. Leibniz Philosophische Schriften.* Edited by the Leibniz-Forschungsstelle der Universität Münster. Vol. VI. Berlin, 1962.
Leland, *Deistical Writers*	John Leland. *A View of the Principal Deistical Writers.* 5th ed., I. London, 1766.
Leuze, *Hegel*	Reinhard Leuze. *Die außerchristlichen Religionen bei Hegel.* Göttingen, 1975.
Lezius, *Der Toleranzbegriff*	Friedrich Lezius. *Der Toleranzbegriff Lockes und Pufendorfs.* Leipzig, 1900; reprint: Aalen, 1971.

L-M	*Lessings Sämtliche Schriften.* Edited by K. Lachmann; 3rd ed. by F. Muncker. 23 vols. Stuttgart and Leipzig, 1886–1924.
Locke, *Works*	*The Works of John Locke.* A New Edition. 10 vols. London, 1823.
Locke, *Two Treatises*	John Locke. *Two Treatises of Government.* Edited by Peter Laslett. 2nd ed. Cambridge, 1970.
Medick, *Naturzustand*	Hans Medick. *Naturzustand und Naturgeschichte der bürgerlichen Gesellschaft.* Göttingen, 1973.
Mendelssohn, *Verzeichnis*	*Verzeichnis der auserlesenen Büchersammlung des seeligen Herrn Moses Mendelssohn.* Berlin, 1786; facsimile reproduction edited by Herrmann Meyer for the Soncino Society, Berlin, 1926.
MGWJ	*Monatsschrift für Geschichte und Wissenschaft des Judentums.* Breslau, 1851–1939.
Mosheim, *Allgemeines Kirchenrecht*	Johann Lorenz von Mosheim. *Allgemeines Kirchenrecht der Protestanten.* Helmstädt, 1760.
Oakeshott	Michael Oakeshott, ed. *Leviathan; or, The Matter, Forme and Power of a Commonwealth Ecclesiastical and Civil by Thomas Hobbes.* Oxford (no year).
p.	Palestinian Talmud.
PAAJR	*Proceedings of The American Academy for Jewish Research.* New York, 1930 ff.
Pfaff, *Academische Reden*	Christoph Matthäus Pfaff. *Academische Reden über das sowohl allgemeine als auch Teutsche Protestantische Kirchen-Recht.* Tübingen, 1742; reprint: Frankfurt a.M., 1963.
Pufendorf, *De jure*	Samuel Pufendorf. *De jutre naturae et gentium libri VIII,* editio secunda. Frankfurt a.M., 1684.
———, *De officio*	———. *De officio hominis et civis juxta legem naturalem libri II,* 1673.
———, *De habitu*	———. *De habitu religionis christianae ad vitam civilem.* Bremen, 1687.
Ravid, *Menasseh ben Israel*	Benjamin Ravid. " 'How Profitable the Nation of the Jews Are': The Humble Addresses of Menasseh ben Israel and the Discorso of Simone Luzzatto." In J. Reinharz and D. Swetschinski,

eds., *Mystics, Philosophers, and Politicians,* pp. 159–80. Durham, N.C., 1982.

Reimarus, *Apologie*   Hermann Samuel Reimarus. *Apologie oder Schutzschrift für die vernünftigen Verehrer Gottes.* Edited by Gerhard Alexander. Leipzig, Insel Verlag.

RGG^3 *Die Religion in Geschichte und Gegenwart.* 6 vols., 3rd ed. Tübingen, 1957–62.

Rüping, *Thomasius*   Hinrich Rüping. *Die Naturrechtslehre des Christian Thomasius und ihre Fortbildung in der Thomasius-Schule.* Bonn, 1968.

Schiedermair, *Leibniz*   Hartmut Schiedermair. *Das Phänomen der Macht und die Idee des Rechts bei Gottfried Wilhelm Leibniz.* Wiesbaden, 1970.

Schlaich, *Territorialismus*   Klaus Schlaich. "Der rationale Territorialismus." In *Zeitschrift der Savigny-Stiftung für Rechtsgeschichte,* Vol. 84, Canonistic Section, LIII, 1967.

——, *Kollegialtheorie*   ——. *Kollegialtheorie, Kirche, Recht und Staat in der Aufklärung.* Munich, 1969.

Schneiders, *Naturrecht*   Werner Schneiders. *Naturrecht und Liebesethik.* Hildesheim and New York, 1971.

Schulz, "Kant und die Berliner Aufklärung"   Eberhard Günter Schulz. "Kant und die Berliner Aufklärung." In *Akten des 4. Internationalen Kant-Kongresses, Mainz, 6–10 April 1974,* II, 1, Berlin, 1974.

Spinoza, *Tract. Theol.-pol.*   *Benedicti de Spinoza Opera quae supersunt omnia.* Edited by C. H. Bruder. Vol. II. Leipsig, 1846.

Stephen, *English Thought*   Leslie Stephen. *History of English Thought in the Eighteenth Century.* 2 vols. (1876). New York and Burlingame, 1962.

Strauss, *Hobbes*   Leo Strauss. *The Political Philosophy of Hobbes.* Oxford, 1952; 6th ed., Chicago, 1973.

——, *Natural Right and History*   ——. *Natural Right and History.* Chicago and London, 1950; 8th ed., 1974.

Sullivan, *Toland*   Robert E. Sullivan. *John Toland and the Deist Controversy.* Cambridge, Mass. and London, 1982.

Thomasius, *Das Recht* — Christian Thomasius. *Das Recht evangelischer Fürsten in theologischen Streitigkeiten.* Halle, 1713.

Wolf, *Menasseh ben Israel's Mission* — Lucien Wolf. *Menasseh ben Israel's Mission to Oliver Cromwell.* London, 1901.

Wolff, *Jus naturae* — Christian Wolff. *Gesammelte Werke,* Section II, Vols. 17–24. Edited by H. Thomann. Hildesheim, 1968.

———, *Philosophia practica* — ———. *Philosophia practica universalis.* In *Gesammelte Werke,* Section II, Vol. 10. Edited by Winfried Lenders. Hildesheim, 1971.

———, *German Ethics* — ———. *Vernünfftige Gedanken von der Menschen Thun und Lassen.* New Edition. Halle, 1752.

Wolfson, *Studies* — Harry Austryn Wolfson. *Studies in the History of Philosophy.* Edited by Isadore Twersky and George H. Williams. 2 vols. Cambridge, Mass., 1973–77.

Zeller, *Philosophie der Griechen* — Eduard Zeller. *Die Philosophie der Griechen in ihrer geschichtlichen Entwicklung.* Sixth Edition. Leipzig, 1919. Reprint (7th ed.), Hildesheim, 1963.

ZGJD — *Zeitschrift für die Geschichte der Juden in Deutschland.* Edited by Ismar Elbogen et al. 7 vols. 1929–36.

Zion — *Zion, Quarterly for Research in Jewish History* (Hebr.), Jerusalem.

APPENDIX

DRAFT OF JERUSALEM [*]

1

Church and State. Borderline disputes between them have caused immeasurable evils—Hobbes—Locke—The latter limits the state to the care for temporal welfare.—A makeshift intended for the protection of dissidents against persecution.—But wrong, for the temporal cannot be separated from the eternal, and ineffective—for the Church employs the secular arm.—The true dividing line is compulsory duties and persuasion. The former belong to the state, the latter is the privilege of religion.—When the church arrogates to itself property and coercive rights, it usurps them.

2

The origin of coercive rights. Only the duties of omission are perfect. The duties to do something become, as a result of contract, duties not to do. Contracts relate to dispensable goods which are used for the benefit of others. Opinions confer no rights nor can they be brought into any connection with rights. Nobody must be asked to testify under oath that he holds a certain opinion. Confirming articles of faith under oath amounts to a misuse of God's name, is a vain oath, never a false oath.— Consolation to all those who confirmed symbolic books or established articles of faith under oath and have a guilty conscience. The state needs religion only as a safeguard of oaths; hence the state presupposes faith and cannot have someone confirm his faith under oath. To the extent that religion does not safeguard the state, it has to limit itself altogether to persuasion.

[*] See Introduction, pp. 11–12, note 27.

247

3

It has been objected to these rational arguments that they run counter
to the Jewish religion—*Searching for Light and Right*. Challenge to
accept the Christian religion as the religion of freedom or else to refute
it.—Inconsistency of this unfair suggestion. He who finds the foundation
of his building to be unsafe will not save his belongings by moving
them from the lower to the upper floor.—Christianity is a yoke in spirit
and in truth—It has transformed thirty-nine corporal floggings into as
many spiritual ones. The modern Reformation of the 18th century is no
longer founded on revelation, leaves everything to reason, yet arrogates
to itself a name in order to use the privileges attached to this name—
Not so Judaism. History of religion. Union of faiths. Divorce of marriage. Faith of my Fathers.

INDEX

Aaron, 120
Ability: natural (physical), 35–37; moral, 36–37, 45
Aesop, 112
Albo, Joseph, 101
Almsgiving, 43
Alphabetical script: origins of, 108–10; effects of, 118–19
American Congress, 139
Anarchy, 42
Anglican bishops, 68
Anglican Church, thirty-nine articles of, 68
Animal worship, 112–13, 116
Animals, social behavior of, 56; in fables, 112
Appetitive urge, 162
Articles of faith: absence of in ancient Judaism, 100; Albo's three, 101; Maimonides's thirteen, 101. See also Anglican Church
Atheism, 63, 116, 136–37n
Athenian philosopher, 75
Athenians, 121
Authority: civil, 33, 35, 38; ecclesiastical, 33, 38; Scriptural, 85; serving as example, 43
Avarice, 60

Bayle, Pierre, 63
Belief: denoting trust, 100; no commandment of, 100; and knowledge, 101
Bellarmine, Robert, 38–39

Beneficence, 47–48
Benevolence, 41–42, 47–48, 57, 61, 122; entailing sacrifice, 41–42, 53, 124; not needed by God, 57–58, 128
Berlin clergy, 80
Blasphemy, 36, 85, 129

Capacity. See Ability
Causality, direct and indirect, 95
Ceremonies. See Commandments prescribed in Mosaic law
Charity. See Almsgiving
Chasdai. See Crescas, Chasdai
Cherubim, 114
Christian Church. See Ecclesiastical law; Ecclesiastical power; Papal authority
Christianity: symbolic books of, 67; based on Judaism, 87; early documents of, 88–89
Church: generically defined, 41; purpose and functions of, 43–44, 61, 70, 72, 74; has no coercive rights, 45, 59–60, 70, 73–74, 77–78; has no claim to property, 59; dispenses no temporal goods, 73; a moral person, 73. See also Excommunication; Ministers of religion; Church and state
Church and state, boundaries between, 35–38, 40–41, 44–45, 56–61, 63, 70. See also Social contract

Excommunication: opposed to the essence of religion, 73–75; right of denied, 73, 77; civil consequences of, 74; in Dohm's view, 77–78; no longer popular in Prussia, 80; in Hobbes's view, 84

Existence, mere, 47; improvement of, 47, 55–56

Experiment, 92–93

Expulsion from the state, 45, 62, 73

Fable. *See* Animals

Faculty, moral. *See* Ability, moral

Fanaticism: religious, 35, 63, 136; atheistic, 136–37

Fear of God, 35, 60, 65, 80

Fear and hope, 43, 62

Felicity, 35, 48, 50, 63, 71, 93–94, 116; temporal, 37–38, 40–41, 45, 52, 90, 97, 119; eternal, 37–40, 90; civil, 43, 62; true, 44, 63; private and public, 127–28

Ferguson, Adam, 55n

First principles, questioning of, 81

Folly. *See* Corruption

Frederick the Great, 78–79

Fuga vacui, 106

Future life, 39, 63

Gentoos. *See* Shasta of the Gentoos

God: omnipotent, 37, 94; supreme judge, 37; creator and preserver, 41, 43, 92, 127–28; will of, 43, 90–91; wants the best for his creatures, 59; all-righteous, 65; intellect of, 90–91; goodness of, 94; eternal, 118, 120, 123; redeemer and lawgiver of the Jewish nation, 118, 127–28; loving and merciful, 121–25; justice of, 124; father, 125; omniscient, 131. *See also* Providence

Gods of the earth, 37

Golden calf, 120

Golden hip. *See* Pythagoras

Goods: definition of, 45–48; exclusive rights to, 47; joint ownership of, 47; intangible, 52, 54–55; immovable, 53; movable, 53; spiritual, 53. *See also* Property

Göttingische Anzeigen, 80–81

Government: form of, 38, 42; notion

of, is inapplicable to church, 62. *See also* Despotism; State

Gravitation, 106

Haller, Albrecht von, 106–7

Happiness. *See* Felicity

Helvétius, Claude-Adrien, 95

Herbert of Cherbury, 101

Heterodoxy, 41

Hierocracy, 131

Hieroglyphic script, 108–10; caused idolatry, 110–13, 115, 118

Hillel the Elder, 102

History: view of, 42, 95–97; of religion, 115–17. *See also* Corruption; Progress

Hobbes, Thomas, 35–37, 84

Homer, 121

Honesty, 44

Honor of God, 59n

Household, rights and duties of, 50–52

Human nature, 103

Hume, David, 95

Hypocrisy, 58, 72, 111, 115–16, 137

Idolatry, 99, 112–13, 115, 118

Independence. *See* Liberty, natural

Indirect bribe and punishment, 61

Individual man, progress of, 97

Industry, 47–49, 53–54

Injury. *See* Injustice

Injustice, 47–49, 52

Inquisition, 38n

Intolerance, 38, 67

Irritability, law of, 106–7

Iselin, Isaak, 78–79n

Jerusalem, 86

Jesuitry, 72

Jesus, 132, 134

Jews, 41, 77, 135; destiny of, 118

Joseph II, 51–52

Judaism: consists of doctrines, laws, and historical truths, 90, 102, 126–27; credal part of, is based on reason but the legislative part is revealed, 90, 97; the true, 94, 100; the ancient, 100, 102; knows no dogmas in the Christian sense, 100–101; principles of, 100–101; its legislation is partly written,

Positive laws. *See* Civil laws
Priestcraft, 116
Priestly nation, 118
Principle of contradiction, 101n
Principles. *See* Convictions
Principles of Judaism. *See* Judaism
Progress, 96–97, 103; abuse of, 103, 110, 128. *See also* Corruption
Property, 44, 47, 53–56, 60
Prophet, the, 104, 116, 127
Providence, 39–40, 63, 94–96, 103, 105, 118, 120, 138
Psalmist, the, 60n, 86, 95, 102, 125–26
Psychology, 91
Public welfare. *See* Common good
Punishment, 43, 61, 73, 123–24. *See also* Eternal punishment
Pythagoras, 81
Pythagorean school, 117

Quality of divine love, 123, 125

Rabbis, the, 39, 60, 123, 130
Reason: moral teachings of, 58; dictates of, 71; Scriptural authority not in conflict with, 85, 130; comprehends and verifies eternal truths, 89, 93–94; truths of, 89; defined, 91; powers of, 94
Reason's house of worship, 88
Reasons motivating the intellect, 40–41, 62, 70
Reasons motivating the will, 40–41, 62, 70
Reformation, 34
Relations between man and God, 41, 57–58, 72
Relations between man and man, 41, 72
Relations between man and nature, 57–58
Relations between nature and God, 57
Religion: inward, 35; vocation of, 43; implies conviction and action, 44; power of, 45, 73; prescribes commandments, not laws, 45; definition of, 58, 70; fundamental articles of, 63–64; sanctions moral duties, 58; must not coerce, 72; divine, 73; true, 73; natural, 87;

revealed, 89–90, 97. *See also* Ministers of religion
Religion of my fathers, 84, 89
Religious disputes, settlement of, 62
Religious society. *See* Church
Render unto Caesar . . . , 132–33, 139
Republicans, 42
Restriction of civil rights, 61
Revelation: supernatural, 90, 94; Sinaitic, 90, 97–98, 127; by word and script, 90, 93, 126–27; befitting ways of, 93; exclusiveness of, 94, 97; direct, 123–24, 126
Reward, 43, 61
Reward and punishment, 43–44; have no persuasive power, 43; are but coercive means to be used by the state for public welfare, 43–44
Right, definition of, 45. *See also* Rights and duties
Right to divorce, 50–52n
Right to kill in war, 46n
Rights and duties: perfect (coercive) and imperfect (noncoercive), 46–48; reciprocity of, 46; transformation of imperfect into perfect, 53, 56–57, 83. *See also* Household, rights and duties of

Sabbath, 85, 129
Sacredness of reason, 58
Sacrifice. *See* Benevolence
Safety, 35, 37, 44
Salvation, 90, 93, 97. *See also* Felicity, eternal
Samaria, 86
Samuel, the prophet, 132
Scientific terms, invention of, 106–7
Script, origin of, 108. *See also* Alphabetical script; Hieroglyphic script
Searcher for Light and Right, 85–87, 130
Security. *See* Safety
Self-love, 41, 57
Self-preservation, 54
Selfishness. *See* Self-love
Senses, external and internal, 66, 71, 91, 104–5

LIBRARY OF CONGRESS CATALOGING-IN-PUBLICATION DATA

Mendelssohn, Moses, 1729–1786.
    Jerusalem, or, On religious power and Judaism.
    Includes bibliographical references and index.
    1. Judaism—Works to 1900. 2. Church and state—Early works to
    1800. 3. Religious liberty—Early works to 1800. I. Arkush, Allan,
    1949– . II. Title.
  BM565.MI3 1983 296 83–40015
  ISBN 0-87451-263-8. ISBN 0-87451-264-6 (pbk.)
  ♾